GALATIANS
and
EPHESIANS

By Lehman Strauss

James, Your Brother

Certainties for Today

The Third Person

The Second Person

The Eleven Commandments

We Live Forever

An Examination of the Teaching
of Modernism

An Examination of the Doctrine
of Jehovah's Witnesses

Devotional Studies in

GALATIANS
and
EPHESIANS

BY

LEHMAN STRAUSS

✳✳

LOIZEAUX BROTHERS
New York

FIRST EDITION, OCTOBER 1957
SECOND PRINTING, FEBRUARY 1958

PRINTED IN THE UNITED STATES OF AMERICA

DEDICATION

To Miss Helen E. Hertzler,
whose faithfulness as a co-worker in the Gospel
of our Lord Jesus Christ has been a source of
encouragement, this volume is gratefully dedicated
by the author.

OUTLINE OF GALATIANS

OUTLINE OF EPHESIANS

Galatians

I. PRELIMINARY

To appreciate and interpret a musical composition one must hear and interpret the prelude. To appreciate and evaluate the main message of a book one must study and evaluate the preface. If the musical student is to arrive at a correct interpretation of the composition, he must understand the prelude in its relation to the whole. If the Biblical student is to arrive at a correct interpretation of any Bible book, he must understand the preface in its relation to the whole.

This outline mentions three suggestions as a prefatory approach to Paul's Epistle to the Galatians. While they do not form a complete introduction to our study, they will, we feel certain, lead us to a clearer understanding of the apostle's message.

A. The Place

It is not an easy matter to decide and declare dogmatically exactly where the churches to which the Epistle was addressed were located. If they belonged to Galatia proper, then they were churches established by Paul in the cities of Ancyra, Pessinus and Tavium on his second missionary journey. If these churches were in the cities of Antioch in Pisidia, Iconium, Lystra and Derbe, they were those churches organized by the apostle on his first missionary journey through Asia Minor as recorded in Acts, chapters 13 and 14.

Galatia proper was not a city nor a village, but a province in Asia, and the present writer is inclined to dismiss the northern Galatian theory in favor of the southern Galatian theory whose cities lay along the main routes of travel. If we are correct we may assume that Paul visited the province of Galatia on three occasions: His first missionary journey (Acts 13 and 14), his second missionary journey (Acts 16:6), and his third missionary journey (Acts 18:23).

We may be certain, however, that Galatia was evangelized and ministered unto by the Apostle Paul. Details such as the places he visited, the length of time he remained, and the nature of the treatment he received while there, are not recorded. We do know from the accurate records of Luke the historian that the mighty apostle to the Gentiles had carried the gospel to that province, and many believed. The Epistle addressed to the saints in that place assures us that local churches had been established there (Gal. 1:2 cf. 1 Cor. 16:1).

No student of Scripture can think of Galatia without recalling the soul-stirring experiences of Paul as he passed through that province. At the hands of its natives he received both beatings and blessings. It was at Lystra that he was severely stoned, dragged out of the city and left for dead. It was somewhere in Galatia that Paul suffered an affliction, possibly a disease of the eyes, which detained him longer than he expected and which brought forth the kindly treatment at the hands of some Galatian Christians (Gal. 4:13-15). Some teachers of God's Word believe that the infirmity of the flesh was caused by the beatings Paul received in Lystra at the brutal hands of certain Jews who were joined by the people of Lystra, and that it was to that experience the apostle referred in 2 Corinthians 12:1-10. If Second Corinthians was written in A.D. 60, and the Lystra experience occurred about A.D. 45 or 46 (Ussher), then Paul's "thorn in the flesh" took place at the time he was in Galatia, for he said that it happened "above fourteen years ago" (2 Cor. 12:2).

Having said this much about the place, we conclude by adding the all-important fact that the workings of the Holy Spirit through Paul's life and labors in Galatia must have been of a strikingly successful character.

B. *The People*

Character study is most fascinating. While human nature is the same in every part of the earth, there are certain traits and characteristics which prevail among one group of people but which may not be noticeable in another.

The Galatians were the sons of the great Celtic family, those migratory tribes which invaded Greece early in the third century before Christ. About 280 B.C. a large number separated from the main body and crossed over into what is now known as Asia Minor. About fifty years later (232 B.C.) their state became known as Galatia, named for the people themselves who were called Gauls. It has been pointed out by some that the Gauls gave the district which they occupied their own names.

When Paul came among them they doubtless were idolators. The Gallic tribes had fought their way through Europe, crossed the Hellespont, and pillaged and plundered as they had gone. By the time of the apostle, however, King Amyntas (35-25 B.C.), the last independent ruler of Galatia, had relinquished his kingdom to Rome and Galatia had become a Roman province. The Roman system had done no spiritual good for the people, so that Paul appeared to them in their ignorance, fear and superstition.

Perhaps the outstanding weakness in the Gauls was their caprice, well known in that day and not eradicated when they accepted Christ, as we shall see later. They were an inconstant people who changed their minds easily. They lacked two essential attributes of Christian character: *spiritual discernment* and *steadfast determination*. That this was their glaring fault is confirmed by secular historians and such passages as Galatians 1:6; 3:1, 3; 4:9. Obviously, they were without deep-seated convictions about divinely revealed truth, a conviction that can be formed only by careful thinking and unwavering faith in the Word of God.

However, we dare not judge the Galatians but remember

our own shortcomings relative to Christian experience. The Galatians had been led astray in doctrinal belief by Jewish proselytes who, while professing to be Christians, had not fully been delivered from Judaistic legalism. Why were they led so easily? No doubt these new converts to Christianity had a sincere desire in their hearts to live a holy life, a desire that very often grips the heart of many a newborn babe in Christ. With such a desire they would be an easy prey to the more experienced and trained Jewish students of the Old Testament. The false teachers were aware of this, hence their approach to the Galatians, telling them that the way for a young Christian to perfect himself in the faith was to be circumcised and keep the Law of Moses (Gal. 4:10, 11; 5:2, 3). The false teachers had the Scriptures on their side and could show these young converts to Christ that the Old Testament supported their claims. The doctrine of works has always appealed to newly saved persons, since their hearts have become fired with a desire to attain to holy living. Thus the Galatians were led in a very subtle way back to the law and to trusting in their own works to commend them to God.

One of the tragedies in church history has been the blight of the Galatian error in the life of the church. A belief in salvation by faith *and* works is not uncommon in our day. There always have been those in our churches who hold that works must be added to faith if one is to be justified before God. But the gospel of pure grace and the doctrine of Judaistic legalism are contradictory systems and will not mix. It is impossible to accept the first and at the same time hold to the second.

Though we cannot dwell any longer here on the inconstancy of the Galatian Christians, we can heed the solemn warnings repeated in the Word of God to beware lest we ourselves fall into the same error. The exhortation to steadfastness is sounded again and again. We need to "hold the beginning of our confidence stedfast unto the end" (Heb. 3:14). "Ye therefore, beloved, seeing ye know these things before, beware lest ye also, being led away with the error of the wicked, fall from your own stedfastness" (2 Peter 3:17). There are many false teachers who are "beguiling unstable souls" (2 Peter 2:14), and of these we must beware.

C. The Purpose

The object of this Epistle to the Galatians is to correct the double error of legalism: namely, that a man is saved partly by faith and partly by good works, and that a man is kept saved and finally perfected by a combination of faith and works.

Moreover, as we shall study in greater detail in the succeeding chapters, it was written to defend Paul's apostolic authority, since the Jews were anti-Paulinists who had sought to discredit both the authority of the man Paul and his message. So Paul wrote this letter to defend his apostleship and to show that the gospel he preached was from God, absolutely free from any taint of human reasoning.

Furthermore, Paul found it necessary to show that salvation was by grace before the Mosaic Law was given, and that the institution of the Law did not supersede grace in the least.

Another problem with which the Epistle is concerned is the relation of Gentile believers to professing Jewish believers and the Jewish ritual. This was a far greater difficulty than one might suppose, for in the very early days of Christianity it was one of the disturbing questions that agitated the Church. Not only in this Epistle but in other of Paul's writings also he shows that the middle wall of partition between Jew and Gentile has been broken down by the substitutionary death of Christ for both, and that the law which separated the two has been done away. Again and again Paul delivers a blow against the fallacy that even though a Jew accepted Jesus as the Messiah, it was necessary for him to continue in observance of the Mosaic ritual. It was this alien propaganda that Paul sought to combat. How he did this is reserved for the study of the text proper.

Another purpose in writing this Epistle to the Galatians was to answer the false claim that Peter was superior to Paul. Mind you, there is not the slightest evidence that Paul was seeking to build up a case for himself. But because Peter was one of the original twelve and was the apostle to the circumcision (Jews), they matched him against Paul who was the apostle to the uncircumcision (Gentiles) (Gal. 2:7, 8). Since the Gentiles were "aliens from the commonwealth of Israel, and strangers from the covenants of promise" (Eph. 2:12), and since Paul was the apostle to the Gentiles, the Jews rejected his message as inferior to that of Peter. In 1930 Dr. William R. Newell published a sixty-four page pamphlet entitled *Paul vs. Peter* in which he expounded the first two chapters of Galatians. At first I was not impressed with the title, but the longer I meditated upon the Epistle to the Galatians, the clearer it became to me that this was a serious problem in the early church. We shall examine Paul's answer to this false claim a little later on.

So far little has been said about any attempt on Paul's part to defend himself, only because the trouble was not primarily personal. Paul had taught that the death and resurrection of Christ comprised the sole ground of the believer in justification before God, that Christ Himself is the sole and sufficient Saviour. The Judaizers did not deny Christ, but they insisted that the death of Christ plus the circumcision of the believer was the ground of salvation. Basically this was the condition that called forth the Epistle.

Epitomizing the purpose of the Epistle, we find it was written to set forth *Grace* in contrast to *Law, Faith* in contrast to *Works,* the *Flesh* and its *Works* in contrast to the *Spirit* and His *Fruit,* the *World* in contrast to the *Cross,* the *True Gospel* in contrast to *Another Gospel, Bondage* in contrast to *Freedom* and the *Old Covenant* in contrast to the *New Covenant.*

There is an unusual tone of severity about this book. In contrast to Philippians and Colossians, there is no word of praise nor request for prayer. How could he praise God for a people who had transferred their allegiance from the grace of Christ to a spurious gospel? How could he give thanks to God with the evidence of their vacillation and forgetfulness so obvious? He could not even call them to pray for others, since they themselves had backslidden and were not walking in fellowship with the Lord. To write words of commendation at a time like this would be deceitful and flattering. The enemies of the Cross had corrupted the gospel of grace, and the false teaching needed to be exposed and condemned. These careless Christians themselves needed to be rebuked and reproved.

II. PERSONAL

(Chapters 1 and 2)

In these two chapters Paul authenticates his apostleship. This is the apostle's personal appeal.

A. The Ascription Is Proclaimed (1:1-5).

B. The Anathema Is Pronounced (1:6-10).

C. The Apostleship Is Proved (1:11-2:21).

A. *The Ascription Is Proclaimed* (1:1-5)

With a sound as firm and full as a trumpet blast, Paul clarions his first strong but clear note of attack to his Galatian friends: "Paul, an apostle." Thus he lays claim to the divinely commissioned office of a messenger from God.

The word *apostle* is the English form of *apostolos,* a Greek word which means "to send." The word is used of a messenger on a commission, with proper credentials to represent another. Literally he is a "sent one," a "messenger" or "minister" or "ambassador." Actually no one of these words fully describes; "apostle" is the total of all these ideas.

Paul's office of apostleship having been challenged, he was compelled to lift up his standard by stressing the fact of his being a divinely appointed messenger. His appointment was "not of men, neither by man." His was not a false office with authority derived from human source.

Today there are men like Paul who are sent directly of God, who serve well in the Christian ministry, but who never had the laying on of men's hands. Prophets in the Old Testament were so commissioned. Then there are other men today who have received their commission from God and yet have been examined by a body of men for recommendation to the church. But the sad plight of the Church is the great number in the ministry who either receive their commission from men and not from God, or else receive no commission at all. Paul's office was that of a true apostle with the divine commission "by Jesus Christ, and God the Father, who raised Him from the dead."

Paul fortifies his argument and himself by linking with himself others whom he calls "the brethren which are with me." These were Christian brethren who were possibly members of some local church, or perhaps Paul's companions in travel. He had some very strong things to say to the churches of Galatia, and he wanted the Christians there to know that all the brethren supported him in what he was about to say. In this way Paul's companions became joint-authors, with their authorization stamped upon his message.

"Grace be to you and peace from God the Father, and from our Lord Jesus Christ." Not once in the Epistles do we find a salutation in which peace precedes grace. God's peace is never enjoyed where God's grace has not been received and retained. Let this be applied to the believer as well as to the unbeliever.

The Galatian Christians had been saved by grace, but they had fallen from grace in that they accepted the erroneous teaching that they must observe the Law of Moses in order to keep saved. In their turning from Grace to Law they lost the joy and peace which came only through believing (faith). Many of our busy church members would be less frantic and less fanatical, enjoying a fuller measure of peace, if they had a new appreciation of the sustaining grace of our Lord Jesus Christ. Both grace and peace have their source in God the Father and their substance in the Person and work of His Son. Grace came down from above in all its plenitude when Christ came into the world (John 1:17 and Titus 2:11), and through the shedding of His Blood He made peace (Col. 1:20), so that joy and peace in salvation is by Christ rather than by character.

Now Paul must remind the Galatians that the grace of God which brought joy and peace was purchased at great cost. The risen Christ to whom he refers in verse one is also the crucified Christ, for He "gave Himself for our sins, that

He might deliver us from this present evil world . . ." The
death and resurrection of Christ are stated at the very beginning, since both of these great truths are essential in a
defense of the doctrine of Justification by Faith. We are
"justified by His blood" (Rom. 5:9), and though He was
delivered for our offenses, He "was raised again for our
justification" (Rom. 4:25).

The apostle states clearly that one of the reasons for the
sacrifice of Christ is our sins. First, He gave Himself for
our sins—our worst sins, sensual and devilish sins, past,
present and prospective. He did not ask us to give *ourselves*,
but He offered Himself as our Substitute and gave *Himself*.
When Christ died, God laid on Him the iniquity of us all
(Isa. 53:6), and in view of such a divine act of grace no
system of law-works could stand.

Then, He gave Himself that He might deliver us from
this present evil age. The world-system is in the lap of the
Evil One, and that system is antagonistic to the work of God
in Christ for sinners. Satan is the god of this age, hence it
must be evil. Here Paul refers to the *age* as a period of time
and not to the physical world. The history of the world is
divided into great periods, or "ages," and this present age
preceding the return of our Lord Jesus Christ is an evil one.

Our deliverance from this present evil age may be understood in two ways: (1) as a present deliverance from the evil
tendencies and characteristics of the world; (2) as a future
deliverance out of this world when the believers are caught
away at the coming of our Lord for His own. It is only
because the Lord Jesus has dealt so thoroughly with the sin
question that we can join the apostle in his ascription of
praise, and say, "To whom [Him] be glory for ever and
ever. Amen."

B. The Anathema Is Pronounced (1:6-10).

No sharper rebuke can be found in the Pauline writings.
This solemn pronouncement is leveled at perverters of the

gospel of Christ. Keep in mind that these are not words of a defendant with an uncontrolled tongue. This Epistle in its entirety is the message from God spoken first to Paul by the Holy Spirit. Paul was writing to the Galatians only that which God told him to write. The private interpretations and human inventions about the gospel are here condemned.

What prompted such stern reproof? False teachers were leading young Christians astray. Said Paul: "I marvel that ye are so soon removed from Him that called you into the grace of Christ unto another gospel." The verb *are removed* used here is in the present progressive tense and suggests that the Galatian Christians were only in the *act* of turning. Their declension was yet in progress. Therefore Paul hastens to arrest them in their downward course away from the truth and to turn them back to it.

Other translations read as follows:

I am amazed that you are so readily deserting for a different gospel Him who called you by the grace of Christ. (*Weymouth*)

I marvel that ye are so quickly removing from Him that called you in the grace of Christ unto a different gospel. (*American Standard Version*)

I am amazed that you are so soon shifting your ground, and deserting Him who called you by the grace of Christ, for another gospel. (*Centenary*)

I am astonished that you are beginning so soon to turn away from Him who called you by the favor of Christ, to a different good news. (*Williams*)

It is indeed a thing to be marveled at that one who has tasted the good word and the grace of God could be led off into erroneous teaching that can never satisfy the human heart. Our Lord ministered in Nazareth, His own country, and "He marvelled because of their unbelief" (Mark 6:6). Actually there is no other gospel to lure us; they are the perversions of the gospel of Christ of which we need to be wary. The spurious gospels, of which there were, and are, many, either *add to, subtract from,* or *change* something *in* the true Gospel. It is the work of the Enemy so to pervert the gospel that those who are young and inexperienced in the faith will be unable to detect the false interpretation and misapplication of the truth.

The word *soon* (verse 6) suggests a possible reason for the failure of the Galatian believers. A better translation would read "quickly," and it would suggest their failure to give time and thought to a diligent study of the facts on both sides. No sooner had Paul left them than the Galatians allowed themselves to be seduced by the Judaistic legalizers. A hasty action taken without careful study led them to accept a perversion of the gospel more readily than they accepted the true gospel as Paul preached it.

And so the Holy Spirit warns us all against any readiness and rashness to accept the teaching of any man. Emissaries of Satan occupy places of importance in Protestant denominations today. "Such are false apostles, deceitful workers, transforming themselves into the apostles of Christ. Ond no marvel; for Satan himself is transformed into an angel of light. Therefore it is no great thing if his ministers also be transformed as the ministers of righteousness; whose end shall be according to their works" (2 Cor. 11:13-15).

Just such a hasty decision, lacking discernment, led the children of Israel to turn to the animal worship of the ancient Egyptians (Exod. 32:8). In our hurried age we need to heed Paul's exhortation to Timothy: "Lay hands suddenly on no man . . ." (1 Tim. 5:22). Much time must be given to prayer and the study of God's Word before we make decisions, especially when our decisions have to do with Christian truth and satanic error. "Beloved, believe not every spirit, but *try the spirits* whether they are of God: because many false prophets are gone out into the world" (1 John 4:1).

And now we must look at the apostolic anathema, a statement more dreadful than any other in the whole Bible. "But though we, or an angel from heaven, preach any other gospel unto you than that which we have preached unto you, let him be accursed" (verse 8). Strong language this! And yet it is God-breathed. Moreover, it is a double curse (verse 9). The word "accursed" is the word "anathema," and it referred originally to animals who were doomed to die as a sacrifice. But later the word came to be used as "a curse," or a "thing devoted to destruction." This is the sense of *anathema* here and throughout the New Testament.

Let it be clearly understood that the apostolic anathema was not an utterance of profanity, but rather *"Let the curse of God be upon him."* Two examples, one from the Old Testament and one from the New Testament, may serve to illustrate this thought (Deut. 11:26-28; Mark 11:12-14, 21). In current language one might say: "Let him be damned."

The anathema in the writings of Paul contains the idea of spiritual death. The apostle used it of himself in Romans 9:3, where he says: "I could wish that myself were *accursed* from Christ for my brethren, my kinsmen according to the flesh." Here the thought is of being eternally separated from Christ, a willingness to lose one's own salvation that others might be saved. Paul's wish could never be accomplished. If it had been possible for him to forfeit his salvation, that forfeit could not have attained the thing Paul desired. (See also Moses' request in Exodus 32:32). Since those who love not the Lord Jesus Christ are to be judged and cast out at His coming (1 Cor. 16:22), how much greater the anathema upon the false teachers who have muddled the minds of those that believe not!

The foundation truths of the Pauline gospel, which is the gospel of God, can be summed up in the words, *"Christ died for our sins according to the Scriptures; and that He was buried, and that He rose again the third day according to the Scriptures; and that He was seen . . ."* (1 Cor. 15:3-5). The vital facts of the gospel, then, are Christ's Vicarious Death, Burial, Victorious Resurrection and His Visible (or Personal) Manifestation. One's faith in the Christ who died to save him and who lives to keep him saved will deliver the believer from lapsing into a legalistic law-works combination, "for as many as are of the works of the law are under the curse" (Gal. 3:10).

Before leaving the thought of the gospel, mark the point of verses six and seven where Paul speaks of *"another* gospel: which is not *another."* The apostle here uses two Greek words, both of which are translated *another* but which have different meanings in the original. The first is *heteros,* which means *another of a different kind or quality,* and from which we derive our English word *heterodoxy.* The second is *allos,* and it means *another of the same kind or quality.* So "another gospel" of the Jewish legalist was another of a different kind and not another of the same kind. Heterodoxy is false opinion, and it differs from Paul's doctrine of the pure grace of God.

A pronouncement as strong as this would hardly come from one whose purpose was to gain personal favor. Paul had no sinful passions as selfish ambition or avarice, therefore his one purpose was to please God and not men. He could say: "For do I now persuade men, or God? or do I seek to please men? for if I yet pleased men, I should not be the servant of Christ" (verse 10). There is no mincing of words here. Paul knew that if he regulated his message so as to gain the favor of man, the blessing of God would not rest upon him or his message. If a man is to devote himself entirely to the service of Jesus Christ, he must renounce every temptation to appeal to the approbation and applause of men.

To "walk worthy of the Lord unto all pleasing" (Col. 1:10) was the constant prayer of the great apostle. When he was in Jerusalem, Paul declared the manner of his conversion and call to the apostleship and then added: "Men and brethren, I have lived in all good conscience before God until this day" (Acts 23:1).

The "servant" has only one person to please, and that person is his Lord. To seek anything other than his Lord's will would make him a traitor. Suppose I did succeed in pleasing men? While striving to do so I could not be a true bondservant (slave) of Jesus Christ. I cannot serve God and man.

It is better to be right in God's eyes than to be popular in the eyes of man. It is more profitable to walk alone with God and know that He is pleased than to have the world at my feet with God's displeasure. Certainly if Paul was concerned with influencing men in his favor, he never would have uttered so severe a pronouncement upon them. No chameleon, this man! If Paul became all things to all men, it was not because he was a trimmer or a twaddler, but that he by every means might save some (1 Cor. 9:22), "not as pleasing man, but God" (1 Thess. 2:4). Christians, beware of pleasing either ourselves or others.

C. *The Apostleship Is Proved* (1:11-2:21)

Paul proves his apostleship by a most convincing threefold argument:

1. His Revelation from God (1:11-21)
2. His Recognition by the Apostles (2:1-10)
3. His Rebuke of and Reasoning with Peter (2:11-21)

At the outset of this apologetic appeal, Paul *assures* them by use of the words, *"I certify you . . ."* (verse 11). In other words, a certified statement of facts is about to follow. His opponents argued that Paul was not of the original twelve who met with the risen Christ before His ascension, therefore he could not possibly be one of Christ's true apostles. It is the old satanic method of discrediting the man. The devil used this same approach against Job (Job 1:9).

So as to leave no doubt in their minds concerning the truth of the statements he is about to make, Paul starts out by saying, "I tell you plainly . . ." Not as though the Galatians had not known before the grounds of Paul's claim to apostleship does he begin thus. To remind them of the facts he says, "I tell you plainly." He was directed by the Spirit to use this same language elsewhere (see 1 Corinthians 12:3; 15:1).

First, Paul based his argument upon his revelation from

God. In the verses now under consideration he used the words "reveal" and "revelation" no less than three times (1:12, 16; 2:2), and then later he speaks of "the faith which should afterwards be revealed" (3:23). The gospel of Christ is not a gospel "after man."

This is particularly true of the gospel according to Paul since he had a unique message to deliver. Paul was exclusively called by God to set forth "mysteries" (hitherto unrevealed truth). Until these mysteries were shown unto Paul they were "hid in God" (Eph. 3:3, 9), therefore he could receive them from no one but God Himself, and that by revelation.*

We are not told how the Lord revealed these great truths of the gospel to Paul, but we may be certain that it was a supernatural revelation. Some modern ministers will not believe in a "revealed religion," but the fact of revelation is clearly stated in the Bible. Revelation is a communication of supernatural knowledge from God; and the Christian's theistic belief in a God who created and controls the universe leads him to believe also that such a One as God can reveal Himself to His creatures. God revealed Himself in *epiphanies* (appearances of God before the Incarnation of Jesus Christ), in dreams and in direct converse with certain of His children. But the finality of God's revelation rests in Jesus Christ (Heb. 1:1), and from Him Paul received these great fundamental truths of the Christian Gospel.

Paul had the plan of salvation revealed to him by Stephen (Acts 7:58-8:1). Then came his marvelous conversion while on his way to Damascus when he saw the glorified Christ in Person (Acts 9:1-6). From then on it was a series of revelations from the Lord Himself directly to Paul. We fail completely if we attempt to account on natural grounds for Paul's conversion, his call to the apostleship and his profound writings. It

---

* The mysteries of (1) Blind Israel (Rom. 11:25). (2) The Faith (1 Tim. 3:9). (3) Godliness (1 Tim. 3:16). (4) Christ and the Church (Rom. 16:25-27; Eph. 3:3-10). (5) The Rapture of the Saints (1 Cor. 15:51). (6) Lawlessness (2 Thess. 2:7).

was God who had separated him (or set him apart) for the work of the ministry. God spoke to him at Corinth (Acts 18:9), at Jerusalem (Acts 23:11), and even in the instructions concerning the Lord's Supper (1 Cor. 11:23). And when any man receives his instructions from the Lord first hand, he can say with the apostle: "Immediately I conferred not with flesh and blood" (verse 16).

Paul did not *conceive* his gospel; he *received* it. After his conversion he did not go up to Jerusalem where the other apostles had learned much, but instead he went into Arabia (1:17) where the Lord met Him. Paul's early education in the rigid school of Jewish ritualism was part of his argument that he did not receive the gospel from man, certainly not the Christian Gospel, since his early training had developed in him a hatred for Christianity (1:13). No human agency could possibly have brought about such a change in the man who at one time relentlessly persecuted the followers of Christ. He was out to ruin and destroy property and people identified with Christianity. Ony God could change such a heart.

Paul had not gone to any school for the apostles, but spent three years with the Lord in Arabia and Damascus, after which he went to Jerusalem to visit Peter (1:18). He could not have been taught by any of the other apostles, since he saw none, save James the Lord's brother (1:19). Having discussed as solemn a subject as this, he wants it understood that he has spoken the truth, for, said Paul: "Before God, I lie not" (1:20).

Second, Paul based his argument upon his recognition by the apostles (2:1-10). Remember, the apostle is not writing an autobiography; he is defending his apostleship, and these details of his personal history are written to strengthen his argument. The incident he is about to relate will support the claim he has made. It will help to prove his apostleship.

When Paul did return to Jerusalem fourteen years later (2:1), he was careful not to affiliate himself too closely with the other apostles there. At least for the first fourteen years of his Christian life he maintained his independence of the others. His visit to Jerusalem was in the company of Barnabas and Titus for the purpose of declaring freedom from the law of Moses. Even there the Gentile believers were being instructed that it was necessary for them to be circumcised according to the Mosaic rite (Acts 15:1-11). Notice that Paul adds for emphasis how he took Titus "also" (2:1).

This choice of a companion was rather significant. Titus was a Gentile who had never submitted to any Jewish rite, but he had been saved through faith in Christ, and that without any thought whatsoever of keeping the law of Moses. Titus might serve as a living demonstration of Paul's argument and be used as a test case in favor of the Gospel of Grace. It suggests somewhat the preparation and determination with which Paul stood his ground in order that the gospel of our Lord Jesus Christ should not be perverted.

This visit to Jerusalem where Paul received apostolic recognition was by "revelation." It was a divinely-directed journey. Even if the other apostles had not been ready to recognize the man Paul and his message, the approval of God was upon both. If it was the desire of the church to have Paul come to Jerusalem (Acts 15:2), that desire was proof all the more that God wanted him there. Paul went, not by human *recommendation* but by divine *revelation*.

A church calling a minister may or may not be in the will of God. But when God directs a church to call a certain minister and at the same time speaks directly to the minister to go to that church, it is certain that He has a plan to be carried out. God prepares a church for His servant and His servant for a church. A good illustration of this is seen in Peter's call to the house of Cornelius. Before the call came to Peter, God was making it plain to Cornelius that he should send for Peter (Acts 10). In the Acts account, Luke, by the Holy Spirit, shows us in detail how God works in such cases, while in Galatians Paul, by the same Spirit, relates the inner experience of the call. One thing is certain, Paul did not have to sell himself to the other apostles. After almost fifteen years of service for Christ, during which time they doubtless watched him intently, they were ready to recognize both Paul and his preaching.

This recognition of Paul by the others was the result of his master-planning which came to him by divine revelation. Realizing that the success of his ministry was at stake, Paul doubtless sought the mind of the Lord in every detail. First, he sought preliminary private interviews with the recognized leaders of the Church (the apostles). He presented God's message "privately to them which were of reputation" (2:2). If there was to be any difference of interpretation, that difference would have to be straightened among the apostles first. If the leaders could not agree, then Paul felt that he would have entered the contest in vain. It was in these private gatherings where this mighty servant of Jesus Christ first won apostolic recognition.

Then, too, Paul gained recognition when they observed his vast knowledge and clear statements of the facts in the case. He was there to refute the erroneous doctrines of false teachers, and in so doing he exposed with accuracy both the method and the message of the legalists.

As to the *method* of the false brethren, they "came in privily to spy out our liberty which we have in Christ Jesus" (2:4). These "false brethren" who may have been unconverted Jews, had slyly and subtly infiltrated the Christian converts to spy out with hostile intention. Like enemies during warfare they had been smuggled in to search out with a view to overthrowing. The end of these men was the complete destruction of the Christian faith and they would stoop to any depth to accomplish it. Paul had thorough knowledge of their method.

As to their *message,* they emphasized the keeping of the Mosaic law, particularly the rite of circumcision. Now circumcision was a national rite enjoined by God upon Abraham and his male descendants. It was also a Jewish religious privilege, so that it was common among the Israelites to refer to the Gentiles as "the uncircumcised" (Judges 15:18; 2 Sam. 1:20).

But circumcision carried with it a moral responsibility which Israel did not always fulfill, and in the time of her spiritual declension God said: "I will punish all them which are circumcised with the uncircumcised . . . for all these nations are uncircumcised, and all the house of Israel are uncircumcised in the heart" (Jer. 9:25, 26). Paul was simply expounding the Hebrew writings when he said: "For circumcision verily profiteth, if thou keep the law: but if thou be a breaker of the law, thy circumcision is made uncircumcision . . . For he is not a Jew, which is one outwardly; neither is that circumcision, which is outward in the flesh: But he is a Jew, which is one inwardly; and circumcision is that of the heart, in the spirit, and not in the letter; whose praise is not of men, but of God" (Rom. 2:25, 28, 29).

In the economy of Grace no merit is attributed to any ordinance performed in the flesh. The true believer neither walks in the flesh nor performs the works of the flesh, and to all who are saved and led by the Spirit, God says: "Ye are circumcised with the circumcision made without hands, in putting off the body of the sins of the flesh by the circumcision of Christ" (Col. 2:11). If any Gentile submitted to circumcision he thereby was forced to assume responsibility to keep the whole law, and in so doing he denied the grace of God in Christ! Messiah died in the flesh, and when He was cut off, all who put their trust in Him should be saved.

When the apostles heard this marvelous teaching they grasped (perceived) the facts of grace, and, writes Paul, "they gave to me and Barnabas the right hands of fellowship" (2:9). Thus Paul was a recognized apostle of Jesus Christ and was invited by the other apostles into a common partnership in the gospel. The only basis of Christian fellowship is in the true knowledge of the Person and work of the Son of God.

Third, Paul based his argument upon his rebuke *of* and reasoning *with* Peter (2:11-21). The rebuke was something

Peter needed and he knew it, for he acquiesced to Paul's remonstrance and gave assent to his doctrinal position. Though men today worship Peter as the infallible first "Pope," he showed, at least in this instance, that he was far removed from infallibility.

Paul withstood Peter to the face (2:11) for his middle-of-the-road position (2:12), and he speaks of that rebuke, not to magnify himself, but to prove his position as an apostle. He had no personal grievance against Peter. The authority of the gospel was at stake, and here he had an opportunity to defend, not only his apostolic authority, but the very heart of his doctrine. Peter attended the Council at Jerusalem when all agreed that the observance of the Mosaic law was not a condition of salvation; therefore, because of his inconsistency Paul resisted him to his face. This was not difficult for Paul to do, since Peter stood condemned by his own conduct.

Peter's conduct was that of a hypocrite. Instead of keeping his eyes on the Lord, he fixed them on man, and the old cowardly fear which he showed the night of Christ's denial overcame him again. He tried in his own strength to be a man-pleaser, changing his conduct without letting each side know what he was doing. When it was convenient for him, Peter would sit at the Gentiles' table and eat the food of the Gentiles that was forbidden the Jews under Mosaic legislation. But when the Jews brought pressure to bear upon him, then Peter would discontinue the practice in order to please them. Poor Peter! He knew better, for God had revealed to him that the work of Christ at Calvary had set aside the Levitical legislation (Acts 10). Paul was not subordinate to Peter, therefore the vacillating course that Peter took called for the rebuke. Paul relates the incident merely to strengthen his apostolic authority.

The sin of Peter did not fail to bring its sad results (2:13). His wrong-doing led others to follow him. Peter's refusal to eat with the Gentile believers split the church. It was bad enough for Paul to see Peter acting as he did, but when

Barnabas and others were carried away by Peter's hypocrisy and withdrew from the Gentiles with Peter, it was doubtless a shocking blow. Barnabas had been Paul's co-worker in the evangelization of the Gentiles, and now to see him join in the role of the hypocrite disturbed Paul greatly.

We may learn from this that not one of us lives unto himself. Both actions and words are bound to have telling effects upon the lives of others. Thank God for Paul's courage. In his rebuke of Peter he defended his apostleship, to be sure. But more than this, he rebuked us all.

Now Paul did not stop with the *rebuke*. He went on to *reason* with his erring brother in Christ (2:14-21). Paul saw the seriousness of the situation plus the stigma cast against the Gentile believers in particular and the whole cause of Christ in general. Since Peter was the chief offender Paul commenced to reason with him, seeking to show to Peter the inconsistency between his belief and his behavior.

Paul's first line of reasoning opens with a question in verse 14. Said he: "Peter, if you, who are a converted Jew, are sitting down to eat with the Gentiles, and not with the Jews, how can you sincerely compel the Gentiles to live after the manner of the Jews?" Certainly this question must have shown to Peter the inconsistency of trimming his sails with the change of the wind. Paul, of course, was referring to Peter's past habit before he was influenced by the legalists. How unfair Peter had been toward the Gentiles when he compelled them to keep the law while he, being a Jew, left himself at liberty! We imagine that with bowed head and shamed face Peter sat in silence as Paul reasoned with him. Peter had been trying to preach what he did not practice.

In verses 15 and 16 Paul reminds his erring brother that they both, being Jews, knew the law and its inability to justify Jew or Gentile. Said Paul in effect: "Brother, we know that no man is justified by the works of the law; moreover, we ourselves had to believe in Jesus Christ in order to be justified by the faith of Christ, and not by the works of the law; for by the works of the law shall no flesh be justified." The claims of Christ had been made clear to both of them, and now if the receiving of Christ had failed to justify them before God, then Christ's claims were false and He was an impostor. In paraphrase Paul says: "If after we have accepted Christ as Saviour (which we did, seeking to be justified) we are still unsaved and in our sins, then Christ is the promoter of sin in getting us to abandon the law, and His promises are untrue. But away with any idea like that. Such a thought is preposterous!"

At the sacrifice of his own life Paul had fought to show the Gentiles blameless apart from their keeping any Jewish ceremonial rite. To attempt to restore now what he had torn down would be folly and would prove him to be a transgressor (2:18). This he could not do since he was now "dead to the law" since the law had convicted and executed him. Since he was dead to the law he was no longer under its authority. He could now "live unto God" (verse 19).

Before closing this chapter, note the word of personal testimony from the pen of that mighty apostle who perceived in the work of Calvary a power both transforming and triumphant: "I am crucified with Christ: nevertheless I live . . ." (2:20). A paradox, do you say? Perhaps. Paul is telling us that he died to live, and his statement is by no means a confusion of words. This is not the only paradox in the Bible. One gives in order to possess. One is placed first by being last. Yes, and one dies to live. None but God's own can understand all this. But Paul is telling us simply that when Christ died, he died; and because Christ lives, he lives. Paul was no longer struggling under Law but he was serenely satisfied in Grace. So precious was the new appraisal and appreciation and appropriation of the divine Presence, that he reckoned the "old man" to have been crucified with Christ (Rom. 6:6).

Yes, and we too died, according to God's reckoning, at Calvary. The law demanded death as the righteous penalty for sin, and its penalty was executed upon us in the Person of Jesus Christ when He died as our Representative. The law that was against us, He took out of the way, "nailing it to His Cross" (Col. 2:14). Being then crucified with Him we are freed from the penalty of the broken law. The demands of the law have been fully satisfied and therefore have no more hold on us.

But thank God we did not remain dead. God was so completely satisfied with the finished work at Calvary that He raised Christ from the dead, and now we too are made alive together with Him (Eph. 2:5). "For if we have been planted together in the likeness of His death, we shall be also in the likeness of His resurrection" (Rom. 6:5). My old *self* was crucified with Christ, but now I have *His* life. No longer do I struggle for life through trying to keep the law, but I "live by the faith of the Son of God who loved me, and gave Himself for me."

Since salvation is by grace and no more of works, Paul says: "I do not set aside the grace of God." If a man can be justified by the law, then Christ went to the Cross and received no reward for His death; that is, He died to deliver us and we are not delivered. But we know better, "For Christ is the end of the law for righteousness to every one that believeth" (Rom. 10:4).

III. POLEMICAL
(Chapters 3 and 4)

Having thoroughly vindicated his apostolic authority, the apostle now proceeds with the doctrinal discussion. The personal discussion prepared the way for the *polemical*. His recognition by the apostles and his rebuke of Peter gave Paul an opportunity for stating clearly his polemic on the doctrine of Justification by Faith. It is this great theme which is set forth in the two chapters we are now considering. Preachers and teachers will profit greatly by studying carefully this argument in defense of the finished work of Christ for the salvation of sinners, to which work nothing can be added. His threefold argument is based on *Experience, Example* and *Explanation*.

A. *The Experience of the Galatians* (3:1-5)

Paul's argument from the experience of the Galatian Christians forms the immediate introduction to his polemic on Justification by Faith. He begins in unusually severe language addressed to believers: "O foolish Galatians, who hath bewitched you, that ye should not obey the truth, before whose eyes Jesus Christ hath been evidently set forth, crucified among you?" (3:1). The men from Jerusalem had come among the Galatians, teaching them that they could not be saved unless they were circumcised and kept the Law of Moses. The Galatian converts appeared to be charmed by this teaching.

The Galatians were not to be excused since the substitutionary death of Christ at Calvary had been depicted so plainly before their very eyes and minds. Paul is not insinuating that the Galatians were naturally stupid and senseless. But there is a tinge of indignant sadness in his heart because Paul himself had graphically portrayed to them the sufferings and death of the Saviour as the only remedy for the sins of the world. Now they had failed to use their powers of perception, or, to put it in modern parlance, they were not using their heads.

Was this issue serious enough to arouse Paul to this outburst of passion? Indeed so! What sanctified mind could refrain from breaking out into indignation upon discovering that those who had heard the gospel preached in such clearness were now considering rejecting it? Paul had preached to them the sufferings of Christ as one who was an eye-witness of His precious blood, and now they were so soon forgetting. Keith Brooks has said: "When the mariner loses sight of his guiding star, the ship may drift into strange waters. The Cross is the central force of Christianity. When it falls from view, or is minimized, Christianity declines." We act foolishly indeed when we turn our eyes away from our Lord Jesus Christ who purchased and paid for us with His own Blood. (See Luke 24:25; Matthew 14:28-31.)

In pressing his argument by appealing to the experience of the Galatians, Paul continues to interrogate. The second of his questions is in verse two: "This only would I learn of you, Received ye the Spirit by the works of the law, or by the hearing of faith?" When they heard and believed th , Gospel of the Grace of God, they received the Holy Spirit. Now Paul would have them testify whether they received the Spirit by observance of the ceremonial law of Moses or by believing in Jesus Christ. There could be but one answer; the gift of the Spirit was an act of God upon those who would receive Him by faith. They knew that the Holy Spirit had not been bestowed upon them because of any amount of works they could have done, for while the law demands works, it was evident that all works required by the law had left them helpless. It is true that man wants to do those things which appeal to him and which fit into his life plans, but works of the law are "dead works" (Heb. 6:1; 9:14) leaving the worker still "under the curse" (Gal. 3:10), for "by the works of the law shall no flesh be justified" (Rom. 3:20, A.S.V.; 4:2-5; Gal. 2:16; 3:11).

While the law demands works, grace requires faith. Grace, upon its demands for works, would cease to be grace. When a believer takes a backward look at his own Christian experience, he must admit that when he believed in the Lord Jesus Christ the Holy Spirit was given by God and it was not on the ground of any personal merit. Both Peter (Acts 10:44-48) and Paul (Acts 15:12) had been witnesses of the Spirit's work in the lives of circumcised Gentiles who had believed. And now Paul argues for Justification by Faith on the ground of this experience in the lives of the Galatian Christians.

The third question follows in the next verse: "Are ye so foolish? having begun in the Spirit, are ye now made perfect by the flesh?" (3:3). Paul's argument is logical since there was a strange inconsistency between their commencement and their continuance in the Christian life. In verse two Paul speaks of the coming of the Holy Spirit into the hearts of the Galatians when they believed; here in verse three he is speaking of the sanctifying work of the Spirit in their hearts as saints. It was foolish for the Galatians to think for even a moment that the work of God in their hearts begun by the Spirit could be brought to perfection in the flesh. The flesh is weak and sickly (Rom. 6:19) and it is the dwelling place of no good thing (Rom. 7:18). How foolish for even believers to think that we can expect any good thing from the flesh! And yet we are guilty. We accept Christ by faith and are born from above by the supernatural power of the Holy Spirit, but too often we settle down to a life of ease, doing those things which are convenient, or we work feverishly in the energy of the flesh. If we have been saved by the Spirit, it is folly to seek development to perfection by joining and attending some church or by practicing ritualistic observances. The flesh is no means at all to sanctification. If we have begun in the Spirit we may say with Paul: "Being confident of this very thing, that He which hath begun a good work in you will perform it until the day of Jesus Christ" (Phil. 1:6).

The fourth question continues to press Paul's argument on the ground of their experience: "Have ye suffered so many things in vain? if it be yet in vain" (3:4). Apparently the Galatians, like many other believers in the early Church, were made to suffer for their stand for Christ. When they received Paul's message they were persecuted (Acts 14:1-7, 19, 22). Was their stand to no avail? Was their suffering all a mistake? Or was their identification with Christ a sham, unreal? Now if they are going back to the very things which, when they abandoned them, caused their persecution, Paul would question the genuineness of their profession. Indeed if they had been truly saved, there could be no advantage now in abandoning the very gospel for which they suffered then. If the gospel of grace had been worth suffering for, then why turn from it?

But there was a doubt in Paul's mind that he had preached to them in vain and that they had believed in vain, for he adds: " . . . if it be yet in vain" (3:4). He is not ready to abandon hope. Looking back on those earlier experiences of the Galatians, Paul says: "I find it hard to believe that you were not truly converted to Jesus Christ. You are being led into false teaching but I desire to see you delivered." The apostle assumes the genuineness of their faith and hopes to lead them to shake off the effects of this false teaching. He could not believe that they were as those "who draw back unto perdition; but [rather] of them that believe to the saving of the soul" (Heb. 10:39).

In concluding the first phase of his polemic in which he argues from the experience of the Galatians, Paul adds his final question: "He therefore that ministereth to you the Spirit, and worketh miracles among you, doeth He it by the works of the law, or by the hearing of faith" (3:5)? We cannot be certain what these "miracles" are because we are not told. They may have reference to some physical wonder wrought supernaturally or to the miracles of regeneration worked by the Holy Spirit in their midst. No matter! The gifts of God in regeneration or the gifts bestowed upon believers for service are the fruits of the Spirit and cannot be attributed to man. The Spirit was supplied, not alone for our salvation, but that He should indwell and energize the believer. The function of the Spirit does not cease with our salvation but He maintains each child of God, meeting all the needs of the new life.

The answer to the question in this verse was inevitable. When the Galatians saw Paul and Barnabas working miracles, they knew that the power was of God and that the blessings of the gospel were imparted to those that "had faith to be healed" (Acts 14:8-15). It was "by grace—through faith" that the abundance of spiritual blessings had come to them. All believers are saved and strengthened by the Spirit through the unmerited favor of God (Eph. 3:16) and not by any works of the flesh (Ironside, pp. 95, 96).

B. *The Example of Abraham* (3:6-18)

Paul has been arguing for Justification by Faith apart from any adherence to Mosaic ritual. He commenced his polemic by illustrating the experience of the Galatians (3:1-5). Now he continues by showing that the principle of faith is not new, but that it is in keeping with God's plan for blessing His people in any age. The Old Testament character chosen by Paul to prove this is Abraham, the father of the Hebrews.

"Even as Abraham believed God, and it was accounted to him for righteousness" (3:6 cf. Genesis 15:6). The reference to Abraham as an example is significantly the work of the Holy Spirit through Paul. The Jewish teachers would proudly point to Abraham as the founder and father of their race and the channel of their spiritual blessings. Such reasoning in the minds of the Jews was anticipated by the apostle who proceeds to prove that only those who live by the faith-principle are the true sons of Abraham and of the promised blessing. Abraham was a Gentile to whom God gave the promise, which promise He continued to confirm until four hundred and thirty years before He gave the Law to Moses, so that Abraham was counted righteous because of faith and apart from the works of the law. No man is declared righteous because of his works. Righteousness can come only by grace through faith. By faith Abraham started, by faith he sojourned, by faith he sought a city which hath foundations whose builder and maker is God, by faith he sacrificed Isaac (Heb. 11:8-10, 17), and by faith "He staggered not at the promises of God through unbelief; but was strong in faith, giving glory to God; And being fully persuaded that, what He had promised, He was able also to perform" (Rom. 4:20, 21). Abraham believed God before his circumcision, and in grace God imputed his faith to him for righteousness (Rom. 4:10-13). It was the Word of God only that made Abraham strong to believe God, and it is our acceptance of God's Word in regard to His plan of salvation through faith in the Lord Jesus Christ that puts us right with Him.

Since the Judaizers had boasted their Abrahamic descent, Paul now will show them what true Abrahamic descent is. "Know ye therefore that they which are of faith, the same are the children of Abraham" (3:7). No Jew is a true son of Abraham merely because he descended by blood generation, but he only who believes God as did Abraham. God foresaw that the Gentiles would ultimately be justified by faith, and He made it clear in His message to Abraham, saying: "In thee shall all nations be blessed" (3:8).

Salvation by grace through faith is not some new thing. God had told to Abraham that very gospel (good news) beforehand. Man is saved by the faith-principle in every age whether he be Jew or Gentile. Contrariwise, if he will not believe, then he is lost even as were those unbelieving Jews to whom Jesus said: "Ye are of your father the devil" (John 8:44). The gospel which God preached to Abraham is the same gospel that Paul preached. Abraham believed in the *promised* Seed (Gen. 15:1-6; 17:19) and that Seed is Christ (Gen. 3:15 cf. Gal. 3:16). Now the Seed has been *provided,* and by the same operation of faith God imputes His righteousness to us when we believe. You see, Abraham was promised a spiritual posterity as well as a natural posterity, and every believing sinner from all the families of the earth becomes Abraham's spiritual posterity (3:29).

To all who relinquish confidence in works, and who, through faith, rest their righteousness and hope of eternal life on the grace and mercy of God, to them I say that God will save even as He saved Abraham. "So then they which be of faith are blessed with faithful Abraham" (3:9), not because we are circumcised as Abraham was circumcised later, nor because of any observance of the law which was given later, but because we believe God as did Abraham who by faith alone obtained the blessing.

"For as many as are of the works of the law are under the curse: for it is written, Cursed every one that continueth not in all things which are written in the book of the law to do them" (3:10). The Galatians were in the act of making a choice to live under the law, and Paul would remind them that when a man chooses to live on the plane of the law he must of necessity accept the consequences if he fails. Or, to put it a little differently, if one places his trust in the works of the law to justify himself, he is exposed to its curse, for the law demands that he who transgresses any part of the law is cursed, "For whosoever shall keep the whole law, and yet offend in one point, he is guilty of all" (James 2:10). It is evident that no man, dead or now living, our Lord Jesus Christ excepted, has fully kept the law, and Paul's argument stands, since that man is as powerless as an infant to fulfill that law, notwithstanding the false teaching of Romish dogma. John Calvin has said that the blessing which the law offers is excluded by our depravity and the curse alone remains.

And what is the curse? The Ten Commandments cannot be the curse, for they embrace the very highest moral and ethical standard for regulating human life. Deuteronomy, chapters 27 and 28, makes it clear that the curse was God's penalty of

death enacted upon any man who did not "keep *all* the commandments" (27:1; 28:15). Paul, quoting the law, said:
"Cursed is every one that hangeth on a tree" (Gal. 3:13 cf.
Deut. 21:23). The Jews put the lawbreaker to death by
stoning, but their custom was to hang the dead body on a tree.
Do you not see how dangerous it is for a man to put himself
under the law? For in so doing he puts himself under a curse.

The curse is twofold: (1) a present condition of alienation
from God in this life, (2) final banishment from His presence
in eternity. A man must render an obedience to the law which
is complete and continuous or else be subject to its curse.
Doing the best we can is not good enough. We are violators,
and since the law is a "ministration of death" and a "ministration of condemnation" (2 Cor. 3:7, 9), all who are under
the law are condemned because they have failed to keep it.

But thanks be unto God for the escape He has in mercy
provided. "Christ hath redeemed us from the curse of the law,
being made a curse for us . . ." (3:13). This is the good
news. Neither Jew nor Gentile could free himself from the
curse of the law. But the difficulty has been solved, for when
Jesus Christ hung upon the Tree, He fell under the curse and
the curse of all men was laid upon Him (Isa. 53:6). This does
not make sense to a legalistic unbeliever, "for the preaching
of the cross is to them that perish foolishness" (1 Cor. 1:18),
but yet it pushes far into the background the wisdom of this
world.

A loving Father could not curse His sinless son whom He
loved, and that Son still remain the object of the Father's love.
The curse of the broken law rested upon all, and Christ, who
alone rendered perfect obedience to the law, assumed the
place of penalty for all. This is the great Biblical truth of the
vicarious sufferings and death of the Son of God who had paid
the price for sins. Christ the perfect Sacrifice offered Himself
to bestow a perfect salvation. The Guiltless One died for the
guilty; the Just One died for the unjust; the Sinless One died
for the sinner. And why did He do it? "That the blessing of

Abraham might come on the Gentiles through Jesus Christ; that we might receive the promise of the Spirit through faith" (3:14). Christ "was made a curse for us" that the blessing of salvation, promised to Abraham, might come to all who believe. When He took our curse He brought to us the blessing promised to Abraham. Christ Himself never violated the law, thus He never came under its penalty; but He subjected Himself to the penalty of that law in our place that we, through faith, might receive the promised Spirit.

Verse 11 contains a statement which seems to be the very heart of Paul's argument. I refer to the words, *"The just shall live by faith."* This tremendous statement appears once before in the Old Testament and twice more in the New Testament as follows: "Behold, his soul which is lifted up is not upright in him: but the just shall live by his faith" (Hab. 2:4).

This secret which God made known to the prophet Habakkuk had its primary application to Israel in those dark days following the cutting-off of King Josiah. Israel's hope was in the coming of Messiah, and it is to His coming that the five "its" of verse three refer. They were to wait for HIM. But the Hope of Israel is also the Hope of all nations in all ages, for the five "its" in the prophecy of Habakkuk become "He" in Hebrews 10:37, where we read: "For yet a little while, and *He* that shall come will come, and will not tarry." If all seemed hopeless to Israel, God would assure His people that there was still hope if they would but believe in Him who was to come. But faith must be exercised. In this vision given to Habakkuk Israel would find food for her faith. Though circumstances all around them seemed to conrtadict their hopes, they would *live* in the present through *faith* in Messiah's coming.

Now very often the New Testament writers by inspiration of the Holy Spirit borrowed from these great passages in the Old Testament. Three times in the New Testament we find the statement which was recorded first by Habakkuk, *"The just shall live by faith."* Let us bear in mind that there are no vain repetitions in the Holy Scriptures. This mighty statement in God's Word is clearly understood only as we study it in the light of each individual context in which it appears. The question arises, "How then can man be just with God?" The answer is given in the three New Testament Epistles where we read, "The just shall live by faith."

The first New Testament passage, referring to the gospel of pure grace, says: "For therein is the righteousness of God revealed from faith to faith: as it is written, *The just shall live by faith*" (Rom. 1:17). Here the emphasis is put upon the first two words so that the answer reads, *"The just* shall live by faith." Who can live by faith? None but the just. The unbeliever cannot live by faith simply because he has not believed. Only the man who has been justified through believing on the Lord Jesus Christ can live by faith. It is only the man that is righteous who possesses life, and that not because of his adherence to the law, but by faith. Hence it is that man and only that man who can keep on living a life of faith. How can a man live by faith? He cannot, unless he has been justified by the blood of Jesus Christ. None but the righteous can live by the principle of faith. It was faith in Messiah's appearing that kept the believing Jew in the time of adversity, and it is also faith in Him that keeps the child of God in this present age. The unjust have nothing to carry them through life simply because they will not believe. Many unbelievers commit suicide, while others exist the span of a lifetime, fearful and hopeless. But *the just* shall live by faith.

The second New Testament passage is the one we are considering in our study of Paul's Epistle to the Galatians, and here we place the emphasis on the middle two of these six monosyllables, and read "The just *shall live* by faith" (Gal. 3:11). The Galatians' error was the false teaching of Judaism which supposed that while a man received eternal life by faith he could retain it only if he did certain works and adhered to the Mosaic ritual. In answering this false claim the point of the quotation from Habakkuk is that a man who has been

declared "just" by "faith" *shall live* apart from works. A life
that is commenced on the faith principle continues on that
same principle. When God declares a man righteous, that man
"shall never die" (John 11:26). Eternal life for the believer is
secured by God the very moment he is justified "through faith
in His Son." Hence Paul's question: "Having begun in the
Spirit, are ye now made perfect by the flesh?" (Gal. 3:3).
There can be but one answer: The just *shall live* by faith, and
that apart from the works of the flesh.

The Epistle to the Hebrews takes up the last two words, so
that we read: "The just shall live *by faith*" (10:38). Here the
force of the argument is an emphasis on the nature and power
of faith. *The just shall live,* not by works but *by faith,* not
because of what he is doing and might do, but because he has
believed. The justified man is declared righteous by God once
and for all when he savingly believes in the Lord Jesus Christ,
and the faith that was exercised in the Lord Jesus the moment
he was saved will keep him justified and alive unto God for-
evermore. Christian faith lives, not only in the visible present,
but in the unseen future. Andrew Murray has said: "Let our
faith so live in the future, that all our life may be in the power
of eternity, and of Him in whom eternity has its glory." The
righteous man will put his trust in God even in the midst of
trial and trouble. Faith is the principle which motivates the
whole life of the believer, and the truly righteous one will keep
on believing.

The argument for Justification by Faith based upon the
example of Abraham is concluded with Paul's explanation of
the Abrahamic covenant. There are at least seven recognized
covenants in the Bible, the Abrahamic covenant being the
third; and this Paul now refers to as a climactic point in his
polemic against the idea of salvation by works of law. God's
covenant with Abraham was actually an unconditional promise.
Notice the frequent use of the words "promise" and "promises"
in the remaining verses of chapter three (14, 16-19, 21, 22, 29).
One's pledge to another to do or not to do something is con-

sidered as sacred, especially inviolable when a document or contract is signed and sealed. Now God pledged Himself to Abraham and to Abraham's Seed, and it is this divine promise the apostle is considering.

"Brethren, I speak after the manner of men; Though it be but a man's covenant, yet if it be confirmed, no man disannulleth, or addeth thereto" (3:15). When men make a covenant they are expected to live up to it, moreover, if it be confirmed, no one could add to it or take from it in any way. But here we are thinking of a covenant between God and man. Now if among men a covenant stands until carried out, how much more will that be true when God is the Covenant Maker! David never violated the covenant he made with Jonathan. Nor has David's God ever failed to keep His promises.

Two thousand years before Christ was born God made a covenant of unconditional grace with Abraham. "Now to Abraham and his seed were the promises made. He saith not, and to seeds, as of many; but as of one, And to thy seed, which is Christ" (3:16). Dr. William Pettingill points out that this covenant was between God on the one hand and two men on the other. These two men were Abraham and Christ. The Seed here refers not to the children of Israel generally, but to Christ and subsequently to all those who are saved by Him. Faith in Jesus Christ who is the promised Seed provides the ground and means of salvation and spiritual blessing. How derogatory for any man even to contemplate the possibility of God's covenant being less binding than that of finite man!

When He gave the promise to Abraham He confirmed it by an oath: "For when God made promise to Abraham, because He could swear by no greater, He sware by Himself . . . For men verily swear by the greater: and an oath for confirmation is to them an end of all strife. Wherein God, willing more abundantly to shew unto the heirs of promise the immutability of His counsel, confirmed it by an oath: That by two immutable things, in which it was impossible for God to lie, we might have a strong consolation, who have fled for refuge to lay hold upon the hope set before us" (Heb. 6:13, 16-18). The two "immutable things" are the promise and oath of God.

For many years Abraham had only these two, but he continued to believe because he knew God would not violate His oath. Actually the promise of God was given to Adam first (Gen. 3:15), but the oath was added to Abraham for his sake and for the sake of all the heirs of that promise. Even as the manslayer, under law, found protection in the city of refuge, so we who have fled to the cross for refuge are assured of eternal salvation through our Lord Jesus Christ. A principle throughout Scripture demands that at least two witnesses are necessary in order to establish a matter legally (Deut. 17:6; 19:15; Matt. 18:15, 16; John 8:17, 18; 2 Cor. 13:1; Rev. 22:16, 18). Thus God's promise and His oath guarantee eternal life to all who believe.

In verses 17 and 18 Paul shows that the Abrahamic Covenant was not set aside by the law of Moses given by God at Sinai. "And this I say, that the covenant, that was confirmed before of God in Christ, the law, which was four hundred and thirty years after, cannot disannul, that it should make the promise of none effect" (3:17). (Paul probably took his figure of 430 years from Exodus 12:40 and would likely suggest the time between the confirmation of the promise to the children of Abraham and the giving of the law.) The teaching here is that the Abrahamic Covenant was unconditional, and since it was not yet fullfilled it cannot be changed nor rendered void by the subsequent giving of the law.

Both Law and Grace came from God. The law was not given first. The first covenant was made by God in Christ in eternity past. It is true that "the law was given by Moses, but grace and truth came by Jesus Christ" (John 1:17), but they were not given in the order in which they are here mentioned. Jesus said to the Jews of His day: "Before Abraham was, I AM" (John 8:58), so that even though the law was given to Moses before the Son of God became incarnate, the covenant of God's grace in Christ was made even before Abraham. God gave his word in the promise which He made, and since His veracity was at stake, nothing could be taken from nor added to that covenant. "For if the inheritance be of the law, it is no more of promise: but God gave it to Abraham by promise" (3:18). The promise given to Abraham was based upon pure grace and its fulfillment did not depend upon anything that Abraham or his posterity could do. Paul is showing the Galatians that they do not need the old ceremonies but that through faith in Jesus Christ they are free. If salvation is to come through human efforts, it is not given by promise at all, "but God gave it to Abraham by promise."

C. *The Explanation of the Law* (3:19-4:31)

Remember now that we are considering Paul's argument for Justification by Faith apart from any mixture of Law-works. Thus far Paul has argued from the experience of the Galatians and the example of Abraham. At this point the apostle foresees and answers a most interesting and thought-provoking question: "Wherefore then serveth the law?" If the law has no place in salvation, why did God bother to give it? If the law cannot justify a person, why was it ordered in the first place? This is an intelligent question when we consider that it is being asked by one who had been all his lifetime in bondage to the law.

The answer to this seemingly baffling question is provided for us in the very Scriptures of the law. Before the Scriptures present to us the law of Sinai, they tell us of the Covenant of Grace, God's free promise to Abraham and to his Seed, which promise is fulfilled in Christ. Yet the Mosaic Code had a divine mission to perform. ". . . It was added because of transgressions, till the Seed should come to whom the promise was made; and it was ordained by angels in the hand of a mediator" (3:19).

The law was given in order that sin might be known for the ugly, despicable thing that it is. The heinousness and seriousness of sin were not rightly known before the law was given.

Now there are advantages and uses of the law other than the one Paul states here, but the apostle is confining Himself to that use of the law which bears on his present subject. The law was given to make sinners see their transgressions. ". . . By the law is the knowledge of sin" (Rom. 3:20). The word here for "knowledge" is *epignosis,* which means "full knowledge." Man is a sinner by nature and practice, yet only as he knows the law does he have full knowledge as to the extent of his transgressions. From the fall of man in Eden the law of conscience was in operation, but between Adam's sin and the time of the Law of Sinai, sin did not take on the character of transgression. Paul himself testified: "I had not known sin, but by the law: for I had not known lust, except the law had said, Thou shalt not covet" (Rom. 7:7). Men were sinners before the law was given, but since there was no law they were not transgressors, "for where no law is, there is no transgression" (Rom. 4:15). Therefore the law was added for the sake of transgression, for "the law entered, that the offence might abound" (Rom. 5:20). The presence of our Lord Jesus Christ in the earth, who was the very embodiment and fulfillment of the law, accomplished the same thing, for He said: "If I had not come and spoken unto them, they had not had sin: but now they have no cloke [or excuse] for their sin" (John 15:22). Responsibility increases with knowledge. (Keen p. 72).

The next phrase, *"till the Seed should come to whom the promise was made,"* shows that the law was a temporary arrangement, extending from Moses to Jesus Christ, for our Lord is that Seed to whom the promise was made (see 3:16). God never intended the law to be a way of salvation. It was a temporary covenant given for temporary purposes, and when Christ the Seed came, He fulfilled the law (Matt. 5:17-20), and He became the Author of eternal salvation to all who would obey Him (Heb. 5:9). The law remains in force to condemn the wicked (1 Tim. 1:8-14) but we who believe are "dead to the law by the body of Christ" (Rom. 7:4). The law had its commencement at Sinai through Moses and its consummation at Calvary through Jesus Christ. For twenty-five hundred years before the law was issued, man carried on without it. The law was in force upon the Jew for fifteen hundred years after it was given until our Lord Jesus came to deliver man from its curse. Now since the death of God's Son at Calvary "ye are not under the law, but under grace" (Rom. 6:14). The whole of the Mosaic administration was temporal until that One Descendant of Abraham, our Lord Jesus Christ, should come, in whom all the promises were to be fulfilled.

Notice further that "it [the law] was ordained by angels in the hand of a mediator" (3:19). The following comment by Dr. Charles R. Erdman is most satisfying on these words of Paul: "It might seem at first that this statement would glorify the law. It might remind one of the majestic scenes amid which the law was given, and of the divine sanctions under which it was enacted. On the contrary, the mention of 'angels' and the reference to Moses intimate that the law was less gracious and permanent than the promise. The latter came directly from God, but the law was given through Moses. Nor did Moses himself receive the law directly from God. It was delivered to him on Mount Sinai by the ministration of angels. Thus in the giving of the law, God is twice removed; but in giving the promise, God stands forth alone, independent, and sovereign. Hence the promise rests on a higher plane than the law." Commenting further on this difficult phrase, Bishop Moule writes: "The law was mediatized, conveyed through Moses, who stood as a third between two contracting parties, God and us. But the Promise was simply *given,* given sovereignly from Him, the ONE Personage in the great act. Without desert, without claim, without goodness on our part, He gave His CHRIST to us."

At this point the apostle anticipates another objection: "Is the law then against the promises of God?" (3:21) Does one contradict the other? Is one competing against the other? If so, then God would be made to contradict Himself since He is the Author of both the promise and the law. Paul himself does not imagine a disagreement between God's law and His promises, but he proceeds to remove any difficulty which might arise in the minds of the Galatians. And to this possible objection there can be but one answer: "God forbid: for if there had been a law given which could have given life, verily righteousness should have been by the law" (3:21).

The answer is clear and conclusive. "God forbid" that any man should ever conclude that the law is against the promise which God made to Abraham. Now there is a righteousness which is of the law and a righteousness which is of faith, but the two are never interchanged in the Scriptures. Rather they are clearly contrasted in Romans 10:5-10. The righteousness of the law says: "That the man which *doeth* those things shall live by them." The emphasis here is on the word "doeth" for the law promised life and righteousness to that man only who should obey the law perfectly.

The teaching of Moses on the righteousness which is of the law is found in Leviticus 18:5 where a man's whole past life is under review. If the Jew could thus perfectly meet every requirement of the law during his entire lifetime and never once fall below God's holy standard, he would thereby escape death—the penalty of sin. But no one, save Jesus Christ, has ever done so, hence the law cannot justify any one of us. Contrariwise, there is justification promised on the faith-principle, for "If thou shalt confess with thy mouth the Lord Jesus, and shalt believe in thine heart that God hath raised Him from the dead, thou shalt be saved" (Rom. 10:9). The emphasis here is upon the word "believe" since the actual order of experience is given in verse 10—faith first, then confession. This is "the righteousness which is of faith." Faith, then, is the ground of justification, and there is absolutely no conflict between God's law and His promises. The Law and the Gospel are not competitive, but complementary, the one to the other, and both play an important role in the economy of God.

The false teachers who had come among the Galation Christians were magnifying the law above the gospel and insist-

ing on the righteous demands of the law, but they had failed
to see that the law had no power in itself to declare the sinner
righteous, much less secure that righteousness for him. If
salvation were found in the law, righteousness could be obtained by it. But the law has no power to impart life or to
justify. How sad! Were the Galatians to leave the gospel of
grace and the completeness of the righteousness of God which
they received by faith alone to return to the bondage and
legalism of those Judaizers? Could they not see that the law
was limited by man's inability to keep it? Did they not know
from experience that the law could not compel a man to obey
its ordinances? We have a law against stealing; still men steal.
Why? Because the law can neither break the habit of stealing
in a man nor can it force him to quit stealing. It can exact the
penalty for its violations, but it cannot change the heart of
man in begetting a desire to keep the law.

"But the scripture hath concluded all under sin, that the
promise by faith of Jesus Christ might be given to them that
believe" (3:22). The answers to the two questions asked in
verses 19 and 21 are not to be found in the reasoning or
philosophy of man, but rather in the Scriptures themselves.
And notice that what the Scripture says is *conclusive!* The
Bible has concluded that all, both Jews and Gentiles, are sinners by nature and practice. This is God's classification of
every member of the human race and it is sufficient to condemn all who reject the promises of God in Jesus Christ. The
promise that God made to Abraham was fulfilled when He
sent His Son into the world. In the Lord Jesus Christ a perfect
and eternal salvation has been provided, and it is "given to
them that believe." Many passages in both the Old and New
Testaments can be adduced in support of these two propo-
sitions, namely, the universality of sin and salvation by grace
through faith. The continued practice of sin in the human race
after the law was given proves the impossibility of keeping the
law of God, and it shows further that the blessings of God are

received on the ground of faith in Christ and not on the ground of works.

"But before faith came, we were kept under the law, shut up unto the faith which should afterwards be revealed" (3:23). We shall understand more clearly the meaning of this statement after we read the American Standard Version, which reads as follows: "But before faith came, we were kept in ward under the law . . ." The words, "we were kept in ward," mean that we were perpetual prisoners under the law before the death and resurrection of Jesus Christ and the coming of the Holy Spirit at Pentecost. The idea expressed is that of a military term, and it suggests that we were held in bondage by the law. Here is a prison scene in which Israel, to whom the law was given, is primarily in view, since the Gentiles were never under the law at any time. As long as Israel was under the law she was guarded as a prisoner in bondage by the law. But during the Dispensation of Law the coming of Messiah was kept before the people as imminent, each generation living in expectancy of this prophesied event. However, when Jesus came and revealed the faith which was once delivered to the saints, He led out from the bondage of the law all who heard His voice and followed Him.

The law could not change the heart of the sinning Jew or Gentile, but because of the sinner's guilt, it could only keep him enclosed in a prison with no possible way of escape. But he could look forward in faith and hope for the coming of the true Deliverer. Hence, "the Law was our schoolmaster *to bring us* unto Christ, that we might be justified by faith" (3:24). By omitting the italicized words, *to bring us,* we learn that the law was our schoolmaster, not to *bring* us to Christ, but rather *until* Christ.

In well-regulated families among upper classes in Greek and Roman homes, it was the custom to employ a child-leader or "pedagogue." This pedagogue guarded the interests of the minor child in the home, watched over the morals of the child and protected it from undesirable associations. Daily he would accompany the child from the home to the schoolroom and then at the end of the day see the child home in safety.

Paul is here teaching the Galatians that the law was for the Jews a child-leader, a code of morals to guide them until Messiah should come. But now that Christ has come we have been brought to God's school of grace, "For the law was given by Moses, but grace and truth came by Jesus Christ" (John 1:17). No longer are we under a child-leader (the Law) (3:25), but we are all the children of God by faith in Christ Jesus (3:26). A man may become a child of God through faith in the risen Christ apart from ever having heard the Ten Commandments. Through faith in Jesus Christ we reach our majority and are no longer under the pedagogue. When those Galatians believed, they were baptized into Christ (3:27), and Paul was teaching them by the Spirit that they were the true sons of God just as much as any descendant of Abraham had been, and that not through the observance of any Mosaic law or ceremony.

Through the finished work of Christ in His death and resurrection all distinctions have been obliterated. "There is neither Jew nor Greek, there is neither bond nor free, there is neither male nor female: for ye are all one in Christ Jesus. And if ye be Christ's, then are ye Abraham's seed, and heirs according to the promise" (3:28, 29). All true believers constitute the Body of Christ (1 Cor. 12:12, 13) with no social, racial or sex distinctions. The Body of Christ is a living organism, a perfect unit, and no one member has any right to think himself better than another. The American Standard Version reads: "Ye are all one man in Christ Jesus." The law had its place until Christ came, but now it is the Lord Jesus Christ, and not the law, who has provided eternal life and justification. All who belong to Him through faith make up Abraham's spiritual posterity and therefore can claim the promised inheritance, for "if ye be Christ's, then are ye Abraham's seed, and heirs according to the promise" (3:29).

At this point the chapter division in the Scripture does not appear to be justified. The paragraph that follows (4:1-7) is a necessary part of the foregoing. In these verses the apostle is still illustrating the difference which exists between the man under law and the child of God through faith in Jesus Christ. Here we are helped to an understanding of the relative place of the Old Testament believers in contradistinction to the place of New Testament believers in this present age of grace.

"Now I say, That the heir, as long as he is a child, differeth nothing from a servant, though he be lord of all; But is under tutors and governors until the time appointed of the father" (4:1, 2). The Jew who lived under the tutelage of the law was a child under age, a minor who had not attained his maturity. As such he had absolutely nothing to say about his inheritance. A minor child might inherit a vast amount of wealth, but so long as he is a minor he dare not exercise any freedom, as an adult, over his inheritance. In many homes the parents are well able to employ servants, but fearing that their own children might miss out on necessary training in housekeeping and domestic arts they have their own sons and daughters do the work of servants. Here Israel as a minor child under the law is still in view. Like a servant, he is under authority, though one day all of God's promises to Abraham's earthly posterity (Israel) will be literally fulfilled through Messiah their earthly King. Israel under the law is but a child, an immature one who can neither speak for himself nor govern his own actions. Both his person and his property are guarded by tutors and governors until the time previously fixed by his father.

We are not to be surprised that Israel's condition under the law is spoken of by Paul as being one of "bondage" (4:3). The Mosaic Law required sacrifices, ceremonies and observances, and as a child sometimes requires correction and punishment during the formative years of his training, even so the law exacted penalties for violations. Under law the Jews were restricted by its many regulations. Old Testament believers were the children of God, but they were under age, and as such they could not enter into the Father's thoughts, nor could they approach God in the same manner as believers do in this present dispensation of grace.

Paul says: "Even so we, when we were children, were in bondage under the elements of the world" (4:3). The word *we* refers to the Jewish believers of whom Paul was one. He uses *we* in contradistinction to *ye* (verse 6), the latter referring to the Galatian believers. The expression, "the elements of the world," is used here and in Colossians 2:8, 20 as a designation for the Mosaic Law, possibly meaning the first principles given to mankind to preserve law and order in the earth.

The question arises as to why Paul says that those things which had a spiritual significance were "of the world." While this system of human government based upon the idea of ruling by law came from God, nevertheless it is a worldly system since God came down to the world's level when He issued the Law of Moses. In Old Testament times the system of legal rites and observances as a means of discipline belonged to that period during which the Jews were being prepared for the coming of Christ. Now Paul would show the Galatian believers that for them to return to these Jewish ceremonies would indicate a relapse into second childhood. Having received Christ they were delivered from legal bondage and were now full-grown sons. It is ridiculous to turn again to that principle of legislatoin employed by the world in its effort to make men do right. The Galatians, like all true believers, were new creations in Christ Jesus (2 Cor. 5:17), created unto good works (Eph. 2:10).

True the Jews were in bondage to Mosaic legislation, but during that time God was making preparation for the greatest event in world history, and "when the fulness of the time was come, God sent forth His Son, made of a woman, made under the law" (4:4). The incarnation of the Son of God was not by chance nor for a single instant before or behind time. It was a scheduled event completing the period of time designated by God, for He alone ordained the time of Messiah's coming.

Christ came "when the fulness of the time was come." (See Wuest p. 114; Erdman p. 81.)

Kenneth S. Wuest leaves us a most interesting paragraph on the word translated *sent forth*. It is *exapostello,* and it refers to the act of one who sends another with a commission to do something, the person sent being given credentials. From this Greek term we receive our English word *apostle,* which means a messenger, a sent one, an ambassador. Well does the author of the Epistle to the Hebrews write: "Consider the Apostle and High Priest of our profession, Christ Jesus" (Heb. 3:1). It was our great Apostle, the Lord Jesus Christ, who was sent by the Father to bring grace from above (John 1:16, 17) to redeem them that were under the law.

It has been stated that Paul never mentioned the Virgin Birth of our Lord. The phrase "made of a woman" certainly refers to the method of the incarnation, namely, the supernatural conception by the Holy Spirit in the Virgin's womb. Christ was born of woman, hence He is true God and true Man. He was the Son of God before His incarnation, for the Son was given before the Child was born. The eternal Sonship of Jesus Christ is proved by the fact that the Son, who was sent, must have existed before He was sent. The teaching of Paul in Galatians 4:4 coincides with Genesis 3:15 where God says that the *woman's Seed* would bruise the Serpent's head.

Notice further that when Christ came He was *"under the Law"* and therefore in subjection under the law. Although He was Lord of the law and its divine Author, He voluntarily placed Himself under the law and permitted it to make its demands upon Him. Now what will He do? Will He, by His omnipotent authority, overcome the law and strike it out of the sacred records? Indeed not! Instead, He took his place with man under the law, subjecting Himself to its restrictions and requirements. And, praise God, He established a perfect record in that He kept the law fully. Thus Christ was an acceptable sacrifice to bear our sins on the cross. He was "made under the law to redeem them that were under the law." By dying under the penalty of the law which we broke He paid our penalty, thus delivering (redeeming) us from any claims which the law would have against us. Since His death and resurrection He has raised every true believer with Himself into a heavenly realm where the law as a legalistic system does not operate.

Christ came, not only to redeem them that were under the law, but *"that we might receive the adoption of sons"* (4:5). In Christ the believer reaches his majority, passes out from under the authority of the law and is placed in the position of a full-grown son. He receives official recognition as a son, as a young man is recognized as a full-grown man on his twenty-first birthday. In Christ we will take our place before the Father as sons of God. The word *adoption* is used in the New Testament only by the Apostle Paul, and in actual experience it is a future transaction. Adoption may be defined as a sovereign act of God (Eph. 1:5), whereby He sets a goal for the believer, a goal that cannot be realized fully in this life. The proof that adoption has also a future aspect attached to it is found in Romans 8:23, where we read: ". . . even we ourselves groan within ourselves, waiting for the adoption, to wit, the redemption of our body." Here it is clearly shown to be that for which the apostle is *waiting*. Believers are already possessed of adoption positionally and have the assurance of their future in that "we have received the Spirit of adoption" (Rom. 8:15), but as sons of God and joint-heirs with Christ we will not be glorified together with Him until He comes again (Rom. 8:17). Now in eternity we will not be the sons of God any more than we are here, but in that day God will put us on display before men, angels, and demons and "shew the exceeding riches of His grace in His kindness toward us through Christ Jesus" (Eph. 2:7).

Our position as sons is realized here and now through the indwelling Holy Spirit, for Paul adds: "And because ye are sons, God hath sent forth the Spirit of His Son into your hearts, crying, Abba, Father" (4:6). The word *Abba* is an

Aramaic term somewhat similar to our English word *Papa* expressing filial relationship to God and an affectionate fondness indicating utmost confidence and trust in Him. Our Lord Himself used this expression in Gethsemane when He prayed: "Abba, Father, all things are possible unto Thee; take away this cup from Me: nevertheless not what I will, but what Thou wilt" (Mark 14:36). The same Holy Spirit who sustained Him in that dark moment would minister to us and have us trust the Father implicitly (Rom. 8:15). None of us will ever fully appreciate in this life the Person and work of our heavenly Father in our behalf, but when we stand before Him in eternity we shall know Him even as we are now known by Him.

"Wherefore thou art no more a servant, but a son; and if a son, then an heir of God through Christ" (4:7). What matchless grace and love! Through the redeeming work at Calvary's Cross we have been delivered from the servitude of the law and have become the bondservants of Jesus Christ, the true sons of God. Moreover, through the sovereign acts of the Triune God, all of His sons are His heirs, begotten again "To an inheritance incorruptible, and undefiled, and that fadeth not away, reserved in heaven for you, who are kept by the power of God through faith unto salvation ready to be revealed in the last time" (1 Peter 1:3-5). May God impress upon each of us, as He impressed upon the believers in Galatia, that our position as sons and heirs of God is due solely and wholly to the grace of God. So personal is all of this to each believer that Paul reverts to the singular, addressing each individual: "no more a servant, but a son." The wealth of this world is but small change in comparison with my heavenly inheritance. Hallelujah! What a wonderful Saviour! (Harrison p. 70.)

Having set forth his argument on Justification by Faith, the apostle now appeals to his readers in a threefold way.

(1) *The Appeal to Arrogance* (4:8-11). The Jewish legalistic teachers took pride in themselves as being the possessors

of a superior kind of religious sanctity. But here Paul thrusts the Sword of the Spirit through their vanity by showing that their condition before they received the Grace of God in Christ was no better than that of the godless pagan. "Howbeit then, when ye knew not God, ye did service unto them which by nature are no gods" (4:8). Actually the reference here in verse eight is to the Gentiles' bondage before they came into the light of the gospel of grace. At that time they "knew not God" and were "without God in the world" (Eph. 2:12), "even as the Gentiles which know not God" (1 Thess. 4:5). Their worship before they were saved was akin to paganism. While doing things to merit divine favor they were actually doing service to idols, for "the things which the Gentiles sacrifice, they sacrifice to demons, and not to God" (1 Cor. 10:20, A. S. V.). All religious rituals, idolatrous feasts and festivals express fellowship with demons, for behind all the idols and images there are demon powers controlling the minds and hearts of the people. When Paul came to the Galatians this is exactly how he found them, enslaved to heathen customs (Acts 14:9-18). Sadly enough, this expresses well the present state of Christendom.

Paul's object in pointing back to their pagan, unconverted past is to show them the seriousness of the backward move they were in the process of making. He wants them to see how awful it is for one who has tasted of God's free grace to turn again to the legalism of the Judaizers. He wants them to cling to the principle of faith, forgetting the sacrifices of beasts, the service of ritual and the earthly priesthood. If there is any religious element in the use of images, paintings, crosses, and similar objects to arouse feeling toward God, it is an idolatrous one. The true believer knows that God desires the inward wooing of the Holy Spirit and not the outward excitement of feeling. We Christians need to realize that the best we can do for poor lost sinners is to show them the power of the gospel in our everyday living and not a multitude of regulations. The world will ridicule our ritual, but it can never repudiate a consecrated, joyous life, lived according to the will of God.

"But now, after that ye have known God, or rather are known of God, how turn ye again to the weak and beggarly elements, whereunto ye desire again to be in bondage?" (4:9). Here is an appeal that must have melted their hearts. They had come to know God. Yet, more wonderful still, God knew them as His own sons. In the face of such a precious and personal relationship with the Almighty, how could they turn back to the beggarly rudiments of the past that could only bring them into bondage again? Is Paul mistaken here when he says that the Galatian believers were turning *"again"* to the weak and beggarly elements, to which they desired *"again"* to be in bondage? Does he mean to compare their turning to legal principles with their former pagan practices? In answer to the first question, Paul is not mistaken. In answer to the latter question, their return to law would be no better for them than would their return to pagan idolatry. Not that the law in itself was idolatrous, but to return now to those rites and observances which were but a shadow of Christ before He came was in God's sight a return to idolatry. Legal observances are but the shadow; Christ is the Substance. By His death and resurrection He fulfilled every Old Testament type. The bondage of paganism was different from, but not less real than the bondage in which the Jews had been held.

Christianity is peculiarly a faith of liberty and a liberating faith. Jesus said: "And ye shall know the truth, and the truth shall make you free", and "If the Son therefore shall make you free, ye shall be free indeed" (John 8:32, 36). But how like the Israelites of old were the Galatian believers! It seems incredible, nevertheless it was true, that Israel, after having been miraculously delivered from Egyptian bondage should desire to return. They lusted after the fish and cucumbers and melons and leeks and onions and garlic of which they ate freely in Egypt (Num. 11:4, 5). And now the foolish Galatians would turn back to be in bondage. And many Christians have not fully learned how glorious is the liberty which is ours in Christ. Many have confessed Christ only to be drawn *again* to the slavery of fleshly desires and personal habits.

But of the various forms of slavery, none is so subtle and so strong as religious slavery. When our Lord dealt with the unbelieving Jews in His own day He ministered to men who were slaves to a system that could not save them. And when He spoke to them of liberating truth, they answered: "We be Abraham's seed, and were never in bondage to any man: how sayest Thou, Ye shall be made free?" (John 8:32, 33). Indeed Jesus saw the men of His day in religious bondage. The history of the centuries has proved that the peoples of India, Asia and the Roman Catholic countries have been the slaves of fear and superstition, devotees of shrines, idols, penance, priestcraft, prayer beads, "days, and months, and times, and years" (Gal. 4:10). Much can be added of the formalism and legalism in our Protestant church. We, too, sometimes take pride in denominational affiliation, mode of baptism or method of observance of the Lord's Supper, feet-washing, keeping of so-called "holy days," and such.

What happened to the Galatians under the influence of legalistic teachers can easily happen to us. In fact, I fear that many have lost their liberty, having returned to those "weak" and "beggarly" elements which are powerless to produce life and powerless to enrich our lives. The religion of cold formalism is without an inheritance, having nothing to offer here or hereafter. When we stand fast in Christian liberty, many will be the uncharitable judgments of others (Rom. 14:5), but we are to let no man judge us for refusing to observe the seasons and rituals of man (Col. 2:16). When our Lord died at Calvary the work of the Cross put an end to the demands of the Law, for He took us out from the bondage of them all, "Blotting out the handwriting of ordinances that was against us, which was contrary to us, and took it out of the way, nailing it to His cross" (Col. 2:14). God does not desire an outward show "in will worship" (Col. 2:23), but rather that we "worship Him in spirit and in truth" (John 4:24). Let us not occupy ourselves with the "shadows" of the "Church year," but let every day be for the child of God a holy day to the Lord.

Little wonder the apostle seems troubled in spirit. "I am afraid of you, lest I have bestowed upon you labour in vain" (4:11). Many a faithful pastor has felt like this after giving himself to the ministry of the Word, seeing some make a good start in Christian experience, only to find later that they have been ensnared by unscriptural doctrine. Let all of this be a warning to every follower of Christ lest these things rob us of our spiritual liberty and place a yoke of bondage on our hearts. Let us not be satisfied with conversion only, but let us seek steady growth and daily progress in the things of God.

(2) *The Appeal to Affection* (4:12-20). The appeal of the apostle continues, but a change in the tone is manifest. He appeals to some of the blessed memories of the past in an endeavor to bring to their minds the bond of love that brought them together and bound them at the first. Thus he addresses them as "Brethren." He would have them think of him as one with themselves. Now it is not easy in these verses to follow the connection of thought since we cannot dogmatically place our finger on all of the history of the circumstances to which Paul refers.

"Brethren, I beseech you, be as I am; for I am as ye are: ye have not injured me at all" (4:12). The word "be" means literally "to become," so that the American Standard Version reads: "Become as I am, for I also am become as ye are." He is simply telling them that there was a time in his own life when, as a devout Jew, he observed all of those Mosaic rites to which the Galatians were turning now. He kept the feast days and observed the Passover and looked upon certain food as unclean. But when he came among the Galatians Paul had been set utterly free from the Law of Moses. He was now a Christian, saved by God's grace, and as such he had laid aside the law for which he was at one time zealous. For many years Paul was prejudiced in favor of the law, "But," says he, "what things were gain to me, those I counted loss for Christ" (Phil. 3:7). In view of the stand he took he appeals to them who are putting themselves under the law to take their place beside him. If he had given up the law after having studied it for years, why should they, who know very little about it, turn to it? If the law had any advantages to offer, certainly Paul would have known it; but after gaining a thorough knowledge of it he turned to Christ. Now he pleads with them not to abandon him when he has left all for them. He made no claim to superiority over them when he came to them, so now he would entreat them to assume no attitude of superior sanctity over him. And lest they feel that Paul has some personal grievance or that he feels ill toward them, he adds: "Ye have not injured me at all." Literally he is telling them that, so far as he is concerned, they did him no wrong.

Then he adds: "Ye know how through infirmity of the flesh I preached the gospel unto you at the first. And my temptation which was in my flesh ye despised not, nor rejected; but received me as an angel of God, even as Christ Jesus" (4:13, 14). Contrary to injuring him, Paul reminds them that he has not forgotten their generous spirit in view of the circumstances under which they first met. When the apostle first came among the Galatians he was a sorry sight with his infirmity of the flesh. His appearance might very well have repelled them, yet they did not despise or reject him because of it but rather received him as the messenger of God even as they would have received Jesus Christ Himself. Paul might not have remained at Galatia when he visited there the first time, but the terrible beatings he received needed attention, and because of his infirmity he remained to preach the gospel to them. And what blessedness then! There was doubtless much rejoicing and praise as they counted themselves happy indeed to have heard the good news of salvation from Paul. Now Paul would like to know what had become of that spirit which was manifested in them.

"Where is then the blessedness ye spake of?" (4:15). What happened to the joy and enthusiasm they showed when they counted themselves blessed to be able to hear him? Legalism had robbed them of the blessings of grace. Their spiritual prosperity was being reduced to a state of spiritual poverty. There is an expression of joy and praise in the early days of conversion which often fades with the passing of time. The church of Galatia was like the church at Ephesus to whom John wrote: "Thou hast left thy first love" (Rev. 2:4). Even today there is that wandering away from the simplicity of the gospel to the legal tendency, observing days and seasons and engaging in ritual. When a man despises the doctrine of pure grace, he throws away the blessings that only God's grace can give. The loss of our first love and the joy of God's salvation should alarm us. May God deliver us from a religion that is merely an empty and heartless mechanical routine. And if we should discover ourselves lapsing into any form of legalism or worldliness, let us come directly to God, as did David, to cry: "Restore unto me the joy of *Thy* salvation" (Psalm 51:12).

"For I bear you record, that, if it had been possible, ye would have plucked out your own eyes, and have given them to me" (4:15). It seems quite clear that, whatever Paul's infirmity was, his eyes were badly affected. His words, "Ye see how large a letter I have written unto you with mine own hand" (6:11), confirm this, the large letters being necessary because of impaired vision. Possibly the incident recorded in Acts 23:1-5 would support the theory that Paul suffered from impaired vision. The point here in Galatians is appealing to their past love and respect for him which made them willing to offer their own eyes to Paul, if by so doing they could have helped him. Some claim that Paul here is using a figure of speech merely to indicate that the Galatians, in gratitude for Paul's message of the gospel, would have sacrificed their sight as an expression of their indebtedness to this servant of Christ. But whether Paul meant what he said to be figurative or literal, he knew they loved him. To that affection he appeals.

"Am I therefore become your enemy, because I tell you the truth?" (4:16). They did not consider Paul their enemy then. Why should they do so now? If they thought then that he was telling them the truth for their own good, why should they think otherwise now? Neither Paul nor the gospel had changed. Why then should they treat him as an enemy? Why should he have to appeal to them so strongly?

The apostle knows the answer. "They zealously affect you, but not well; yea, they would exclude you, that ye might affect them" (4:17). The words "they" and "them" refer to the false Judaistic teachers. Actually the legalists were jealous of the Christian liberty the Galatians were enjoying, and they showed a warm interest in them, but "not well" or literally, "in no good way." The motives of the Judaizers were selfish and were never calculated on for the welfare of the Galatian converts. The Jews were seeking converts to the circumcision party in their own selfish interests. It was a dishonorable and contemptible move on the part of the Jews to win the Galatians away from the Gospel of Grace. The Jews subtly pretended to exclude the Galatian believers from their fellowship on the ground that the Galatians were on a lower spiritual plane than they themselves, hoping thereby to persuade them to adopt the Mosaic ritual. Paul exposes their evil method of proselyting.

Then he adds: "But it is good to be zealously affected always in a good thing, and not only when I am present with you" (4:18). He would encourage them to receive the attention and ministry of any true messenger whose motives and messages are divinely approved. This they should do at any time whether Paul is among them or absent from them. He is not jealously objecting to their listening to a minister other than himself, but rather instructing them how to discern between the true and the false. If they were zealous for the truth at all times, his presence or absence would make no difference. Paul himself was both jealous and zealous for the Galatian Christians, but with an intent dissimilar to that of their enemies.

The appeal becomes stronger and the expression of affection deeper as Paul continues: "My little children, of whom I travail in birth again until Christ be formed in you" (4:19). This is the only place in which Paul uses the words "My little children," and it is employed here to make the appeal more tender. It is the warm-hearted appeal of a teacher toward his disciples. Our Lord used it when speaking to His disciples toward the close of His earthly ministry (John 13:33). Paul was experiencing again that anguish of soul through which he passed when he preached the gospel to them at the first. He had led them to the Lord Jesus, hence he uses that metaphor, mentioned elsewhere in Scripture (1 Cor. 4:15; Philem. 10), which speaks of a believer leading sinners to the Lord as one who gives birth to spiritual children. Birth-pangs bring one close to death's door and are an expression of love. Few ministers carry the burden for lost souls (Rom. 9:3) and wrestle in prayer for their salvation as Paul. Hence there are few who know the joy and rejoicing of a soul-winning ministry.

Now the Galatians had already been conceived and brought forth, but because of their lapse into legalism they needed to be restored to the joy and fellowship in the gospel. Christ was in their hearts, but only in a passive way. The blessed Lord was not having His way in their hearts. The Holy Spirit was being grieved and quenched so that He was not at liberty to glorify the Son in them. There was no outward expression of the Lord Jesus Christ in their lives. It was Paul's blessed privilege and duty to form not himself but

Christ in his hearers. This he proceeds to accomplish in the pain and agony of his own soul. Will they resist him? Will they ignore his affectionate appeal?

(3) *The Appeal to Acuteness* (4:21-31). The apostle concludes his appeal by calling upon his hearers to use their intelligence. Surely they possessed some power of discernment and could make some distinction between truth and error. So he asks them: "Tell me, ye that desire to be under the law, do ye not hear the law?" (4:21). "Have you comprehended the meaning of the law? Do you realize the demands of the law upon you when you put yourself under it?" Their minds needed to be stirred up, for while they insisted on being under the law they were not heeding the full demands of the law.

"For it is written, that Abraham had two sons, the one by a bondmaid, the other by a freewoman" (4:22). This combination of words, *it is written,* is used to introduce a quotation or a brief summary of some portion of the Old Testament. Here the apostle is about to summarize the history of Ishmael and Isaac, sons of Abraham, as recorded in Genesis, chapters 16, 17, and 21. Ishmael, Abraham's son, was born of Hagar the bondmaid (or slave girl), while Isaac, also Abraham's son, was born of Sarah the freewoman and the wife of Abraham's love. Since the Galatians claimed to understand the law and were about to place themselves in bondage to it, then surely they would see the force of Paul's illustration drawn from the experience of Abraham. Abraham lived before Moses and therefore before the giving of the moral and ceremonial Code at Sinai. But here "the Law" refers more generally to the writings of Moses and Paul now illustrates his point with a familiar story from the Scriptures themselves, and shows them what that bondage which they desired would do to them.

Note the force of verse 24: "Which things are an allegory: for these are the two covenants [or testaments]; the one from the mount Sinai, which gendereth to bondage, which is Agar" (4:24). In speaking allegorically Paul is merely applying the facts of a literal historic narrative to illustrate a principle. It was forcefully said by Hogg and Vine that "the presence of an allegorical meaning does not deprive the narrative of its literal meaning." Great care must be exercised in an attempt to use this method of treating the narratives in God's Word.

Abraham, two of his sons, and their mothers are now before us as real persons of history. To these the apostle refers to illustrate and illuminate the doctrine of Justification by Faith. God had made a promise to Abraham when He said: ". . . In thee shall all families of the earth be blessed," and "he that shall come forth out of thine own bowels shall be thine heir" (Gen. 12:3; 15:4). The promise is clear. Abraham and Sarah were to become the parents of a son who was to be the precursor of the coming Messiah, the Seed in whom all the nations of the earth should be blessed. But time passed and to Abraham and Sarah it seemed that God forgot His promise or else failed to keep it. At this point Sarah herself suggested that her servant-girl be given to Abraham, not to take the full status of a wife, but merely to serve as a concubine to bear Abraham a child. No doubt Sarah thought that she was assisting God, but actually she and Abraham were stooping to one of the common customs of the heathen nations around them.

In the process of time Ishmael was born to Hagar the "bondmaid." Of him it is written that "he who was of the bondwoman was born after the flesh" (4:23). No doubt Abraham continued for a while in hope that Ishmael would prove to be the promised child through whom the Seed should come. He went as far as to pray: "O that Ishmael might live before Thee!" (Gen. 17:18). But God could not permit this. Only evil came from the disobedience of Sarah and Abraham. Ishmael, the son of the bondwoman, became the progenitor of the Arabs, from whom came Mohammedanism, a curse to the Jew and to all mankind ever since. Ishmael's birth was after the order of nature, but not according to God's plan. It was wrong for Sarah and Abraham to think that God could be hindered or hurried.

In God's time "He of the freewoman was [born] by promise" (4:23). The birth of Isaac was according to the divine plan in spite of the old age of Sarah and Abraham. From a natural standpoint they could not become parents. But Isaac was a child of promise. His birth was a miracle, hence he was a child of grace. What was humanly impossible was brought to pass by the power of God in fulfillment of the divinely-given promise.

Why does Paul recount all this? "Which things are an allegory: for these are the two covenants; the one from the mount Sinai, which gendereth to bondage, which is Agar" (4:24). Paul's use of the word "allegory" does not in any way cast doubt upon the literalness and trustworthiness of the historic narrative. He is simply illustrating truth. The two women, Hagar and Sarah, represent the two covenants (or testaments), Law and Grace. The new covenant (or testament) began with the death of our Lord Jesus Christ, for He said: "This cup is the New Testament in My Blood, which is shed for you" (Luke 22:20 cf. 1 Corinthians 11:25). The Old Covenant of the Law which was given at Sinai is allegorically identified with Hagar, and its children are definitely in a state of bondage. The legal covenant, or the covenant of Law, can only make slaves. Ishmael was born fourteen years before Isaac, but that did not make him Abraham's heir. If it did, by that same token the Mosaic Law would have a greater claim upon us than would the Gospel of Christ. The sons of these two mothers, Hagar and Sarah, are the children of the covenants as represented in the respective mother of each. In the days of slavery here in our own United States of America, before the Civil War, the national law entitled a child born to a woman in slavery the status of his mother. The father might be a free man, but if the mother was a slave woman she could bear only slave children. Hagar is a type of Sinai, and Sinai, when Paul wrote this Epistle, "answereth to Jerusalem . . . and is in bondage with her children." Hagar represented the Jerusalem of Paul's day which was the center of legal religion, the existing Judaism which held men in bondage.

"But Jerusalem which is above is free, which is the mother of us all" (4:26). Observe here how Paul speaks of two Jerusalems, *"Jerusalem which now is"* and *"Jerusalem which is above."* Hagar symbolizes the former with its Judaistic legal religion, while Sarah symbolizes the heavenly Jerusalem, the true spiritual city of which all Christians are members. Christians are not under bondage but are brought into liberty through faith in the Gospel of Jesus Christ. The earthly Jerusalem with its Judaistic system is not our mother. Jerusalem above is our mother. Our Lord and Saviour has gone up to take His place at the right hand of the Father, hence Heaven is our home. John writes: "And I John saw the holy city, new Jerusalem, coming down from God out of heaven, prepared as a bride adorned for her husband" (Rev. 21:2). The full force of the allegorical contrast between the two Jerusalems is seen in Hebrews 12:18-24 where the last contrast is drawn between the Old and the New Covenants—*Mount Sinai versus Mount Zion.* The difference between them is the difference between the earthly and the heavenly, between Law and Grace, between the natural and the spiritual. In the first we see the law with all its claims; in the second we see the blood by which the claims of the law have been vindicated.

Paul now makes reference to the prophecy of Isaiah. "For it is written, Rejoice, thou barren that bearest not; break forth and cry, thou that travailest not: for the desolate hath many more children than she which hath an husband" (4:27).

This prophecy looks forward to Christ's coming in glory when Israel will recognize the great truth contained therein. Sarah was barren, yet she brought forth One through whom all the families of the earth have been blessed. Israel, the nation that had the law, is said to have God as her husband (Isa. 54:5), and is referred to in Hosea as the wife of Jehovah. But the children of the desolate, the Gentiles without the law, among whom the Galatians were numbered, are more than those (Jews) who had a husband (God) and the law. While Israel who had the law is temporarily set aside, God is calling out from among the Gentiles a people for His name. In this verse we see the hope of the Gentiles. The preaching of the gospel of grace, which the world calls barren, is the one saving message that is bringing forth children to God.

"Now we, brethren, as Isaac was, are the children of promise" (4:28). Like Isaac, we have been supernaturally born into God's family by the operation of the Holy Spirit. Isaac was a child of promise and of faith, and as such he is a type of every true believer who has his standing before God, not on the ground of being a descendant from Abraham, but upon the grace bestowed to Abraham.

"But as then he that was born after the flesh persecuted him that was born after the Spirit, even so it is now" (4:29). In Abraham's household Ishmael ridiculed Isaac. The child after the flesh was antagonistic toward the child after the Spirit. The one born by natural power is the antithesis of the one born by supernatural power. *Even so it is now.* This persecution expresses the attitude of the natural man toward the children of God. Such was the attitude of men toward our Lord and, at the time when this Epistle was written, toward the Apostle Paul. We believe that, until the end of the age, those who have been saved by grace through faith in the finished work of our Lord Jesus Christ will suffer at the hands of those who seek salvation by law and works. The man who takes pride in doing his religious duty can easily become the judge of the duty of others. The religion of self-effort envies the religion of the man who quietly rests in the promises of God's Word. Paul himself, before his conversion, was an example of this very thing. Saul of Tarsus actually thought that he was doing God a service when he persecuted the Christians (Acts 26:9, 10). Legalism appeals to the old nature so that "even now" we find "the old man" persecuting "the new man" which was born after the Spirit. The flesh and the Spirit are opposed to each other, continually at war (Rom. 7:22, 23).

But what is God's will in the matter? Shall legalism triumph? Must the new nature succumb to the attacks of the flesh? "Nevertheless what saith the Scripture?" The mind of God in this as in all matters is to be found in God's Word. He says: "Cast out the bondwoman and her son: for the son of the bondwoman shall not be heir with the son of the free-woman" (4:30). Actually these were the words of Sarah (Gen. 21:10), but they were endorsed by God (verse 12). There could be no room in one family for both law and grace, bondage and freedom. One must be cast out.

We too are either under law or under grace. God's children are children of promise. There is no place in the Church for legalism. The expulsion of Ishmael from Abraham's house is God's condemnation upon all who seek heaven by the legalistic principle of law-works; and those who take pride in their denominational birthright and the performance of religious duties may be missing the spiritual inheritance that can come only through Jesus Christ.

This is the climax of Paul's argument, and it points to the utter rejection of the children of Abraham after the flesh in contrast to Abraham's spiritual posterity through faith. The law and the gospel cannot co-exist. They will not mix. Therefore to seek to keep the law in order to add to one's faith is sinful and must ultimately result in eternal separation from God. He who trusts in his own merits for salvation will find himself cast out.

"So then, brethren, we are not children of the bondwoman, but of the free" (4:31). The difference between law and grace, bondage and liberty, has been fully established, and that will serve as a basis for the practical teaching which is about to follow. We will now pass on from doctrine to duty in order that we might learn how to live out our freedom.

IV. PRACTICAL
(Chapters 5 and 6)

A. *The Privileges of Liberty* (5:1-12)

That the believer in Christ is not in bondage but is rather a free man was Paul's closing word in the doctrinal section of his Epistle. He has adduced his evidence. Now he will apply the truth. Having instructed them in doctrine, he now exhorts them in duty. The freedom which was theirs in Christ ought not to have been lightly despised. The liberty procured by Christ at Calvary exempted them from the ceremonies of the law, but it did not stop there. How little He would have actually accomplished in His death if that were all! There is more to our being delivered by His grace, for we are now free to do the right thing. Grander than freedom from the demands of the law and the power of Satan is our liberty to grow in Christian experience, in grace and in the knowledge of our Lord Jesus Christ.

"Stand fast therefore in the liberty wherewith Christ hath made us free, and be not entangled again with the yoke of bondage" (5:1). There is suggested here the method by which the Christian lives his life. Under law a man depended on his own effort in an attempt to obey the law. Under grace a child of God depends upon the liberty and leading of the Holy Spirit. The wondrous provisions of grace continue to operate in the life of the Christian. Grace saves us; grace sustains us.

Since Christ died to purchase this freedom for us, we are here exhorted to *"stand fast."* We are to live our lives independent of the claims of the law, but dependent upon the indwelling Holy Spirit. The exhortation to the Galatians was to beware lest they become *"entangled again."* They had formerly been ensnared by heathenism and were in slavery to its customs and practices. At that time Paul had preached Christ to them, and through faith they had been delivered from the net of the enemy. Now why should they return to another form of bondage (the Law) which could offer no more toward saving them than did their former pagan idolatry? The mesh of legalism in any form, Jewish or Gentile, tends to make us self-conscious instead of Christ-conscious. It is from this endless round of self-effort that Christ delivers us.

The Christian is God's free-born man saved by divine grace, and in that grace the child of God stands (Rom. 5:2) and grows (2 Peter 3:18). Dr. Norman B. Harrison has said: "Christian liberty is a life so lived that these provisions of grace continue to operate." Our God is the God of all grace (1 Peter 5:10), and if we revert to legalism we place ourselves under another "yoke." The yoke can be anything that joins two objects together so that neither can operate independently of the other, and it is nearly always used of bondage or servitude of some kind. The only "yoke" the believer knows anything about is the will of God (Jer. 5:5). It is the service of the Lord, and Jesus Himself refers to His yoke as being "easy" and "light" (Matt. 11:29, 30). When the servant is under the same yoke as His Master, it is far different from the cumbersome requirements of any legal system. "Viewed religiously all men are in bondage, the Jews to a law . . . the Gentiles to their own ideas of what God must be . . . their own conceptions . . . the creation of their own minds, not the revelation of God in Christ . . . To the unregenerate the law is an instrument of bondage, for it commands him to abstain from the things to which he is naturally inclined, and to do those things for which he has no desire" (Hogg and Vine).

"Behold, I Paul say unto you, that if ye be circumcised, Christ shall profit you nothing" (5:2). When a man rejects the grace of God and places himself under law he faces problems. Do not confuse the problem here. Paul is not implying that a circumcised person cannot be saved. He himself had been circumcised (Phil. 3:5). Greek students tell us that the tense of the verb is present continuous, so that the apostle is warning them of the danger of continuing the practice of the law as a Christian obligation. If the Galatians were to put themselves under law and submit to the rite of circumcision, they would deprive themselves of the effects of the ministry of the risen Christ. While their Christian standing before God would not be affected, their state would. If righteousness is sought through circumcision, or through any legal system, it cannot at the same time be received through Christ on the ground of grace. If salvation and justification and the promise of eternal life are obtained by the works of the law, then there was no need for God to send His Son to procure these blessings for us. Paul is not directing derogatory remarks against the law, nor is his reasoning directed against the outward rite or ceremony as such, but rather against the false teaching that those things are necessary to salvation and the worship of God.

For emphasis he repeats what he told them in 3:10, namely, the law is a unit, hence the offender in one point is the offender of the whole law and is guilty of all. Success in keeping one part of the law will not compensate for failure in another: "For I testify again to every man that is circumcised, that he is a debtor to do the whole Law" (5:3). If any man assumes the responsibility of the entire legalistic system, he is unquestionably condemned and Christ can render him no service. Paul expresses the truth of this in the words, "Christ is become of no effect unto you, whosoever of you are justified by the law" (5:4). There are professing Christians in our churches today who are unaffected by the Person and work of our Lord Jesus Christ. Legalism has put them in such a position that they are unable to derive any spiritual benefits of the risen Lord. Their religious experience is disassociated from Him. He has no effect upon them whatever.

It is an awful thing when the sacrificial work of Christ on the Cross, His bodily resurrection, and present intercessory ministry are meaningless to an individual.

Paul's next words, "Ye are fallen from grace" (5:4) have become a bone of contention between various groups. It is unnecessary to say that there is such a thing as "falling from grace." Those who refuse to accept what the Bible teaches about the eternal security of the believer in Christ tell us that falling from grace means losing one's salvation. But are we to conclude here that when a believer sins, he ceases to be a Christian? Certainly not! If such were the case there would be no Christians in this world, for all would have ceased to be Christians soon after salvation was received. Paul is not now dealing with Christian behavior nor is he warning against moral declension. The issue here is doctrinal and Paul is dealing specifically with defection in doctrine. Dr. Marion McH. Hull has pointed out that this word as it occurs in the original (which gives it its basic meaning) means "to make inoperative, of no effect." Adding law to faith in Christ creates paralysis of the spiritual development. Arrested development is all too common in the lives of believers, and the cause is usually the same, namely, self-deprivation of daily grace for growth in the knowledge of our Lord Jesus Christ. When a man serves notice on God that he prefers to depend on what he can do for himself rather than on what Christ has done for him, that man is falling from grace. When a man decides to live in the energy of the flesh, he cuts the supply-line of God's Grace (Dr. N. B. Harrison).

The attitude of all true believers is now described by the apostle: "For we through the Spirit wait for the hope of righteousness by faith" (5:5). The Dispensation of the Law had its consummation with the death of Christ, so that Pentecost ushered in the Dispensation of the Holy Spirit. It is through the Spirit that the righteousness of God is imputed to the believer. Moreover, the Holy Spirit is the source of the Christian's hope, and since He inspires the hope, there can be no hope for the man under law. Our hope rests upon faith in Christ, not upon the flesh.

The phrase, "the hope of righteousness," does not reflect in any way upon the present experience of justification. All believers are justified (or declared righteous) immediately upon acceptance of Jesus Christ. But there is a completed hoped-for righteousness for which we wait. It is entirely by faith in Christ. "For in Jesus Christ neither circumcision availeth any thing, nor uncircumcision; but faith which worked by love" (5:6).

There is plain talk and practical truth in Paul's next words: "Ye did run well; who did hinder you that ye should not obey the truth?" (5:7). The important lesson here for us all is that as long as we are obeying the truth we are getting along well; we are running the race well. The obedient child of God has joy and peace in Christian experience. But it is tragic when a believer in Christ, after having made a good start in the Christian life, is hindered through disobedience to God's divine truth. Beware of Satan's attempts to hinder you. Beware lest the things of this world hinder you. Beware lest the temptations of the flesh hinder you. The Galatians were being hindered in their spiritual life because of reverting to the "do-religion" of the law.

"Who did hinder you?" Paul asks. Satan had been busy working through the Jewish teachers. The Galatians were making progress in their faith and growing in grace until they gave ear to these false Judaistic teachers. It was then that legalism retarded their progress. They were running the Christian race well until they were intercepted by the enemy. When they accepted the false message, they disbelieved the truth. Had they continued to believe God they would have continued to obey God, for obedience is the only possible evidence of a heart-belief in God. In the case of the Israelites their disobedience is said to be the evidence of her unbelief (see Hebrews 3:18, 19).

The Galatians were not led by the Holy Spirit into legalism, for, writes Paul: "This persuasion cometh not of Him that calleth you" (5:8). The influence that was winning them over was not of God to be sure. The Holy Spirit calls men to Christ through the Gospel of Grace (3:2, 3), therefore they were now listening to another voice. Having been deceived by the enemy they needed to know that this new doctrine was not of God but of the Evil One. Any voice that seduces from grace is hostile to the truth of God.

The false teaching of the Judaizers is here compared with leaven: "A little leaven leaveneth the whole lump" (5:9). Leaven in the Scripture is always a symbol of corruption. A very small lump, operating on the principle of fermentation, will permeate and corrupt the whole. Perhaps some of the Galatians felt that there could be no harm in turning just a little from the doctrine of Justification by Faith, but, like leaven, legalism would spread throughout the province of Galatia and endanger the spiritual life of the entire church. When the woman hid leaven in the three measures of gospel meal, the whole became affected by it (Matt. 13:33). A little later when our Lord warned His disciples against the legalism of the Pharisees and Sadducees He used leaven as a symbol of their false doctrines (Matt. 16:6-12).

We need to guard ourselves against the influence of false teachers, for when evil begins it quickly spreads to great proportions. We can see today how the false doctrines of Modernism have affected the whole lump of Christendom. Let the enemies of God's Word put us down as being contentious and uncharitable if they will, but let us never despise the day of small things. Some years ago our newspapers published a story of how a single case of scarlet fever brought death to nine families in one community. Even so can one false teacher confuse an entire company of believers. Whether leaven is used of doctrine, as in the case before us, or of moral evil such as occurred in 1 Corinthians 5:6-8, we need to beware of its persuasive and pervasive power.

In spite of the attack of the legalists upon the Galatians,

Paul expresses his belief that those saints in Galatia will remain true to the Gospel of Jesus Christ. "I have confidence in you through the Lord, that ye will be none otherwise minded . . ." (5:10). Even though they may have been forming new opinions Paul believed that God would keep them and that they would eventually resist the Judaizers. If they were truly saved, Satan could not pluck them out of God's hand (John 10:28-30).

However, those who were responsible for the trouble would not escape divine judgment, for, writes Paul: "He that troubleth you shall bear his judgment, whosoever he be" (5:10). He who touches God's anointed must suffer for it. God will judge the man who disturbs the faith of His children, and that judgment will be twofold (1:8, 9). Satan's ministers may transform themselves to appear as ministers of righteousness, but their "end shall be according to their works" (2 Cor. 11:13-15). Judgment is coming at the hand of God, for "By Him actions are weighed" (1 Sam. 2:3). In that day all false teachers will be unmasked and punished.

Paul's persecutors might have told the Galatians that the apostle himself preached circumcision. Such a report against Paul could not be true. He says: "And I, brethren, if I yet preach circumcision, why do I yet suffer persecution? then is the offence of the cross ceased" (5:11). Paul was preaching the cross, and it was that message which was a stumbling-block to the Jews. On the truth of redemption through Calvary the mightly apostle stood, and upon that he exhorts the Galatians to stand with him.

B. *The Prohibition of License* (5:13-26)

This section of the Epistle is most essential in its relation to the teaching of grace. Too often there are those professing Christians who do not understand grace and are therefore unrestrained in the indulgences of their natural desires. Paul had faced this reaction before on the part of others, for he anticipated such questions as the following: "Shall we continue in sin, that grace may abound?", and, "Shall we sin, because we are not under the law, but under grace?" (Rom. 6:1, 15). Though the Christian has been delivered from the demands of the law, he has the indwelling Holy Spirit who exercises a superior control over every thought, word and deed. While he is no longer under the control of any legal system he is in complete submission of God the Holy Spirit.

Hence the expostulation: "For, brethren, ye have been called unto liberty; only use not liberty for an occasion to the flesh, but by love serve one another" (5:13). Here is a caution signal lest the believer's freedom which has been purchased for him by Jesus Christ becomes a springboard for sin. The old nature has not been eradicated. We need to beware of its assertion. Christians are free, but Christian liberty does not mean exemption from all temptation. Our liberty in Christ is freedom to do right, not freedom to do what our old nature desires and dictates. Liberty in the Lord is not license to sin. While a Christian does not have the law, he does have the Lord; and his position in grace puts him on a much higher spiritual plane than the Mosaic legal system. No true believer in Jesus Christ will think of his freedom from law as leaving him without obligation to the righteous demands of a holy God.

The normal conduct of the child of God is a complete effacement of self. Love is the constraining motive of all his actions. Christians should not use liberty for an occasion to the flesh, *"but by love serve one another"* (5:13). Because we are born from above and are partakers of the divine nature, we are to esteem others better than ourselves (Phil. 2:3) and be willing to lay down our lives for the brethren. Paul had exhorted the Galatians to answer God's call to liberty; now he warns them against abusing their privilege. They are not free to serve themselves, but rather to serve others. They should never renounce their liberty, but they must be willing to forego the use of it for the sake of others, if they are called upon to do so. The perfect law of liberty (James 1:25) is the royal law of love, and it is fulfilled in obeying the words, "Thou shalt love thy neighbor as thyself" (James 2:8). Liberty is one thing, the use of liberty is another thing; and our exercise of freedom is governed by our relationship to men.

"For all the law is fulfilled in one word, even in this; Thou shalt love thy neighbour as thyself" (5:14). Love is greater than all the law, for it is the constraining principle and power in the Christian's life. Love will make us considerate of others and less self-centered. Such love will never proceed from the law but from the Cross. When our actions toward God and others are motivated by the constraining love of Christ, we are fulfilling all that the Mosaic Law could require of us. Elsewhere Paul refers to love as "the fulfilling of the law" (Rom. 13:8, 10).

One may be very punctilious in observing ceremony and ritual but not have the love of God in him. Calvin has said that "none are more zealous and regular in observing ceremonies than hypocrites. God therefore chooses to make trial of our love to Himself by that love of our brother, which He enjoins us to cultivate." A lawyer asked Jesus concerning the law, and out of the law our Lord taught him that love to God and to his fellowmen constituted the two great commandments (Matt. 22:34-40). And to His own followers the Lord said: "A new commandment I give unto you, That ye love one another; as I have loved you, that ye also love one another" (John 13:34). The newness lay in the standard of Calvary's Cross, as expressed in Christ's words, *"as I have loved you."* Divine love never remains idle, but manifests itself in service to others.

"But if ye bite and devour one another, take heed that ye be not consumed one of another" (5:15). The apostle here warns against any demonstration of the flesh in the place of true liberty. Since Christian liberty expresses itself in mutual love, great care must be exercised against false liberty which is self-centered. When the believers in a given assembly are at each other's throats, that assembly will soon be broken and scattered. Wild animals bite one another by nature, but it is a strange sight to see sheep bite each other. Here the word "devour" suggests the idea of exploiting one another, using one another selfishly. The scribes (legalists) were known for exploiting even the widows (Mark 12:39, 40), but such action is the direct opposite of love. When believers expose and condemn each other, they are soon consumed. Men who clamor for freedom are sometimes seeking deliverance from restraint to do as they please. It is sad to hear of Christians snapping and snarling at one another. Possibly the Galatians had some disputes among themselves about doctrine. If so, they were to guard against slander, accusations and reproaches, for disputes and disagreements within the Church are of Satan, and they will lead to destruction of the organic community life of the local church. One side may think it has won, but both have lost.

Now follows the remedy: "This I say then, Walk in the Spirit, and ye shall not fulfil the lust of the flesh" (5:16). By "the lust of the flesh" is meant the sinful desires of the "Old Self" before conversion. Right here we arrive at the crux and climax of the Christian's problem—the Spirit versus the Flesh. As sons of Adam we inherit the flesh; as sons of God we are given a new life and nature which is subject to the Holy Spirit. The two are contrary since their aims and purposes are diametrically opposed (5:17). Dr. Harrison has suggested that in one sense, the Christian has a harder time than other folks. If I am an unsaved man and want to do a thing, I go ahead and do it. If I am a saved man, I may want to do it and the Spirit may say, "No, you are not to do it." Now by walking in the realm of the Spirit we can obstruct the desires of the flesh. We are to be occupied with the Spirit, guided by the Spirit, filled with the Spirit, for He is the One who can help us. A holy life is never produced by ourselves through our own strength, but by the power of the indwelling Holy Spirit. Our deportment is not guided by the old nature. If it were, we could only fulfill the desires of that evil nature; but the Holy Spirit has been given to us to liberate us from the enslavement to sin, and free us to choose the right.

The conflict spoken of in 5:17 doubtless had been the experience of the Galatians. They discovered that the Christian life could not be maintained without a struggle, the flesh lusting against the Spirit, and the Spirit against the flesh. Paul describes this struggle more fully in Romans 7:7-25. Now the believer must choose his master. Will his master be the law, which can produce only the works of the flesh? Or will his master be the Spirit of God?

The Works of the Flesh. In the following three verses (19-21), Paul gives us a list of the *works* of the flesh. In verse 16 he speaks of "the *lust* of the flesh." There he has in mind "the inner motions of the soul, the natural tendency of men in their fallen estate toward things evil and toward things forbidden." But here, beginning at verse 19, he describes the actual display of those inner motions in word and deed. A man's character is manifested in his works. As he thinketh in his heart, so is he (Prov. 23:7). A man can be no better outwardly than what he is inwardly. Moreover, no man can hide his real self. He may hide his lusts for a season, but his works are "manifest." They are easily obvious and recognized. It is not difficult to distinguish between the man who fulfills the lust of the flesh and the man who is being led by the Spirit.

While Paul's list of fleshly works is not complete, it is quite comprehensive in that it includes sensual sins, religious sins, religious sins, social sins, and personal sins. The following comments on the works of the flesh are much as they appeared in the author's book, *This Is the Victory.*

Adultery. This is sexual unfaithfulness on the part of two persons, when either of them is married to a third person. It seems difficult to believe that a Christian would be guilty of such a violation, yet the writer knows of just such a case at this time, and it is affecting not only the life of the pastor, but also the spiritual condition of the church. How solemn are these words of our Lord Jesus: "But I say unto you, That whosoever looketh upon a woman to lust after her hath committed adultery with her already in his heart" (Matt. 5:28).

Fornication. This is sexual relationship, the incontinence or lewdness of unmarried persons. Though shocking, yet it is true that a fundamental pastor says he has officiated already at two "forced" marriages (of course not until after he had dealt with both couples in the light of God's Word).

Uncleanness. This is any thought, word, or deed of impurity or lewdness.

Lasciviousness. One who acts without regard or restraint in his brutish and lustful desires is lascivious. Webster defines it: "Looseness; irregular indulgence of animal desires." It is tragic, nevertheless true, that human beings are devoted to the gratification of the senses or the indulgence of a lewd and voluptuous appetite.

Idolatry. In a strict sense idolatry is the worship of deity in a visible form, whether the image worshiped is the symbol of the true God or a false divinity. Golden calves, fetishes, the sun, moon, and stars may be objects of idolatry, but Paul is not referring to these ancient forms of idol worship. He is concerned with another kind of idolatry which is just as destructive and devastating. It is that "little" god which relegates the Lord Jesus Christ to a secondary place in the believer's life. It may be an automobile or an ambition; it may be a position or a pleasure; it may be politics or people; it may be a loved one or an associate. Whatever is placed in our affection before God becomes an object of idolatry. What is your first consideration? Are you so utterly abandoned to the Lover of your soul that He receives first consideration in your life? If not, then you are carnal—an idolatrous Christian.

Witchcraft. Dealing with the practice of evoking spirits to produce results which are apparently supernatural is witchcraft. It is this element in the flesh that leads some children of God to teacup readers, palmists, spiritualists, and fortune-tellers when they ought to be consulting God in prayer. We have known Christians to refuse to walk under a ladder or to raise an umbrella in the house. Others carry rabbits' feet or miniature horseshoes, while still others cross their fingers when making a decision or spit when a black cat crosses their path. Any child of God who has to "trust luck" while refusing to trust his loving Heavenly Father is guilty of carnality, and is guilty before God of "minding the things of the flesh."

Hatred. This word means antipathy, aversion, or abhorrence. To hate is to dislike or detest another. A Christian who is horrified at another's sins of adultery, fornication, idolatry, or uncleanness, often nurtures a dislike against another Christian. That believer is as guilty of manifesting the deeds of the flesh as is the adulterer or the idolater. God does not distinguish or differentiate between these "deeds of the flesh." They are related to each other and are contrary to the law of love and devotion to God.

Variance. Again the Christian worker is guilty before God, for some of the choicest "servants" of the Lord can be charged with causing discord or dissension among brethren.

Emulation. It means competition or rivalry. When, because of jealousy, you strive to equal or surpass the achievement of your Christian brother, you are carnal.

Wrath. This means violent anger, vehement exasperation, or a raging resentment. Too often we have seen this prisoner break forth within and angrily attack another believer.

Strife. Not a few pastors must take valuable time to referee a contest for superiority between two of the brethren, each of whom claims "super-spirituality" but is as fleshly as the first Adam himself.

Sedition. A sedition is a factious commotion within the Church of Jesus Christ, making for insurrection and rebellion. It causes what is commonly known as "church splits." It always arises from within a carnal or fleshly Christian, for sedition is a deed of the flesh.

Heresies. This is any school of thought which is contrary to the recognized, fundamental doctrines of the Christian faith.

A schismatic in the church who tends to subvert the faith once delivered to the saints is likewise guilty of being carnal. All "parties" and "factions" are caused by some Christian who has been conquered by the self-life or the flesh.

Envyings. Here is another of the more common sins of the Christian. One becomes discontented as he looks upon another's superiority or success. His envy will cause him even to injure or do other harm. Are you a carnal Christian?

Murders. This is the unlawful, intentional killing of a human being by another human being of sound mind. But listen to the Holy Spirit of God: "Whosoever hateth his brother is a murderer" (1 John 3:15). And again: "But he that hateth his brother is in darkness, and walketh in darkness" (1 John 2:11).

Drunkenness. Usually this has reference to being drunk or intoxicated with strong drink. But it further refers to any intemperate, worldly indulgence which is nothing less than fleshly frivolity; and this intoxicates also.

Revelling. This has to do with carousing, engaging in loose, boisterous behavior such as "celebrating" with unruly merriment and revelry; a worldly outing, a worldly house party, or a carnival.

The "deeds of the flesh" mentioned above do not exhaust the long list from which we have drawn only in part, but they suffice to show us that many of our churches are overrun with carnal Christians. Every Christian should have a burning desire to be delivered from these deeds which emanate from within the heart where the flesh has not been "reckoned dead," and where the deeds of the flesh have not been mortified.

Note the apostle's repeated warning. ". . . of the which I tell you before, as I have also told you in time past, that they which do such things shall not inherit the kingdom of God" (5:21). There is no thought here of a believer losing his salvation and being cut off from the kingdom of God because he has reverted to one of the above-mentioned works of the flesh. Rather does the verse carry the idea of one who *practices* such things. When a man names the Name of the Lord he departs from the habit of unrighteous acts, if he is truly regenerated. The mere professor is still a partaker with the unsaved children of disobedience, and upon all such cometh the wrath of God (Eph. 5:6, 7).

The Fruit of the Spirit. The caution to stand guard against license is continued in verses 22 and 23 where the manifestation of the Spirit is set forth in contrast to the works of the flesh. How refreshing just to read these Christian virtues as they stand arrayed against the vices of the flesh. "But the fruit of the Spirit is love, joy, peace, longsuffering, gentleness, goodness, faith, meekness, temperance: against such there is no law" (5:22, 23). The word "fruit" is singular as against "works" (plural). Fruit is an outward expression of inward life and power. Just as *all* of the fruit on any one tree is developed by the life in that tree, even so is *all* of the Spirit's fruit developed in the child of God. These Christian virtues are not a part of the natural man. They belong to the "New Man" and are manifest in the believer because of the Holy Spirit's indwelling. The "New Man" is the "Good Tree" of Matthew 7:17-20, and the Holy Spirit may be compared to the sap that produces fruit.

This ninefold fruit springs from the new nature as one is born again of the Spirit. The character of the fruit shows clearly the character of the power that produced it, for, said our Lord: "Ye shall know them by their fruits" (Matt. 7:16). When the Holy Spirit is not hindered in a believer's life, His fruit will develop.

Love. While there often appear remarkable instances of human affection in an unregenerated man, none but those born of the Spirit can demonstrate the love here mentioned. The fruit of the Spirit is love since "God is love" (1 John 4:16). When we become regenerated the seed of divine love is planted in our hearts. Paul expresses it thus: "The love of God is shed abroad in our hearts by the Holy Ghost which is given unto us" (Rom. 5:5). When our Lord commanded His disciples, "That ye love one another" (John 13:34). He was not asking them to merely show human affection for each other. Our

Lord wants His own to yield to the Holy Spirit that He might work His love in us. Many churches are weakened by members who cherish ill-will in their hearts. Others have wronged them and they hate because of it. The command in the Bible to allow the Holy Spirit to love through them is completely ignored. This evil comes from the old nature, not from the Holy Spirit. None but those with the Holy Spirit within them can show forth His fruit of love.

Joy. Calvin says the "joy" here is that cheerful behavior toward our fellow men which is the opposite of moroseness. Luther suggests it is the cheerful heart with sweet thoughts of Christ. Friend, do you have this joy? In His well known discourse on fruit-bearing our Lord said: "These things have I spoken unto you, that My joy might remain in you, and that your joy might be full" (John 15:11). Elsewhere the Scripture commands us to "Rejoice always" (1 Thess. 5:16, A.S.V.). Nehemiah comforted the people by reminding them that "The joy of the Lord is your strength" (Neh. 8:10). Notice it is *His* joy. Circumstances and events may be against us, but if we abide in Him, the Holy Spirit will make us joyful. The Apostle Paul was not without sorrow, yet he could testify: "I am exceeding joyful in all our tribulation . . . as sorrowful, yet alway rejoicing" (2 Cor. 7:4; 6:10). If we are to bear good fruit, care must be given to cultivation. So then, rejoice. We are not speaking here of happiness, for happiness depends upon happenings, but rather the "joy of the Holy Ghost" (1 Thess. 1:6). A "worrying Christian" is a misnomer. Do you have the Lord? If you do, then "rejoice in the Lord" (Phil. 3:1). There is not a single verse in the Bible that will permit a child of God to worry. Joy is strengthening to the spiritual life, but sadness and worry paralyze the soul, rendering it too weak to face up to life's problems. The distraught and downcast Christian soon becomes weary in the work of the Lord. Are you one of His? "Let all those that put their trust in Thee rejoice: let them ever shout for joy, because Thou defendest them: let them also that love Thy name be joyful in Thee" (Psalm 5:11). Yes, joy is an everlasting fruit manifested in the life of the child of God, even when there seems to be no cause to rejoice.

Peace. These first three virtues are somehow linked together in a particular way. Love is the foundation of our Christian faith (see 5:13, 14), and where there is *love* in the heart, *joy* is sure to follow, and this will bringe *peace.* Our Lord desires His own to possess His peace. He bequeathed it to believers, saying: "Peace I leave with you, My peace I give unto you: not as the world giveth, give I unto you. Let not your heart be troubled, neither let it be afraid" (John 14:27). In chapters 14 and 16 of the Gospel according to John the Holy Spirit is promised and His ministry is explained. Then Jesus said: "These things I have spoken unto you, that in Me ye might have peace. In the world ye shall have tribulation: but be of good cheer; I have overcome the world" (John 16:33). Since the Spirit's coming at Pentecost, every believing sinner is assured of Christ's peace. The Son of God is the Prince of Peace (Isa. 9:6), and coming to earth He brought heaven's peace with Him (Luke 2:14) and made it available to us through the shedding of His blood (Rom. 5:1; Col. 1:20). Too many Christians worry. And why? They live in the energy of the flesh; they attempt to live apart from the leading of the Spirit. Important issues calling for careful decisions will arise in our lives to be sure. But there is no cause for worry. "Let the peace of God rule [arbitrate, settle all questions] in your hearts" (Col. 3:15). You worry only when you refuse to yield to the Holy Spirit. Let us hearken to God's commandments (Isa. 48:18), keep our minds stayed on Him (Isa. 26:3) and love His Word (Psalm 119:165) if we would enjoy tranquillity of mind.

Longsuffering. The word means simply *to suffer long.* It is a special virtue that has its origin with God (Exod. 34:6) since it is one of the divine attributes. It is not something we generate within ourselves, but rather that forbearance and patience with joyfulness according to *His* power (Col. 1:11). Are you sweet and serene under provocation? Can you endure patiently under distrust? Or are you quick-tempered and easily provoked? The Holy Spirit seeks to develop the image of Christ in us, "Who, when He was reviled, reviled not again; when He suffered, He threatened not . . ." (1 Peter 2:23). When Christ is formed in us, longsuffering will enable us to pray for those who injure us and to wait patiently until God has vindicated Himself. Some of us are too easily offended and need to learn how to suffer long.

Gentleness. Some students of the Bible translate this word to mean *kindness.* The English word "gentleman," while it does not fully cover the meaning, does cover it partly. Gentleness is thoughtful consideration, courteous and kindly action, the delicate ministering of love. When David praised the Lord for His manifold blessings, he said: "Thy gentleness hath made me great" (Psalm 18:35). The Lord's kindly consideration of David had multiplied His servant. God is rich in goodness toward us (Rom. 2:4), and that goodness found its full manifestation in Jesus Christ (Eph. 2:7). When we are not quenching the Holy Spirit in our lives He brings forth His fruit of gentleness in us and we cease to be unkind to others. "Love suffers long and is kind" (1 Cor. 13:4). Even though others may tax our patience we will be "kind one to another, tender-hearted, forgiving one another, even as God for Christ's sake hath forgiven you" (Eph. 4:32).

Goodness. Most of us have been guilty of looking for goodness in the natural man, but each of us must learn with Paul: "For I know that in me (that is, *in my flesh,*) dwelleth no good thing" (Rom. 7:18). But in conversion we are God's workmanship created in Christ Jesus unto good works (Eph. 2:10). "If any man is in Christ he is a new creature, the old things are passed away" (2 Cor. 5:17, A.S.V.). Paul says of the Christians in Rome that they are "full of goodness" (Rom. 15:14). God has supplied the new man with all that is necessary for every good work (2 Tim. 3:17). We are to be ready unto every good work and careful to maintain good works (Titus 3:1, 8, 14). Oh, dear reader, the Spirit of God longs to do good to others through you and me!

Faith. The word means *faithfulness* and signifies the abandonment of self and complete confidence in God. Faith "believeth all things" that are of God and knows that all things work together for good to those who love Him (Rom. 8:28). To doubt the providence of God at any time is a work of the flesh. The Christian grace of faithfulness needs to be cultivated in our lives. We surrender too easily. Some Christians pledge themselves enthusiastically to do a service for God, but, alas, their faithfulness is short lived. Some affiliate themselves with a local church and show a degree of constancy for a while, but soon yield to the flesh instead of to the Holy Spirit. "Consider the Apostle and High Priest of our profession, Christ Jesus; Who was faithful to Him that appointed Him" (Heb. 3:1, 2). Then heed the word of the Spirit of God: "Moreover it is required in stewards, that a man be found faithful" (1 Cor. 4:2). "Be thou faithful unto death, and I will give thee a crown of life" (Rev. 2:10).

Meekness. Meekness does not mean weakness. It is the fruit of power. Why did our Lord display meekness? Certainly it was not because He could not help Himself. He had the infinite resources of God at His command. But there were times when He deliberately refused to assert Himself, for while He understood the hatefulness of His enemies He purposed to remove it. Regardless of the treatment of friend or foe He was never cast down nor depressed, yet He was meek in heart (Matt. 11:29). Let us put to death that false humility which is a work of the flesh and allow the Holy Spirit to bring forth in us His fruit of self-forgetfulness. Wherever you find a man pushing himself to the forefront you may be sure he is walking after the flesh. Meekness does not mean that we underestimate our own abilities, but it is the unselfish view toward the ability of others. We are naturally proud, but the Spirit can subdue our natural tendency and produce in us "the meekness and gentleness of Christ" (2 Cor. 10:1).

Temperance. This word contains the idea of having the mastery of self-control. I am responsible to walk not after the flesh but after the Spirit (Rom. 8:4). Self-control is the fruit of the Spirit. He takes over and controls from within. When the flesh rules the life we lose control of ourselves, but as we yield to the Spirit we are Spirit-controlled. If there is to be victory over the natural impulses it can be only as the Spirit of God empowers a man to rule his own spirit.

These nine graces make up the cluster of the Spirit's fruit, and "against such there is no law" (5:23). They are above and beyond the realm of the law. No law can make a man love, give a man joy, guarantee a man peace, nor form in him such fruits. When a man is walking in the Spirit he does not need any law. Life by the Spirit is far above anything the law could make possible. Under law man utterly fails and produces the works of the flesh (5:19-21). Under the control of the Holy Spirit he rises above the very standards of the law. While the law seeks to restrain the evil tendencies natural to man it is powerless to produce righteousness within. Right living is the fruit of the Spirit, and the fruit of the Spirit fulfills the whole law. While we are not under law as the rule of life, the Holy Spirit in us can fufill the requirements of the law. The fruit of the Spirit is the fruit of God, therefore against such there is no law. That which is of God does not violate the law of God, hence one in whom is the fruit of the Spirit, in him the law of God is fulfilled.

Are we Christ's property? Have we been redeemed by His Blood? If we are truly Christians, then says Paul: "They that are Christ's have crucified the flesh with the affections and lusts" (5:24). Here Paul refers to a definite act accomplished in the case of each believer when he receives Christ as Saviour. He does not ask the Christian to crucify the flesh (or old man), but rather declares to the true child of God that the old man was crucified. Co-crucifixion with Christ is something we must reckon on (Rom. 6:6, 11). When we were born again we confessed that Christ's crucifixion was ours, therefore we can say: "I am crucified with Christ" (Gal. 2:20). Since we now have a new life and are vitally united with Christ in His resurrection we need to walk in the Spirit and allow Him to control our ways. You see, the work of the Spirit in us is based upon the work of Christ at Calvary for us. Now then, since "we live in the Spirit, let us also walk in the Spirit" (5:25).

Chapter five closes with a warning to beware of self-praise. "Let us not be desirous of vain glory, provoking one another, envying one another" (5:26). We are to guard against conceit which only promotes a spirit of competition, which in turn may result in envy and division. Such action toward one another is not in keeping with the Spirit's leading. Before we were saved we enjoyed a show of the flesh to provoke and rritate others. But now we are to enjoy true freedom and not permit our Christian liberty to be perverted as license to show off and set ourselves above our fellows. There is no spiritual pride, no "holier-than-thou" attitude, no overcritical spirit in the life where the fruit of the Spirit is manifested. We can glory in nothing save the Cross and what we are by the Grace of God. Does my daily life bear out my profession of Christ? May God help me to stand guard against license.

C. *The Practice of Love* (6:1-10)

It has been clearly pointed out by the apostle that the life in which the fruit of the Spirit is in evidence, is a life that loves. While he argues for liberty, he also argues for the law which every Christian must obey. It is the law of Christ, which is the law of love. In verses one to ten this law is applied to the conduct of the believer in relation to a fallen brother.

"Brethren, if a man be overtaken in a fault, ye which are spiritual, restore such an one in the spirit of meekness, considering thyself, lest thou also be tempted" (6:1). Christians are brethren and constitute the only true brotherhood. There are "brethren" in families, lodges and secret societies, but the word never reaches its fullest meaning until it is used in its

relation to true Christian brotherhood. Beloved, we are brethren, and as such we have a mutual relationship in the Lord.

Now Paul supposes a case in which a brother in Christ is
suddenly seized upon by the Enemy and led into some act of
sin. The sinning one did not cease to be a Christian; he did not
become unsaved. He was not severed from the Body of Christ
but merely dislocated. In the original the word "restore" means
"to set in joint, as a dislocated bone." It is a surgical term and
it suggests the work which must be done when a bone is frac-
tured or a joint is dislocated. When we dislocate some member
of our human bodies, the aggravation prevents the body from
functioning normally. There is discomfort until the bone is
set or the dislocation put into place. The Galatians who were
still being led by the Spirit and who had not turned to legalism
are being urged to exercise skill and gentleness in restoring their
erring brethren. The genuinely spiritual believer manifests the
fruit of the Spirit when he leads the sinning brother back into
the Way. Criticism and censoriousness will be put aside. Just
as an injured limb is sensitive to the touch of another, even
so the erring brother is difficult to deal with. Those who deal
with sinning saints must do so in the spirit of meekness. Very
often a harsh attitude drives the erring one farther from God.

The task of dealing with the fallen one belongs to those
"which are spiritual." The spiritual man is one led by the Holy
Spirit, and only such can qualify for this delicate work. We are
exhorted to deal gently, meekly and delicately with the erring
brother, "considering thyself, lest thou also be tempted." We
are not to judge, for even the spiritual are subject to temptation.
Sometimes it is the very one who, like Peter, displays self-
confidence that commits the sin he boasted he would never
commit. My brother fell today; I may fall tomorrow. Spiritual
pride itself is sinful and very dangerous, "Wherefore let him
that thinketh he standeth take heed lest he fall" (1 Cor.
10:12). It behooves us to beware lest we fall into temptation
and make license of our liberty in Christ.

"Bear ye one another's burdens, and so fulfil the law of

Christ" (6:2). The law of Christ is the law of love, and love always comes to the rescue of another who is in distress. Our Lord bore the burden of our sins in His own body, hence it is Christlike to undergird our brother's burden. Each of us should assume a responsibility for the spiritual well-being of our fellow believers. Christians are burden-bearers, and while we cannot bear the burden of sin as Christ bore it, we can share His warm-hearted and sympathetic interest in others.

Here is one of the hindrances to becoming a successful burden-bearer: "For if a man think himself to be something, when he is nothing, he deceiveth himself" (6:3). Here is sound advice: Never look upon our erring brother as if he were less spiritual than ourselves. The conceited man is a deceived man and is in no condition at all to restore a sinning brother. The misfortunes of others do not suggest in the least that we are superior. There is no good in the flesh, the old nature, and what we are in Christ we are by the grace of God. When we stand upon our own dignity we deceive our own minds. When a man has a high regard for his own moral goodness he has a false estimate of himself. Satan has deceived him and he has deceived himself.

"But let every man prove his own work, and then shall he have rejoicing in himself alone, and not in another" (6:4). This is spoken of the New Man in Christ—the new self; as Paul says "I of myself with the mind, indeed, serve the law of God" (Rom. 7:24, A.S.V.). The idea here is that every man is called to self-judgment. Let each of us impose the acid test of God's Word upon ourselves and not upon our brethren. We should gauge our own lives by God's standard and not our neighbor's. "Let a man examine himself" (1 Cor. 11:28). When a Christian minds his own business, he will receive from God the commendation that is due him. The approval of a good conscience is likewise satisfying. Beloved, we have our individual responsibility and each must give an account of himself to God (Rom. 14:12).

Individual responsibility is further enjoined upon the believer in Paul's next statement, where he says: "For every man shall bear his own burden" (or *load*) (6:5). While there are certain kinds of burdens we can share with one another, such as those mentioned in verse two, there are certain moral and personal responsibilities that each must bear alone. In a certain sense my life is linked up with others, but at the Judgment Seat of Christ I must face my Lord alone. As a husband, father, pastor and citizen, there are certain inalienable responsibilities that I must bear. If I fail to bear my moral obligations while here on earth, then I must bear the shame of neglect and failure when I stand before God. In verse two I am told to aid my brother who has failed in carrying out his responsibility, while in verse five I am exhorted not to fail to carry out my "own" personal, private responsibility. My task is my own, hence I have no right to expect someone else to assume it for me. I am to avoid being lazy and careless about my own obligations, and at the same time be ready to assist him who may need my help. In the armed forces each soldier must bear his own pack. But when a buddy is wounded on the field of battle the soldier who has not been struck by the enemy comes to the aid of the wounded one. Verse two suggests an opportunity to serve others; verse five reminds us that before God every one will bear his own load.

An example of the burden the spiritual man will seek to share is cited for us in verse six: "Let him that is taught in the Word communicate unto him that teacheth in all good things." Perhaps Paul has in mind here the extra load which rests upon some of the ministers of God's Word. If a man gives himself to teaching others, he should be supported by those who have been the recipients of his teaching. The word "communicate" conveys the idea of sharing, of having things in common. The teacher and the taught are sharing in the blessed fellowship of giving and receiving. The teacher passes on the great truths of God's Word which are the fruit of his labor; the taught acknowledge this by communicating to him "in all good things." The saints at Philippi displayed the fruit of the Spirit, for they excelled in the grace of giving (Phil. 4:15). When we support the Lord's servants, whether on the foreign mission field or at home, we advance the cause of our Lord Jesus Christ. No man has a right to put a price on his ministry, but he does have the right to expect that God will supply his needs through His children. Christians must not expect to be on the receiving end all the time; they must be on the communicating end as well. "Even so hath the Lord ordained that they which preach the gospel should live of the gospel" (1 Cor. 9:14). Is God using your pastor to instruct you in the way of life? If He is, then share that good teaching with others and pray for God's servant. (Ironside p. 217. Luther p. 272.)

The teaching in verse six concerning giving and receiving is followed by the closely related law of sowing and reaping: "Be not deceived; God is not mocked: for whatsoever a man soweth, that shall he also reap. For he that soweth to his flesh shall of the flesh reap corruption; but he that soweth to the Spirit shall of the Spirit reap life everlasting" (6:7, 8). No allowance is made here for the man who is deceived, for in the light of verse three, he deceived himself. This fundamental law to human life should be self-evident. A man is a fool who thinks that he can break God's laws and escape the consequences. When a man plants wheat he expects to harvest a crop of wheat, simply because like begets like. And yet a man breaks God's laws and expects to escape the results. It can never be! "He which soweth sparingly shall reap also sparingly; and he which soweth bountifully shall reap also bountifully" (2 Cor. 9:6). When Israel sowed the wind she reaped the whirlwind (Hosea 8:7). No man can gather grapes of thorns, or figs of thistles (Matt. 7:16, 17). No man can turn his nose up at God and treat the Almighty with contempt. Let us sow bountifully. What we pass on to others in the name of the Lord is not lost. Paul could say: "I will very gladly spend and be spent for you . . ." (2 Cor. 12:15). We are God's stewards, and as such we will reap a harvest in proportion to our sowing—not what we intended to sow, or thought we had sown, or knew what we should have sown, but that and only that which we actually did sow. One can give and enrich himself, another can keep and yet impoverish himself. We cannot live one kind of life and expect to harvest another. The Christian who ignores the teaching of God's Word will have to answer at the Judgment Seat of Christ; the sinner who defies God must answer for his unbelief at the Great White Throne.

The idea of sowing and reaping continues in verse nine: "And let us not be weary in well doing: for in due season we shall reap, if we faint not." Let us not retreat in the battle nor give way to the heat of the day, for in its own time the harvest will come. Brethren, let us be patient and persevering unto the coming of the Lord. "Behold, the husbandman waiteth for the precious fruit of the earth, and hath long patience for it, until he receive the early and latter rain. Be ye also patient; stablish your hearts: for the coming of the Lord draweth nigh" (James 5:7, 8). Just as God gave promise to Noah that in the earth there would be that unending procession of seasons and times of harvest (Gen. 8:22), even so shall it be for the believer who faithfully sows to the Spirit. Continue witnessing, working, praying and giving. The harvest will come just as certainly as the Lord Himself will come.

Now in view of the certainty of the harvest: "As we have therefore opportunity, let us do good unto all men, especially unto them who are of the household of faith" (6:10). The fruit of the Spirit in the life of the believer will be communicated to all men with whom we come in contact, but in a particular way to fellow believers. The Christian should patronize other Christians whenever possible. Before we endeavor to show a benevolent spirit to the unbeliever, there must be a genuine display of the family spirit within the family of God. In so doing we will be imitating our blessed Lord who went about doing good to the thankless as well as to the thankful. This is the proof of love.

D. *The Postlude* (6:11-18)

This last section of the Epistle contains Paul's final warning against the false teachers as well as his closing words to the churches in Galatia. Despite his infirmity Paul did not employ an amanuensis (very much the same as a stenographer to whom one would dictate), but rather did he pen the manuscript himself, the "large letters" betraying the extent of his visual handicap. Paul considered the defense of his apostleship and the authority of the gospel important enough to write to the Galatians with his own hand at the cost of pain and effort (6:11).

He would warn them finally that the Judaizers were not concerned for the spiritual well-being of the Christians in Galatia. Their motives were not pure. They merely sought to make a fair "shew in the flesh," preaching circumcision only to escape the persecution that came to those who preached salvation through faith in Christ's death on the Cross (6:12). The legalists, like their posterity in some churches today, wanted the crown without the cross. They were unwilling to take a stand with Jesus Christ despite the cost. Their insistence on the circumcision of the Galatians was pure selfishness on their part. They had identified themselves with the church, but they compromised the truth so that they might remain in good standing with their Jewish brethren.

Paul exposes them further (6:13) by pointing out that the Judaizers who were not keeping the law were merely trying to save face because of their own failures. While they lived in sin they boasted of having succeeded in persuading others to become circumcised. How like some of our denominational churches today! They boast an increase in membership, in finances and in multiplied activities while there is not the reality of God's power in their midst. Many people are deceived into believing that because they are members in good standing of such churches they are saved. They fail to see that the keeping of special days and the observance of ordinances can never bring salvation.

In contrast to the self-effort and self-glorying of the legalizers, Paul adds his personal testimony: "But God forbid that I should glory, save in the cross of our Lord Jesus Christ, by whom the world is crucified unto me, and I unto the world" (6:14). By the cross here Paul does not have in mind the wooden beams on which the body of our Lord was fastened. To Paul the Cross was a revelation of the meaasure of man's hatred against God and of God's love for mankind. The Cross of Christ was the place where the love of God for sinners was poured out. There man did his worst against God while God did His best in behalf of man. When the Judaizing teachers gloried in their success of persuading a Gentile to observe the Mosaic Law, Paul exalted the finished work of Christ at Calvary for sinners. They denied the Cross so that they would not have to bear a cross; Paul identified himself with it notwithstanding the persecution which resulted from such a stand. Paul knew that in heaven the believer's boast will be in God's redeeming grace and that all glory will be ascribed to the Lamb of God. Let others despise the Cross if they will, but let it be the fixed purpose of every true child of God to find his highest expression of praise in the atoning work of the Lord Jesus Christ. It is only as we thus take our stand that the world-system is rendered unattractive to us and we are rendered unattractive to it. Faith in Christ and acknowledgment of what He has done for us will not allow for any compromise on our part with the world. Let the Cross separate us from the world and the world will no more appeal to us.

Now to the point of the matter. "For in Christ Jesus neither circumcision availeth any thing, nor uncircumcision, but a new creature" (6:15). Circumcision can add nothing to the salvation of the Jew; nor can the lack of circumcision take anything away from the Gentile. But the redemption offered through the blood of Christ can make both Jew and Gentile "a new creature." Yes, that is the point: Ye must be born again.

There can be no substitute for the regenerating power of the Holy Spirit when a man savingly believes in the Son of God as His Substitute and Saviour. The only thing that matters is not whether a man is circumcised but whether he is born again. The outward ritual will affect the body, but it is the soul of man that must be reached. God alone can meet this need, and meet it He did in Jesus Christ. Now "if any man be in Christ, he is a *new creature* . . ." (2 Cor. 5:17). The mere external formalism in religion may have a form of godliness, but it is without the power (2 Tim. 3:5). The new birth is the necessary experience that will avail anything. "And as many as walk according to this rule, peace be on them, and mercy, and upon the Israel of God" (6:16).

The subject has been fully and satisfactorily dealt with. His apostleship has been proved and the authority of the Gospel of Grace has been vindicated. Paul had become God's chosen vessel to utter His final word against legalism. Now he will be troubled about the matter no more. He had given God's Word, and with it the promise that the message would not return void. In his body he bore the brand-marks of his devotion to Jesus Christ (6:17). The scars testified of his loyalty to his Lord. Yes, he belonged altogether to the Lord Jesus Christ. At one time he was proud of the mark of circumcision, but now he can point to those scars received in the service of a new Master. He was no inexperienced recruit, but an old veteran of the good fight of faith. Thank God for Paul! And more than this, let us praise Him for His matchless grace whereby we are justified in His sight.

"Brethren, the grace of our Lord Jesus Christ be with your spirit. Amen" (6:18).

Ephesians

INTRODUCTION

Paul was one of a long list of godly men and women, beginning with Joseph in Egypt, whose prison experience was used by God to bring forth His praises. Here is solid evidence that God makes the wrath of men to praise Him. So testified Asaph in Psalm 76:10.

W. M. Taylor has written what he calls *The Prison Literature of the Christian Church*. Beginning with the era immediately preceding the Reformation, Taylor cites such worthies as Savonarola who, during his month of imprisonment before his execution, wrote his commentaries on the Thirty-first and Fifty-first Psalms; and gentle Anne Askew who, holding that in the Lord's Supper the bread, after consecration, remained bread, wrote on the night before she was burned at Smithfield:

> Like as an armed knight
>   Appointed to the field,
> With this world will I fight,
>   And faith shall be my shield.
>
> Faith is that weapon strong
>   Which will not fail at need;
> My foes therefore among
>   Therewith will I proceed.
>
> I now rejoice in heart,
>   And hope bids me do so,
> That Christ will take my part
>   And ease me of my woe.

William Tyndale, to whom perhaps our English Bible is owed more than to any other one man, while imprisoned at Vilvorde, requested his Hebrew Bible, Hebrew Grammar, and Hebrew Dictionary. Defying the Pope and all his laws, he said: "If God spare my life, ere many years, I will cause a boy that driveth the plough to know more of the Scriptures than thou dost." Thus Tyndale became known as "the man who hath translated the New Testament into English."

Lady Jane Grey, on the eve of her execution, sent her Greek Testament to her sister with the prayer that God would give her sister grace to live in His fear and die in the true Christian faith.

Some of us cannot forget *Pilgrim's Progress,* the fruit of John Bunyan's labors while in the Bedford Jail; nor the letters of Samuel Rutherford, written from his confinement in Aberdeen; nor the hymns of Madame Guyon, written in similar circumstances, of which the following lines are but a sample:

> My cage confines me round,
>   Abroad I cannot fly;
> But though my wing is closely bound,
>   My heart's at liberty.
> My prison walls cannot control
> The flight, the freedom of my soul.

These saints of God and countless others, like Paul, had learned to be content in whatever state they found themselves (Phil. 4:11). They proved that the grace of God is sufficient in every circumstance (2 Cor. 12:9). Realizing what God in grace had done for him, Paul accepted his long hours of confinement as an opportunity for a wider ministry for Him through the written word.

The city of Ephesus was the seacoast capital of proconsular Asia, and was one of Asia's great religious, political, and commercial centers. The famous temple of Diana, one of the seven wonders of the ancient world, was situated in Ephesus. This mighty structure had taken more than 200 years to build and was the center of Diana-worship, concerning which we read in Acts 19:23-41. As a huge temple it served as a fitting illustration to Paul, when he wrote his Epistle to the Ephesians, of the true Church of Jesus Christ, the abode of the Holy Spirit. The substance of the epistle is, indeed, the calling and conduct of the Church. When Paul wrote from his prison in Rome, he would show the saints that in the invisible Church they had a temple, not made with human hands, infinitely more glorious than Diana's. Worshipers of Diana gathered in Ephesus from all over the Roman Empire, believing that their image of Diana had fallen from heaven (Acts 19:35).

Such was Ephesus, a religious center; and, as is every great religious center, it was a hotbed of cults and superstitions. Silver images of various sorts were made and sold at a profit. Magical arts were practiced, even the Jews erecting a synagogue in that place (Acts 18:19; 19:8). But one day something of supernatural origin happened in that great seaport city. The Gospel of Jesus Christ was preached and a smashing blow was dealt the pagan metropolis. From this it never recovered.

A. The Commencement in Asia

We cannot be dogmatic on all of the details as to just when and by whom the church in Ephesus was founded. Several possibilities exist. First, on the Day of Pentecost when the Holy Spirit descended in power, seventeen nationalities were represented, among them men from Asia, of which Ephesus was the capital (Acts 2:9). Possibly these men were the first to carry the gospel back to the region round about Ephesus. In the second place, there is a possibility that Paul's visit to Ephesus, on his return from Europe during his second missionary journey, was the occasion for the founding of the church there. We do know that at that time he entered into the synagogue and reasoned with the Jews and, while he did not remain for any extended length of time, he left Priscilla and Aquila, well-taught Christians, to carry on there. A third contribution of Christian truth made to Ephesus was through Apollos, a converted Jew of Alexandria, who visited the city, speaking and teaching diligently the things of the Lord (Acts 18:24-26).

How or when the seed of God's Word was first sown at Ephesus we cannot tell, but we may be certain that Paul's three years' stay there (Acts 20:31) made deep and abiding impressions upon the inhabitants. It was during the great apostle's extended visit to that wicked city that the mighty power of the gospel was demonstrated through his life and ministry.

When Paul arrived at Ephesus, he found "certain disciples" (Acts 19:1), professed followers of Christ who had received the teaching of John the Baptist but who were ignorant of the full message of the gospel and the Person and work of the Holy Spirit. These men were about twelve in number. Paul was quick to discern their lack of understanding and propounded two questions to them.

His first query was: "Did ye receive the Holy Ghost when ye believed?" (Acts 19:2). I have quoted the American Standard Version here, since Paul's question was not, as the King James Version would suggest, whether at some time after their belief they had received the Holy Spirit. Actually Paul wanted to know if they had been born again. The answer was a sure indication that Paul had proper discernment in the matter, for they replied: "We did not so much as hear whether the Holy Spirit was *given*." Again I have used the American Standard Version because the word "given" is added, and that word is necessary to complete the sense.

This small group had missed the real meaning of Pentecost. The condition of the Ephesian "believers" was akin to that of many church members today. They had a belief that was not unto salvation, since it lacked the genuine supernatural experience of regeneration by the Holy Spirit. Some of my readers may want to differ with me here and tell me that these "disciples" were saved but, like the Jews today, they were out of date. Indeed the basis of their faith and baptism was not in the Redeemer who had already come and died on Calvary's cross for the remission of sins and had come forth from death and the grave. They did not know the true gospel, and that the Holy Spirit was the one who saves a man the moment that man trusts the Saviour.

Paul realized that he could not build a church at Ephesus on such flimsy material. Nor can we! The presence of the

Holy Spirit in a man's heart is the test of true Christianity, for "if any man have not the Spirit of Christ, he is none of His" (Rom. 8:9). A fragmentary gospel is a spurious and dangerous gospel of another kind. If a man, upon his believing, does not receive the Holy Spirit, he has not believed unto salvation at all.

Eager to help the Ephesians, Paul asked his second question: "Unto what then were ye baptized?" (Acts 19:3). They answered: "Unto John's baptism." Notice, he did not ask if they had been baptized. He took that for granted. The unsatisfactory answer to his first question raised suspicion in his mind about their their baptism. What might have prompted his question concerning baptism? I see an answer that is highly probable. Paul could not conceive of any one receiving true Christian baptism and yet being so ignorant about the new birth. If they had received the true believer's baptism, they should have known something about the gospel and its power to save.

Now we are not to hold these disciples responsible for their ignorance. They were doubtless willing to learn but had been taught by Apollos who, while an eloquent man and mighty in the Scriptures, knew only the baptism of John (Acts 18:24, 25). With all of this man's knowledge, all of his eloquence, all of his fervency, and all of his boldness, he was sadly lacking in the truth of the finished work of our crucified, risen, and ascended Lord.

Apollos taught a preparatory baptism unto repentance, which looked forward to the coming of the King. Christian baptism looks back to His coming and sees the accomplishments of our salvation in Christ's virgin birth, virtuous life, vicarious death, victorious resurrection, and visible ascension to the Father's right hand. Christian baptism is the identification of the true child of God with his Lord in death, burial, and resurrection.

The result of Paul's kind and straightforward approach is disclosed in these words: "When they heard this, they were baptized in the name of the Lord Jesus" (Acts 19:5). At first thought I was inclined not to comment upon this verse at this point. But as I pondered it more I was impressed with the many who have been robbed of the truth of the gospel, yet who have submitted to certain rites such as infant baptism, confirmation, and the like. Perhaps it might help someone who reads these lines and who has come to a personal knowledge of the Lord Jesus Christ, but who was baptized before conversion, to look further into this matter. Many persons have asked if they should be re-baptized. I shall quote from J. C. Macaulay who has written well on The Acts: "I doubt the validity of an ordinance administered apart from personal, living faith. Therefore, while I cannot lay down a law of procedure, I should point to this incident and encourage a following of the impulse of the renewed heart." This has been well said and it expresses fully the mind of the present writer.

Paul's next move at Ephesus found him in the synagogue where he spoke boldly for three months, reasoning and persuading concerning the things of the kingdom of God (Acts 19:8). Here he witnessed to his Jewish brethren but they only hardened their hearts and refused to believe. His action at this point is of interest. Luke says: "He departed from them, and separated the disciples" (verse 9). Paul refused to linger where Christ was denied. Any true servant of Christ would hesitate in fear and trembling before dividing a church, but light can have no communion with darkness (2 Cor. 6:14), hence the only action remaining is to come out from among those in darkness and be separate. Personally, I believe it quite likely that this might have been the formation of the local assembly at Ephesus. Many local evangelical churches that are greatly blessed of God today exist as the result of some such movement. When men are determined to oppose the teaching of God's Word, it is useless to continue with them.

The church at Ephesus continued for two years in a schoolhouse (Acts 19:9, 10), of which one Tyrannus was the headmaster. Many a rural church in our own country had its beginning in a public schoolroom. God wanted Asia to hear the gospel and the matter of a meeting place was no problem with Him. A man like Paul needs no fancy edifice in which to preach. For two years the ministry of teaching and preaching God's Word flowed ceaselessly to all Asia from the local schoolhouse. Mighty spiritual movements need not emanate from great cathedrals. A Spirit-filled man may be the instrument of revival, no matter the evironment in which you place him. Such was Paul.

The seal of God's approval was obviously upon this zealous apostle in the notable miracles which were performed through him (Acts 19:11, 12). The very handkerchiefs which he touched brought healing to the sick. From other victims demons were cast. Observe please that these are called "special miracles" and that "God wrought" them. This was not God's usual method but rather a special demonstration in a transition period before the Bible was completed, and the Jews were neither on legal ground nor on full New Testament ground.

B. The Conflict in Ephesus

Not until "divers were hardened, and believed not . . ." did Paul begin to feel satanic resistance. After that, some who heard Paul speak the gospel "spake evil of that way before the multitude" (Acts 19:9).

Before examining more closely the conflict in Ephesus, recall Paul's mention of it in the following descriptive words: "I will tarry at Ephesus until Pentecost. For a great door and effectual is opened unto me, and there are *many adversaries*" (1 Cor. 16:8, 9). Later, in his second epistle, he adds: "For we would not, brethren, have you ignorant of our trouble which came to us in Asia, that we were pressed out of measure, above strength, insomuch that we despaired even of life" (2 Cor. 1:8).

Two antithetical reactions to the preaching of the Word in Asia appear. Be assured that God's Word did not return unto Him fruitless. It never does. When we come to examine the conquests in Asia we shall see, then, how the Word of God grew and prevailed. But the sword of the Spirit is two-edged (Heb. 4:12), affecting those who will not accept it as well as those who do. The antagonism between light and darkness, truth and error, is always sharp wherever and whenever a man preaches the whole council of God. Because he preached only a half-truth, the ministry of Apollos never created a stir, although he spoke boldly. But when Paul came among them they heard the Word of the Lord Jesus in all its fullness, and the struggle between the force of righteousness and sin became more open.

In the city an attempt to imitate the work of God was begun by one of the evil priests and his seven wicked sons. "Then certain of the vagabond Jews, exorcists, took upon them to call over them which had evil spirits the name of the Lord Jesus, saying, We adjure you by Jesus whom Paul preacheth" (Acts 19:13). Little did those imitators, dealing in sorcery and witchcraft, know how terrible is the name of our Lord Jesus Christ against those who misuse that holy name. They thought they imitated the ministry of Paul, but they were ignorant of the fact that Paul did nothing of himself. God wrought the miracles by the power of the Holy Spirit. God did not tolerate those blasphemous imitators but dealt a hard blow to Satan's emissaries and their sinister practice of the black arts. Paul had many adversaries, not the least of these being "the rulers of the darkness of this world" (Eph. 6:12).

The apostle faced opposition in still another form. Professional sculptors made silver images of the goddess Diana and sold them for profit in Ephesus. The leader of the silversmiths' "union" was Demetrius, who seemed to have the power to call together those workmen of like occupation (Acts 19:24, 25). When Paul went throughout Asia teaching that "they be no gods, which are made with hands" (verse 26), sales for the silver shrines dropped and a trade riot broke out. Gaius and Aristarchus, Paul's companions in travel, were dragged to the public theatre to be made a spectacle of (verse 29). Since the preaching of Paul had not only hurt the sale of images but had challenged the right of the Ephesians to worship Diana, wild excitement continued for the space of two hours amidst the shout of the natives of Ephesus: "Great is Diana of the Ephesians" (verse 34). Note their chief concern. When Demetrius spoke to his fellow-craftsmen, he said: "Sirs, ye know that by this craft we have our wealth" (verse 25). The honor of their goddess Diana was a secondary interest; finanacial gain was their main concern. Pious and religious shouts were but a cover-up for their real interests. Into the midst of this frenzied mob Paul would have gone to defend his companions, but some of his friends, who resided in Asia, restrained him (verses 30, 31).

Such are the conflicts where the true gospel is preached. Unfair and illegal business enterprises cannot survive where the Word of God goes out in power. As A. B. Simpson has said: "A gospel that goes down to the heart of Wall Street and turns business upside down must have some power in it." The incident with the tradesmen and the public demonstration climaxed the conflict in Ephesus.

C. The Conquest in Ephesus

We will conclude our introductory study to the Book of Ephesians by glancing briefly at the extent of the victory wrought by God through Paul in Asia. First, "all they which dwelt in Asia heard the word of the Lord Jesus, both Jews and Greeks [Gentiles]" (Acts 19:10). The conquest reached far beyond the city limits of Ephesus. Even Demetrius testified that "not alone at Ephesus, but almost throughout *all Asia,* this Paul hath persuaded and turned away much people" (verse 26). Such geographical gains are not appreciated until one realizes that it was to those seven churches in Asia, Ephesus being one of the seven, that the ascended Lord sent those last letters through John in the Book of The Revelation. To witness to Ephesus alone would never satisfy the heart of the Apostle Paul. This aggressive missionary of the early Church would not rest until all within reach of the gospel had heard. The noteworthy advance of the gospel in a pagan land was a remarkable stride in the founding of the church at Ephesus. The Church in our day cannot boast of such an accomplishment. Multitudes have not yet heard.

The measure of the conquest is seen in a demonstration of supernatural power in the performing of miracles. This was brought to our attention earlier in this chapter when we considered the conflict, namely, Satan's attempt to imitate the work of the Lord (Acts 19:13).

Through Paul, God had wrought special miracles in healing the diseased and casting out evil spirits. All miracles are the exercise of the direct power of God, performed sometimes through various instruments, and at other times apart from any instrument. In the case before us, God wanted to bear witness to both His messenger and His message, so He worked the miracles of healing through His servant. Thereby He authenticated the message in a special way. Any attempt on man's part to duplicate these miracles is a poor imitation indeed.

The people at Ephesus had been held in superstition and trickery for many years, so God exhibited His might in a manner that would both confirm Paul's ministry and condemn as preposterous the work of the exorcists and the evil powers of darkness. This was a mighty victory for the gospel. The victory is seen still further in the punishment which had fallen upon the wicked sons of Sceva.

A final glance at the extent of the conquest brings us to the great consecration service where "many that believed came, and confessed, and shewed their deeds. Many of them also which used curious arts brought their books together, and burned them before all men: and they counted the price of them, and found it fifty thousand pieces of silver" (Acts 19:18, 19). Thus these new converts showed the sincerity of their confession. The gospel had triumphed and they got right with God without weighing the cost. "So mightily grew the Word of God and prevailed" (verse 20).

It was with genuine believers, such as some of these, with whom Paul had the joy of working in the day of the church's beginning in Ephesus. Oh, that a mighty wave of conviction of sin might sweep through our congregations today, and that men and women might destroy openly their tools of sin and vice!

I. THE CALLING AND
DESIGN OF THE CHURCH
(Chapters 1-3)

The Epistle to the Ephesians, along with those letters to the Philippians, the Colossians, and Philemon, is a Christological Epistle. Careful examination unfolds the grandeur and the glory of the Person and work of our Lord Jesus Christ. While it is true that this book of six chapters is a treatment of the design and destiny of the Church, we must be careful to observe that the Church has her calling and consummation "in Christ." All of her blessings are in Him. All of the purposes of God toward the Church are related to the Lord Jesus Christ, so that the Church, in its *calling as an organism* and in its *conduct as an organization,* is seen from the Christocentric standpoint. The most significant phrase in the epistle is made up of the two words, "in Christ." If one is not "in Christ" he can know nothing experientially of these "spiritual blessings." R. W. Dale has said: "The doctrinal teaching of this epistle is very little more than a development of the single expression, 'in Christ'." Except a man be "in Christ," he can claim none of the blessings of God as his redemption rights. We cannot by-pass Jesus Christ to get to God.

A. *The Christian's Present Possessions in Christ* (Chapter 1)

The first three chapters of the epistle deal with doctrine; the last three chapters, with duty. In the first half Paul explains the riches of God's grace; in the last half he exhorts the recipients of God's grace.

Two verses give Paul's usual method of opening a letter. In this, the salutation, the writer designates the author and the addressee: "Paul, an apostle of Jesus Christ by the will of God, to the saints which are at Ephesus, and to the faithful in Christ Jesus" (1:1).

There are no serious doubts among commentators concerning the Pauline authorship of this epistle. Confined in a prison in Rome, well stricken in years, Paul writes a letter different from his other epistles. Controversy is absent. Warning against any particular error of doctrine is missing. Yet this particular difference causes no concern, for both the external and internal evidence are convincingly strong.

Paul designates himself as "an apostle of Jesus Christ." He was alike Christ's possession and His representative. The risen Lord having both saved and sent him, Paul became God's minister to the Gentiles. Having completely surrendered his life to the Lord Jesus Christ, his learning, zeal, and teaching ability were all consecrated to the service of his Master. He was truly an apostle "by the will of God."

"By the will of God" gives additional authority to Paul's position as an apostle. When a man is sent by the will of God, then his hearers will do well to heed his message. Right here we might notice that the will of God is mentioned four times in this first chapter (verses 1, 5, 9, 11). The will of God reaches far back into eternity past, long before the foundations of the earth were laid. What a blessed privilege every servant of God has when he is called to make this known to others! Let us exercise the greatest care lest we interpose anything between the will of God and ourselves while we are here on earth. The human will has no place or function in redemption or in active service apart from the divine will. Every exercise of the spirit, mind and body reaches its loftiest position only when it is motivated by God's will.

The letter is addressed "to the saints which are at Ephesus, and to the faithful in Christ Jesus." The word for "saint" is *hagios,* and it means *a holy one.* Paul usually applied this term to the true child of God. The primary meaning of the word is *separated* or *set apart.*

The Roman Catholic Church has tainted the word "saint"

with so much superstition that it is almost impossible to restore it to its original and intended use. Today its application is to any who exhibit an exceptional, artificial type of piousness, or to those whose own works merit the Pope's canonization. According to the Bible, all Christians are saints (Heb. 10:10, 14). The temple was at one time holy, not because of its materials and magnitude, but because it was a set-apart place for the service of Jehovah. The altars were holy, the vessels were holy, the sacrifices were holy, the priests were holy, all because they were divinely chosen to discharge the function of holy service to the Lord. People in their ignorance call theirs the "All Saints Church," and refer to the apostles as "Saint Peter" and "Saint Paul," but God calls all who have been washed in the blood of the Lord Jesus and born again by the Holy Spirit "saints" (1 Cor. 1:2).

It is God who sanctifies us. He sets us apart; we do not consecrate ourselves. "Saint" suggests no personal merit on man's part, but a condescending act of Almighty God in setting apart those who believe in His Son. H. A. Ironside has said: "We do not become saints by saintliness, but we should be characterized by saintliness because we are saints."

The letter, moreover, is intended for "the faithful in Christ Jesus." The "faithful" are not mere professors but those who demonstrate their sainthood by their saintliness. Faithfulness to Him whose name is held, bears witness to others of God's calling. Faith in Christ is much more than intellectual assent; it includes a surrender of the intellect, the heart, and the will to Jesus Christ as Saviour and Lord. The name and fame of a church and its testimony will remain only so long as its members are "faithful in Christ Jesus." When a man truly has faith in Christ he will keep faith with Christ. If one is not true to Christ, then he has exercised no faith in Christ.

The typical Pauline salutation continues with the words: "Grace be to you, and peace, from God our Father, and from the Lord Jesus Christ" (1:2). Paul combined the two forms of salutation used by the Greeks and the Hebrews to send his

Christian greeting. Here is a twofold blessing from two persons. The Father sends His grace and peace; the Son says: "Give them Mine, also." It could not be otherwise, since the Son shares the exalted position with the Father "in the heavenlies." God and Christ are One, thus they are the one source of "grace and peace." The gospel that Paul preached is always known as the gospel of grace, the gospel of the ill-merited favor of God.

Notice that God will not offer peace apart from grace. Nor can any man have peace before he accepts God's grace. These two words form no mere conventional courtesy, as the Greeks and Hebrews might use them, but rather are they a rich Christian blessing.

Are we saints? Then let us receive and appropriate what is ours, for what is sent to us we have a right to possess. All through the pages of the New Testament the grace and peace of God in Christ shine gloriously forth. To accept His grace is to know His peace—peace not only with Him but with others also. Ephesians will unfold for us "the riches of His grace" (1:7). Twelve times in this one epistle Paul uses the word "grace." May each of us lay claim to our possessions.

All of the following blessings are ours because of *grace:* (1) salvation (Eph. 2:8), (2) justification (Rom. 3:24), (3) victory over sin (Rom. 5:20), (4) power to testify (Rom. 12:3, 15:15; Col. 4:6), (5) strength for service (2 Tim. 2:1; Heb. 12:28), (6) a spirit of generosity (2 Cor. 8:7), (7) sweetness in singing (Col. 3:16), (8) ability to stand (1 Pet. 5:12), and (9) strength in suffering (2 Cor. 12:9). There are doubtless many more, but these will suffice to show us the greatness of our need in appropriating God's grace.

1. *Paul's Praise to God for What We Received* (1:3-14)

The next verse is the key verse in the first half of the epistle, since it introduces us to the source of our wealth in Christ. It is definitely a word of praise: "Blessed be the God and

Father of our Lord Jesus Christ, who hath blessed us with all spiritual blessings in heavenly places in Christ" (1:3).

The adjective translated "blessed" means *to celebrate with praises*. At the very outset Paul magnifies the grace of God toward the Ephesians so that they, too, might be filled to overflowing with praise. God is said to bless us when He bestows upon us every provision for our spiritual peace and prosperity. We are said to bless God when we offer praise and thanksgiving for His provision.

More than twenty-five years had passed since Paul met the Lord Jesus Christ near Damascus. Still he was counting his blessings and praising God for them. Paul is not praising God because God *desires* to bless him, nor because God has *determined* to bless him at some future time, but because God *"hath"* blessed him. Yes, and "us"! God is the Blesser, and the blessed are those, and those only, who have received His Son as *"our* Lord Jesus Christ." The "us" here are the "saints," and as God's set-apart ones we are eligible for the blessings.

The nature of the blessings is said to be "spiritual." There is possibly more than one explanation of this. First, Paul might have intended to distinguish the blessings from those mercies of God that are material, physical, and temporal, that are intended particularly for the body. Second, Paul possibly meant by "spiritual blessings" those blessings pertaining to the Holy Spirit and intended to minister to the human spirit. The saint's citizenship is in heaven, hence he no longer sets his affection on things in the earth. Moreover, his principal needs are spiritual so that he must be "strengthened with might by His [God's] Spirit in the inner man" (3:16).

Too many of us place the emphasis upon those things that are temporal and transient while we neglect the values that are spiritual and eternal. The Father designed every spiritual blessing for the Church. They are ours "in Christ," and are delivered to us by the Holy Spirit. The lasting joy that God bestows upon us is not in the things of this world, but rather in "heavenly places" or, better still, "in the heavenlies." Ours are heavenly experiences and heavenly privileges conferred upon us by God in Christ. They originate among the eternal and unseen things.

The first of the believer's possessions for which Paul praises God follows: "According as He hath chosen us in Him before the foundation of the world, that we should be holy and without blame before Him in love" (1:4). We must see at the outset that all that God had done for us in Christ is "according to the *eternal purpose* which He purposed in Christ Jesus our Lord" (3:11). In eternity past, God had certain settled purposes which He accomplished at various times during the dispensations of human history, and here we are carried back into the remotest ages of past eternity where, says Paul, God was loving us and planning that all who are "in Christ . . . should be holy and without blame before Him." God's eternal choice, then, was that all who are in Christ should be a holy people.

The phrase "chosen us in Him" could be rendered "chose us for Himself." Chose us for what? Not to everlasting life, but that we should be spotless for Himself! The election in the divine Mind was that all those in Christ should be "holy ones," free from every defilement of sin.

It is not difficult to see how God should purpose in His heart, before the world came into existence, that He was going to have a holy people who would be to the praise of His glory and grace. To that end God created Adam, and in spite of the fall of man, God is still going to carry out His purpose in Christ. The divine choice will find its consummation when Christ returns for His bride "to present you faultless before the presence of His glory with exceeding joy" (Jude 24). Temporarily we are in this world, but not of it. We were chosen to be holy before its foundations were laid; we are merely passing through it to another world. We might fail to practice holiness here, but the eternal purpose of God will be fulfilled when our Lord returns and "we shall be like Him" (1 John 3:2).

God has selected a people to be His holy habitation. Are you in that company, my friend? You are, if you are "in

Christ." If you are not, you may this very day join that holy band by trusting Him as your Saviour. Then you, too, will be a part of the true Church of God's creation and design which, on the great presentation day, will be presented a glorious Church, "holy and without blemish" (Eph. 5:25-27).

The ultimate purpose of God's choice is not salvation but sanctification. John Calvin stated that it is wrong to say that any of us may attain perfection in this life; nevertheless, this is the goal to which the whole course of our lives must be directed, even though we cannot reach it till we have finished our course. Let us grow in grace and in the knowledge of our Lord Jesus Christ, saying with Paul: ". . . neither count I my life dear unto myself, so that I might finish my course with joy" (Acts 20:24). And let us praise God that we have been chosen to be a part of the completed structure, a perfect Church throughout all eternity.

When God designed His Church in eternity past He "predestinated us unto the adoption of children by Jesus Christ to Himself, according to the good pleasure of His will" (1:5). The American Standard Version makes it clear that the verb translated "predestinated" is "foreordained." It means *to appoint,* or *to determine beforehand.*

To what have we been predestinated? Neither this verse nor any other verse in the Bible teaches that God decrees that some men are foreordained to everlasting life while others are foreordained to everlasting death. Christ "gave Himself a ransom for *all*" (1 Tim. 2:6), and "this is good and acceptable in the sight of God our Saviour; who will have *all* men to be saved, and to come unto the knowledge of the truth" (1 Tim. 2:3, 4).

Notice, please, that we have been foreordained *unto* adoption as sons. The word "adoption" is used only by Paul. To understand its meaning, you must lay aside the idea of the word as used today when, by a legal act, an adult person takes a minor, not his own, into the relation as his child. The adoption of the believer is still future, being a divine act whereby

God sets a goal for the believer. Paul states clearly that our adoption is something for which the believer is "waiting" (Rom. 8:23), having been foreordained *"unto"* adoption. Although we do have here and now the Spirit of adoption (Rom. 8:15), His Presence in us is merely the seal, or guarantee of a future act of son-*placing*. Adoption does not mean son-*making,* for in eternity we shall be sons no more than we are now but, rather, at that time, we shall be properly placed in God's show-case and displayed as sons. God has predestinated us unto the adoption—it is future. Therefore, His sovereign act of adoption can have nothing whatever to do with His choice of us.

In the Epistle to the Galatians, Paul explains how Jesus Christ secured our adoption for us by His death at Calvary in order that "we might receive" it (Gal. 4:5). Our present standing is that of sons; for, "beloved, now are we the sons of God." And how wonderful this is! But, adds the Apostle John: "It doth not yet appear what we shall be" (1 John 3:2). The fact of our present son-*making* and our future son-*placing* were all "according to the good pleasure of His will." Our future position, which was God's choice, was not only His will but His enjoyment. The mightiest angel in heaven will not share in the glory of the believer's future position.

If you, dear reader, are not a son of God, your future is dark indeed. But even now there is time. If you trust Jesus Christ as your Saviour, God will make you His son now and place you in an exalted position as His son in eternity. Then you, too, will join in praise to God for His goodness.

Verse six teaches us that every true believer has been foreordained to be such a trophy of the grace of God as to cause men to praise the glory of His grace. Paul writes: "To the praise of the glory of His grace, wherein He hath made us accepted in the Beloved" (1:6). These words, not to be considered by themselves, are just a link in a golden chain of thoughts beginning with verse 3.

God has blessed us with every spiritual blessing because He

chose us in Christ before the foundation of the world, that we should be holy and without blame before Him, one day to place us on display as His glorified sons. Then His holy and unblemished Church will cause men and angels to acknowledge the wonders of His infinite love and grace toward sinners.

God has foreordained that men shall extol and praise His grace in all its eternal glory. This is the terminus of His kindness toward sinners. Today this is demonstrated only meagerly in the lives of His true followers, but in the end of the age "He shall come to be glorified in His saints, and to be admired in all them that believe" (2 Thess. 1:10).

The Lord of heaven and earth will be wondered at by all when the Church Age has run its course and the last member has been added to the Church. With mingled surprise and admiration, the spectators of earth and hell will marvel at the monument of divine grace. All who have put their trust in the Lord Jesus Christ are certain to be present and a part of that magnificent exhibition, for, adds the apostle: "He hath made us accepted in the Beloved." We are already accepted in the Father's presence because we are in Christ. What condescending love and grace! We are accepted, but only because the Father has "made us" so. Let us continue to praise God, not only for what we have been saved *from,* but for what we are saved *to.*

These verses (1:3-14) are referred to by Charles R. Erdman as a hymn of praise consisting of three stanzas. He says that the first relates to the past: God the Father is the subject, and the refrain closes with the words, "To the praise of the glory of *His* grace" (1:6). The second stanza relates to the present: God the Son is the subject, and it concludes "to the praise of *His* glory" (1:12). The third stanza relates to the future: God the Holy Spirit is the subject, and it concludes "unto the praise of *His* glory" (1:14). And then Dr. Erdman shows that the three stanzas are bound into a harmonious unity by recurring references to Christ: "In the Beloved," "In Christ," "In Whom."

We have come now to the second stanza of Paul's wonderful hymn of praise (1:7-12). The first stanza makes clear the work of God in grace in eternity past. The second shows God's grace manifested toward us now in Jesus Christ's earthly ministry. Paul continues: "In whom we have redemption through His blood, the forgiveness of sins, according to the riches of His grace" (1:7). Before the sinner becomes saved he is a captive in the slave-market of sin. He is sold out to the world, the flesh, and the devil. As a slave in bondage he needs to be freed. Someone must purchase him and take him out of the market of sin. Christians, once bondmen, now have redemption.

The word "redemption" appears three times in Ephesians, and it means *to set free by the payment of a ransom*. The ransom price of the slave is the blood of Jesus Christ, and if any man is to be released from the power and penalty of sin it must be "through His blood." The penalty for sin is death (Gen. 2:17). Death is sin's wages (Rom. 6:23). Only a substitute life will satisfy the righteous demands of God. Since the life of the flesh is in the blood (Lev. 17:11), and the Son of man gave His life a "ransom" (Matt. 20:28), all who trust in Him are assured of release from sin's power and penalty, but only "through His blood." In the first stanza, the Father plans our redemption (1:4-6); in the second, the Son provides it. We shall never be able to overestimate the worth and power of the death of Jesus Christ. God displayed His wisdom and power in creation, but only in the death of His Son do we see a manifestation of divine compassion for sinners, and the only responsibility imposed upon sinners is that of believing. Redemption is a present fact: "we *have* redemption."

Paul includes in the same sentence, "the forgiveness of sins." To "forgive" is *to release from guilt*. God holds resentment against the unbeliever, the resentment being justly provoked by a violation of His holiness; but when the sinner comes to Christ, guilt is removed and resentment ceases. A man may forgive a friend who has wronged him, but the forgiveness cannot cancel the guilt. But when God forgives a sinner He actually remits the sin and removes the guilt. Forgiveness for the believing sinner is an act of God whereby He sets aside absolutely and eternally, by judicial decree, all condemnation and guilt. Judicial forgiveness, in contradistinction to the Father's forgiveness of His sinning child (1 John 1:9), covers all sin, and by it the believing sinner is pardoned forever. It forever absolves and acquits the sinner. But forgiveness was dear to the Forgiver. It cost the life of God's Son.

Observe the measureless abundance of divine forgiveness— "according to the riches of His Grace" (1:7). No adequate explanation of divine forgiveness can be made apart from those beautiful and precious words. Only the view of the depth and degradation of our sin will cause us to appreciate in any degree the limitless ill-merited favor of God. The word "according" shows the measure of God's grace in forgiveness. "Riches" suggests the inexhaustible springs of liberality. Have you ever tried to estimate how rich God is in grace? He has grace enough for every sinner and riches to spare. And to think He gives liberally to all in proportion to His riches!

That we might know the eternal purpose of God provided for us in His Son, "He hath abounded toward us in all wisdom and prudence" (1:8). God makes His purpose known and then gives His children the capacity to understand and appreciate it. The truths of God are deep truths, but "God hath revealed them unto us by His Spirit" (1 Cor. 2:10). The desire in the Father's heart is that His Church should know the secret things of His divine plan. The Word of God is the revelation of His counsels, and all who search the Word may have an intelligent understanding of His wonderful plan. We, as the redeemed saints of God, "have the mind of Christ" and can foresee the ultimate destiny of the whole creation.

How does God abound toward us in all wisdom and prudence? The answer comes to us in the next verses: "Having made known unto us the mystery of His will, according to His good pleasure which He hath purposed in Himself: That in the dispensation of the fulness of times He might gather together in one all things in Christ, both which are in heaven, and which are on earth; even in Him" (1:9, 10). This is the manner in which He made His grace to abound toward us in all wisdom and intelligent understanding. He made known unto us the mystery.

A mystery is a truth once hidden but now revealed. A mystery is not mysterious in the present connotative meaning of the word but a *secret now revealed by God.* There are a number of mysteries in the New Testament, the true meaning of which God disclosed to Paul. In confidence God has much to tell His own concerning His plan for Israel, the Church, and the world. All of the purposes of God find their fulfillment in Jesus Christ. This present dispensation began with the revelation of God in the virgin birth and virtuous life of His Son. The revelation reached its climax at Calvary. And He continued to reveal Himself in His bodily resurrection and ascension into heaven.

At this moment the authority of Jesus Christ is not fully acknowledged in the earth, but in the end of the age all things in heaven and in earth will find their headship in Christ. In Colossians, Christ is seen as "the Head of the body, the Church," but when He comes again, by Him God will reconcile all things unto Himself, whether they be things in the earth or things in heaven. God will head up all things in Christ. Many military leaders have dreamed of world empires, but God has "highly exalted Him, and given Him a name which is above every name: That at the name of Jesus every knee should bow, of things in heaven, and things in earth, and things under the earth; And that every tongue should confess that Jesus Christ is Lord, to the glory of God the Father" (Phil. 2:9-11).

The "times," or seasons, suggest that God is developing His plan through a series of definite and successive stages, the fullness of which has not yet come. However, it is God's intention in the final important season to send His Son to earth again to sum up all things in Him. This divine intention was at one time unknown, even to the prophets, but according to God's good pleasure He has made it known to us now. Our Lord's first coming was in the fullness of time. However, *in that day* He will not merely offer Himself but will establish His throne and rule with a rod of iron.

When speaking of the future glory of Christ, the apostle is reminded again of the believer's position, for in Christ "we have obtained an inheritance, being predestinated according to the purpose of Him who worketh all things after the counsel of His own will" (1:11). The real meaning of this verse is missed entirely if we hold to the King James Version. Let us see it in the American Standard Version—"In whom also we were made a heritage . . ." (1:11, A.S.V.). We just saw in verse 10 how that everything in heaven and earth will be unified in Christ. Now Paul adds that, in Christ, the believer is God's chosen portion or private possession. The saints are predestinated to be His inheritance. Of Israel it was said: "Yet they are Thy people and Thine inheritance"; "For the Lord's portion is His people; Jacob is the lot of His inheritance" (Deut. 9:29; 32:9). When Christ returns in glory to establish His kingdom, all history and creation will be combined in a glorious and harmonious consummation as His inheritance, but the apex of His inheritance will be those whom He has redeemed with His own blood along with regathered Israel. This is God's eternal purpose, and He works all thing after the counsel of His own will. What majestic beauty and simplicity in the purpose of God! It is not merely that Christ shall receive the earth and all that is in it, but that we have been made His heritage.

Only as we are "in Christ" are we God's inheritance, and the reason He made us His inheritance is "That we should be to the praise of His glory, who first trusted in Christ" (1:12). Though now we are the objects of His love and mercy, eventually we shall be the subjects of His glory.

Speaking through the Prophet Malachi, God said: "And they shall be Mine . . . in that day when I make up My jewels" (Mal. 3:17). Here the word "jewels" means *special treasure,* and it is used first of David who, upon setting his affection on the house of the Lord, stored away his treasure of gold and silver for the building of the temple. Even so God is storing away His special treasure, building a holy temple, "In whom all the building fitly framed together groweth unto an holy temple in the Lord" (Eph. 2:21). As God looks down upon this sinful earth He sees a company of despised followers of His Son, and He says: "They shall be Mine when I make up My special treasure."

We are of greater worth to God than angels. We are His costly treasure! Someone has said: "When God found me, I was no better than a cobblestone—not worth picking up. But He took me into His laboratory of grace, and by the chemistry of atoning blood He processed me, and I came out as His jewel—a bit rough, I'll admit, but after a few years of cutting, buffing, and polishing, He will present me at last before His throne absolutely flawless." How wonderful it all is! Thus the second stanza of this wonderful hymn of praise concludes "to the praise of His [Christ's] glory."

We come now to the third and last stanza of Paul's hymn of praise (1:13, 14). In the first stanza (1:3-6), we saw *the plan of the Father* wherein we were chosen, predestinated, and adopted that we might be to the praise of *His* glory. In the second stanza (1:7-12), we saw *the provision of the Son* wherein we were redeemed and forgiven that we might be to the praise of *His* glory. Now we are to look at the last stanza (1:13, 14), wherein we see *the pledge of the Spirit* unto the praise of *His* glory. The Father finished His plan. The Son finished the work which the Father gave Him to do. Now the Holy Spirit is in the world fulfilling His pledge.

Verse 13 contains three prominent words, each essential to the other. They are "heard," "believed," and "sealed." Here we shall see the work of the Holy Spirit in the divine plan. All three Persons in the Godhead have had a pertinent part in man's redemption.

What is the Spirit's work? All men being spiritually dead

in trespasses and sins, man needs new life. Since the Holy Spirit is "the Spirit of life" (Rom. 8:2), He quickens us from spiritual death.

How does the Spirit accomplish this quickening? The instrument He uses is the Word of God. In Ephesians it is called "the Word of truth, the gospel of your salvation." Elsewhere we are reminded that "faith cometh by hearing, and hearing by the Word of God" (Rom. 10:17). Paul says: "Ye heard," and "ye believed." It is through the Word that men are born again, "For the Word of God is living, and active, and sharper than any two-edged sword, and piercing even to the dividing of soul and spirit, of both joints and marrow, and quick to discern the thoughts and intents of the heart" (Heb. 4:12, A.S.V.). Only when we hear the gospel are we born again by the power of the Spirit (John 3:5), "not of corruptible seed, but of incorruptible, by the Word of God, which liveth and abideth forever" (1 Pet. 1:23). The written Word of God is the living, active, sharp, penetrating, discerning sword of the Spirit by which men are brought face to face with God's plan of salvation. The duty of the sword of the Spirit is to bring life, but all who refuse it are slain by it. We cannot adequately explain our salvation apart from the Spirit's ministry through the Word.

Upon "hearing" and "believing" the Word, immediately "ye were sealed with that Holy Spirit of promise" (1:13). When we hear the gospel our part is to believe; it is God's part to seal. We are not sealed *by* the Spirit but, rather, *with* the Spirit. Better still, the Spirit is the seal. It is "God who hath also sealed us, and given the earnest of the Spirit in our hearts" (1 Cor. 1:21, 22).

A seal is a mark of authenticity or genuineness. "Forasmuch as ye are manifestly declared to be the epistle of Christ ministered by us, written not with ink, but with the Spirit of the living God; not in tables of stone, but in fleshy tables of the heart" (2 Cor. 3:3). True believers are the credentials of

Christ, His letters of recommendation to a lost world. A letter is the written expression of the writer; hence the children of God are not those whose names are written in ink or engraved in stone, but those upon whose hearts the Holy Spirit has written the evidence of the power of God's Word. The distinguishing mark between the false professor and the true Christian is the indwelling Holy Spirit.

Furthermore, a seal is the mark of ownership. God knows us by His seal. Jesus said: "I am the good Shepherd, and know My sheep, and am known of Mine" (John 10:14). As livestock are distinguished by the owner's brand, even so God has His own special brand whereby we are marked out as His possession, and "if any man have not the Spirit of Christ, he is none of His" (Rom. 8:9). The stamp of validity is God's seal, the gift of the Holy Spirit, which is the sign that we are His people and members of the true Church of Jesus Christ.

Then, too, the seal is the mark of security, for the Spirit "is the earnest of our inheritance until the redemption of the purchased possession" (1:14). Here is the answer to the problem some men have regarding the preservation of the believer. Wherein does our security lie? The word "earnest" denotes *a down payment,* or a pledge that an agreement will be kept. Now God has offered us eternal life upon belief on His Son. But can we be certain that we shall enter into that life after we die? Yes, indeed! The earnest bound the bargain, and the deposit will not be returned until the remainder of our redemption, which is the redemption of our body (Rom. 8:23) is fully realized. The Holy Spirit is in the earth as God's deposit, or guarantee, until Jesus Christ comes again to receive His own unto Himself. The indwelling Holy Spirit is our guarantee of a finished transaction and a safe delivery of spirit, soul, and body to heaven. Our future inheritance of glory is assured, for the sealing with the Spirit is designed to give us certainty that the future will bring a completed redemption, and that "unto the praise of His glory."

2. Paul's Prayer to God for What We Require (1:15-23).

The epistles of Paul are noted for their prayers offered to God in the interest of the saints. W. H. Griffith Thomas has said that there are few more precious subjects for meditation and imitation than the prayers and intercessions of the great apostle. The greatness of the man and his ministry can be attributed in a large part to his prayer life.

There are two prayers of Paul recorded in Ephesians. The first prayer is before us; the second is to be found in 3:14-19. If prayer for others is a test of one's own spiritual life, then Paul ranks high among the godly leaders in the history of the Church. Most of our prayers are taken up with ourselves or with those nearest and dearest to us. Needs of others occupy a small place in our prayer life. Paul's prayers are included by the Holy Spirit as a corporate part of the epistle.

First, consider the *occasion* of the prayer. It commences with the word "wherefore," which literally means *on account of this*. In the preceding verses Paul has issued, by the Holy Spirit, some profound teaching on the work of the triune God in making plans for the completed redemption of all believers. Now, because of this, he desires that they should possess an experiential knowledge, having the doctrine transmitted into actual experience. He would have them enjoy the full scope of their inheritance in Christ.

Paul's heart is filled with thanksgiving for the saints at Ephesus, for, says he: "I heard of your faith in the Lord Jesus, and love unto all the saints" (1:15). Two things about the Ephesian Christians were conversational pieces: (1) their faith in the Lord Jesus, and (2) their love to all the saints.

The object of their faith was the Lord Jesus Christ. They were not ashamed of Him, for obviously others were hearing of their faith. Paul says: "I heard." Where people are soundly saved they will not hide their light under a bushel, but will proclaim the joys of salvation found in Christ. Then, too, where faith is genuine, love will be in evidence. One of the unmistakable signs of the new birth is one's conduct toward "all the saints." True Christian love is shed abroad in our hearts by the Holy Spirit (Rom. 5:5). Where He is in control, there must be love to all the saints. Love is the fruit of faith in Jesus Christ, for "We know that we have passed from death unto life, because we love the brethren" (1 John 3:14). While true love embraces all men, it reaches out in a particular way to those who belong to our Lord Jesus Christ (see Galatians 6:10). Faith begets love.

Let us consider further the *objectives* of the prayer. Paul's earnestness made his prayers intelligent and specific. He knew that general prayers could expect general answers, so why pray if there was nothing to pray about? But he did pray, and the Holy Spirit has preserved for us one of the most profound petitions in all of the apostle's writings.

The prayer is addressed to "the God of our Lord Jesus Christ, the Father of Glory" (1:17). This suggests to us that the Christian's God, the God and Father of our Lord Jesus Christ, is the Father to whom glory belongs, for He is "the God of glory" (Acts 7:2). And to think that the Father to whom glory belongs, who is the "Father of mercies" (2 Cor. 1:3), the "Father of [our] Spirits" (Heb. 12:9), and the "Father of lights" (Jas. 1:17), is *our* Father! O Christian, rejoice! How can a Christian ever think of calling any man his holy father, as Romanists do, when he has God as his Father? Our heavenly Father is the source of every blessing. To Him be all glory!

The first request in the prayer is for "wisdom and revelation" (1:17). When Paul requests for the saints "the spirit of wisdom and revelation," he is not praying for the gift of the Holy Spirit's Presence. They have already received the Holy Spirit as the divine seal (1:13). Paul desires for them that heavenly wisdom and revelation which is imparted by the Holy Spirit.

"Revelation" is the important word here, for revelation is the key to all knowledge. The ministry and office work of the

Holy Spirit is to reveal to the Christian the meaning of all truth, whether historical or prophetical (John 14:26; 16:12-15). The Christian has no excuse for ignorance, since the Holy Spirit was given to reveal even "the deep things of God" (1 Cor. 2:10). Some men are wise in Hebrew and Greek grammar and the mechanics of Bible interpretation, but Paul is not praying for the tools of knowledge. He covets for them a wise and understanding spirit that none can impart but the Holy Spirit Himself.

Why do Christians not have a wise and understanding spirit in things pertaining to God's Word? The answer lies, in part, in the last phrase of verse 17, namely, *"in the knowledge of Him."* Christ is true wisdom and true knowledge. Three other translations of this verse make the deeper meaning clear:

> That the God of our Lord Jesus the Messiah, the Father glory-clad, may, *in bestowing the full knowledge of Himself,* bestow on you the Spirit which is manifested in divine illumination and insight into the mysteries of God (*Way*).

> For I always beseech the God of our Lord Jesus Christ—the Father most glorious—to give you the spirit of wisdom and penetration *through an intimate knowledge of Him* (*Weymouth*).

> That the God of our Lord Jesus Christ, the glorious Father, may grant you the Spirit to give wisdom and revelation *which come through a growing knowledge of Him* (*Williams*).

Surely you have caught the force of Paul's statement. Wisdom and revelation come to us only by intimate associations with our Lord. A growing knowledge of the Author of the Bible guarantees a wise and understanding spirit in discernment of His Word. Paul would have us seek to know God, for then we shall have a Spirit-given knowledge which is accurate and thorough (Phil. 1:9; Col. 1:9), not merely an intellectual knowledge. Human philosophy says: "Know thyself." Our Lord said: "And this is life eternal, that they might know *Thee* the only true God, and Jesus Christ, whom Thou hast sent" (John 17:3). Ordinary knowledge may be acquired; spiritual insight into the deep things of God is a gift (Jas. 1:5).

The prayer continues: "The eyes of your understanding being enlightened" (1:18). The American Standard Version reads: "the eyes of your *heart*," not *mind*. The "heart" is the inner man, including the emotion and will; it is the whole self, man's inward being. This marvelous faculty of spiritual sight is lacking in the unregenerated man. He is powerless to apprehend spiritual things. "But the natural man receiveth not the things of the Spirit of God; for they are foolishness unto him: neither can he know them, because they are spiritually discerned" (1 Cor. 2:14). Now the eyes of the believer's heart must be continually taken up with his Lord in order that his knowledge of spiritual truth might increase.

Paul requests for the saints the spirit of wisdom and revelation in the knowledge of Christ that they might know three things:

(1) "The hope of His calling." God has called us, but to what purpose? He has called us to perfection in the likeness of Jesus Christ (Rom. 8:29; 1 John 3:1, 2). He has called us to a completed righteousness and to the completed redemption of our bodies. He does not call a believer to hope for the forgiveness of his sins: they are gone. The hope of His calling is to see Him and be one with Him. One day our Lord will come again, and we shall all be changed to see Him as He is and to be like Him. Such a glorious hope inspires to holy living and to a hatred of all that is of this world. "Every man that hath this hope in *Him* purifieth himself, even as He is pure" (1 John 3:3). All Christians have the same hope. It is Christ's coming to take His own to be with Himself.

(2) "The riches of the glory of His inheritance in the saints." Here Paul prays that we might have a full appreciation of our worth to God. Already we have noted that God made us His heritage that we should be to the praise of His glory (1:11, 12). God has an inheritance. His inheritance is in His saints. The gold and the silver and all the universes are

His. He has riches untold. But His riches are not in the universes that He possesses, nor in the substance of the earth that is His, but in the saints that He purchased at infinite cost, namely, the precious blood of His only begotten Son (1 Pet. 1:19). Beloved Christian, think not of what you can get from God but, rather, think of what you mean to God. The Christian Church is precious to God. He purchased it and paid for it with the blood of His Son. Paul would have us appreciate our dignity. I cannot understand how this can be, but I know that God has an inheritance even in me.

(3) "And what is the exceeding greatness of His power to us-ward who believe" (1:19). What an objective in prayer! That men might know the measure of God's power. The Christian needs supernatural power, and God would have us see how great is His power to accomplish His purposes in us. How much spiritual strength is available for me in my daily life? How much divine energy is at my disposal? The power that God has made available to the believer is "according to the working of His mighty power, which He wrought in Christ, when He raised Him from the dead, and set Him at His own right hand in the heavenly places, far above all principality, and power, and might, and dominion, and every name that is named, not only in this world, but also in that which is to come" (1:19-21). Here is the inexhaustible strength of God in taking His crucified Son who was dead and buried, and raising Him from among the dead to His present majestic position in heaven. What power! The same continuous current of His mighty power stands available to the faithful, to all who will believe.

Can you conceive this? The power which raised Christ from the grave, lifted Him to heaven, put all things under His feet and made Him the Head over all to the Church, is to us-ward who believe. How can we fail with Him as our Head and with such power at our disposal?

Now consider the last phrase. God "gave Him to be the head over all things to the church, which is His body, the

fulness of Him that filleth all in all" (1:22, 23). Jesus Christ
has been exalted to absolute authority over His Church, hence
through His sovereign Person and exalted position the Church
takes her orders. He is the exalted Head over *all*. The order
of the Church must be His will and every activity must exalt
Him, since it is in the capacity of Head over all that God gave
Him to the Church. When the members of the Church recognize this, then there will be no lack, for the Church will receive
its fullness from Him. As the recognized Head He imparts the
needed strength to accomplish every task. When the visible
body of Christ on earth recognizes the invisible Head in
heaven, the gates of hell will not prevail against the Church.
Popes, cardinals, and bishops are merely men; and when any
man sets himself up as the head of Christ's Church, it is sacri-
lege of the basest sort. Beloved, let us take our position in
subjection to our Lord Jesus Christ, that we may enjoy victory
all along the way, for we cannot be complete without Him
(Col. 2:9, 10).

B. *The Christian's Past Position in the World* (Chapter 2)

The theme of Ephesions is Christ and His Church. In chapter
one, the Church is likened to a body of which Christ is the
Head. The Head is in heaven, and through the ministry of the
Holy Spirit in the world, the Body, which is Christ's purchased
possession, is being formed. The Head without the Body is
incomplete. When the Body is complete, the Head will come to
unite the Body to Himself, never to be separated.

The symbolism is beautiful. In chapter two, the Church is
likened to a building. Paul speaks of its foundation as being
"the apostles and prophets," its chief Corner-Stone is "Jesus
Christ Himself," and believers fitly framed together form "an
holy temple in the Lord . . . for an habitation of God through
the Spirit" (2:19-22). Such is the creation and design of the
Church.

Ephesians is the thrilling story of how God creates anew
the man that He created originally in His own image and like-

ness, but who, through disobedience, fell from his lofty position. The plan involved a perfect Head for the Body and a perfect Head-Stone for the Building. So in the fullness of time God sent His Son in a human body, and through His virgin birth, virtuous life, vicarious death, victorious resurrection, and visible return, He is restoring to the Father His fallen creature.

In our present chapter Paul shows the need for being made a new creation by reviewing the believer's past history before he became saved. He shows the unregenerated man to be separated from God both by death and distance. It is a portrait of what every unsaved man is, and what every saved person was before trusting in Christ.

1. *Separated by Death* (2:1-10)

These verses are marked by a series of triplets. The three's of the Bible make for interesting and instructive teaching. Bible triads represent strength and completeness. The Scripture says that "a threefold cord is not quickly broken" (Eccl. 4:12). The verses before us contain a triad of evil and a triad of good: (a) the three ravaging forces are the world, the flesh, and the devil (verses 1-3); (b) the three redeeming facts are mercy, love, and grace (verses 4-6); and (c) the three resulting features are that the saints are made alive together with Christ, raised up together with Christ, and made to sit together in heavenly places in Christ.

(a). *Three Ravaging Forces* (2:1-3). The believer's past position in the world was that of every unsaved man, "dead in trespasses and sins" (2:1). The clearer the picture of our destitute condition before we were saved, the greater is our appreciation of what God has undertaken to do for us. The natural man is dead, a state into which he has come through trespasses and sins. "Man is separated from God because the life-cord has been severed."

God had warned Adam: "In the day that thou eatest thereof thou shalt surely die" (Gen. 2:17). Our first parents ignored the warning, and "by one man sin entered into the world, and death by sin; and so death passed upon all men, for that all have sinned" (Rom. 5:12). Sin and death came through Adam. In Adam's sin all sinned; therefore in Adam's sin all die. Because of the solidarity of the human race, no man has escaped sin. Therefore, death is universal.

Never in Scripture does death mean annihilation. H. S. Miller defines death as the separation of a person from the purpose or use for which he was intended. There are three kinds of death: (1) *physical*, the separation of the soul, or life, from the body (1 Cor. 15:21, 22; Heb. 9:27); (2) *spiritual*, the separation of the spirit from God (2:1; 4:18; 1 John 5:12); and (3) *eternal*, the everlasting banishment from the Presence of God. (1 Cor. 6:9, 10; 2 Thess. 1:9).

In Ephesians Paul speaks of spiritual death. The unsaved man may be physically and mentally alive to all of the pleasures of this world but dead spiritually (1 Tim. 5:6). How foolish for someone who is spiritually dead to try to live the Christian life! It cannot be done. Suppose a person allows himself every indulgence and says to himself: "Ah, this is the life." Then he comes to church occasionally to imitate the Christian life. Such effort is futile. You see, we are all born as dead men, and we live as dead men until we are made partakers of the life of God. Someone has said: "You cannot live a life for God until you receive life from God." In physical death, the function of the body ceases; in spiritual death, there is no function of man's spirit toward God. As far as the relation of the nations of the earth toward God is concerned, we live in a world of dead men. There is a state of intense physical activity, but until a man passes from death unto life (John 5:24), he remains alienated from the life of God (Eph. 4:18).

Three opposing forces of evil are responsible for holding man in the state of spiritual death. The first of these is the *world:* "Wherein in time past ye walked according to the course of this world . . ." (2:2). Here the word "world" should be translated "age." The course of this age Paul describes in Galatians as "this present evil age" (Gal. 1:4). The nature of the unregenerate man responds to the direction of the age, and the god of this age is Satan (2 Cor. 4:4). This vile world is no friend to grace to help us on to God. Be not conformed to this age (Rom. 12:2) nor court its friendship (Jas. 4:4). Certainly "love not the world" (1 John 2:15). The unsaved will follow the course and traditions of this world, but the Christian never! The world may answer the requirements of the unregenerate heart, but God's true children seek those things which are above.

The second of the opposing forces responsible for holding man in the state of spiritual death is the *devil.* Paul said that in times past we walked "according to the prince of the power of the air, the spirit that now worketh in the children of disobedience" (2:2). It has been pointed out already that a personal devil is the god of this age. The saints who have been born again were born into God's kingdom (John 3:3), having been rescued from the power of darkness and transferred into the kingdom of God's Son (Col. 1:13). The unsaved man is still in Satan's kingdom and therefore is Satan's slave. Satan separates men from God by blinding their minds, lest the light of the glorious gospel of Christ, who is the image of God, should shine unto them (2 Cor. 4:4). Of course their blindness is self-chosen. They refused to believe. By rejecting their Deliverer, they fell into the clutches of Satan.

The great spiritual struggle in the world is the control of the soul of man—the God of light and life versus the god of darkness and death. If you are a rebel against God, then you are ruled by Satan, and he will continue his evil work in you to keep you separated from God. I shrink from the horror of my past, but I praise God for His remarkable delivering power.

The spiritually dead are held in separation from God, not only by the world and the devil but also by the *flesh:* "Among whom also we all had our conversation in times past in the lusts of our flesh, fulfilling the desires of the flesh and of the mind; and were by nature the children of wrath, even as others" (2:3). With our sin-controlled nature we formerly behaved ourselves according to our sensual appetites. Beloved Christian, this was our past. When I look at the pleasure-mad, lust-craving throngs today, I see myself as I was before God saved me by His power. And all Christians, Jews and Gentiles alike, yielded to the desires of the flesh and the cravings after those things that were not good for them. I was a corpse in the cesspool of corruption when the Lord Jesus found me, but, praise God, He has given me His life and now my desires are toward Him. I was worthy to be judged, but now I am justified in Christ.

(b). *Three Redeeming Facts* (2:4, 5). After Paul shows how three ravaging forces of evil separated us from God, he lists three redeeming facts: the fact of God's *mercy*, the fact of His *love*, and the fact of His *grace*. The transition is marked with the words, "but God" (2:4). These words mark the turning point of man's destiny. We were separated from God by the world, the devil, and the flesh, *"but God!"* God intervened and, were it not for His divine intervention, we would still be dead in our sins and separated from Him. Against the dark picture of human ruin we see divine redemption. Doomed to wrath, *but God!*

There is the fact of His *mercy:* "But God, who is rich in mercy . . ." (2:4). Praise God for His mercy, for it was mercy we needed. What is mercy? It is God's exercise of pity and compassion upon the sinner with a forbearance he does not deserve. The whole of our salvation is ascribed to the mercy of God, and He is "rich in mercy." Indeed, the Lord is merciful, full of mercy (Psalm 103:8). When the holy and eternal God who hates sin, loves and saves the sinner, that is mercy. He is the "Father of mercies" (2 Cor. 1:3), and we need only come to His throne of grace to obtain mercy (Heb. 4:16). In chapter one we saw "the riches of His grace" (1:7) and "the riches of His glory" (1:18), and here we read that He is rich in mercy. Let us say with the Apostle Peter: "Blessed be the God and Father of our

Lord Jesus Christ, which according to His *abundant mercy* hath begotten us again unto a lively hope by the resurrection of Jesus Christ from the dead" (1 Pet. 1:3).

Then, too, there is the fact of His *love:* ". . . for His great love wherewith He loved us" (2:4). Abundant mercy and great love! Oh, the love of God! Who can fathom it? Who can explain it? We can do nothing better than ponder His own Word: "For God so loved the world, that He gave His only begotten Son, that whosoever believeth in Him should not perish, but have everlasting life" (John 3:16); "But God commendeth His love toward us, in that, while we were yet sinners, Christ died for us" (Rom. 5:8); "In this was manifested the love of God toward us, because that God sent His only begotten Son into the world, that we might live through Him" (1 John 4:9).

> Could I with ink the ocean fill,
>   Were the whole sky of parchment made,
> Were every blade of grass a quill,
>   And every man a scribe by trade;
>
> To write the love of God above
>   Would drain the ocean dry;
> Nor could the scroll contain the whole
>   Though spread from sky to sky.

Finally, there is the fact of His *grace:* "By grace ye are saved" (2:5, 8). Grace is everything for nothing. It is helping the helpless, going to those who cannot come in their own strength. Grace sets aside my unrighteousness and demerit and gives me a righteousness I do not merit. God owes me nothing but He offers me complete salvation. That is grace. Man could do nothing whatever to plan his own salvation. It was planned by God before the foundation of the world. The world, the devil, and the flesh separated me from God; but by His mercy, love, and grace, He saved me.

(c). *Three Resulting Features* (2:5-10). We are to see now, in part, what God's mercy, love, and grace accomplished for us. First, with Christ we were made alive—

"quickened together" (2:5). We were spiritually dead; now we have been made spiritually alive. The believer passes through the same experience spiritually that the Lord Jesus did physically. We were crucified with Christ (Rom. 6:6; Gal. 2:20). We died with Christ (Rom. 6:8); we were buried with Christ (Rom. 6:4; Col. 2:12); we have been made alive with Christ. Since He died our death, we died with Him. When you were saved, a dead man became alive, and to you was given a life you never possessed before. The same life-giving power that was demonstrated when our Lord gave life to the dead, when He Himself came forth from the dead, and when He will yet call forth from the graves all who have died, is the power at work in giving new life to the sinner who is spiritually dead. Our Lord Jesus said: "The hour is coming, and now is, when the dead shall hear the voice of the Son of God: and they that hear shall live" (John 5:25). That is the power at work when one is born again. The voice of God is the voice of power, and when a man hears and believes the Word of God, he "is passed from death unto life" (John 5:24).

Men do not get life through baptism, or the Lord's supper, or church membership, but through hearing and believing the Word of God. And if the Word of life goes unheeded, the same God who offers new life to the sinner will one day banish the unbeliever from His presence forever. "Hear, and your soul shall live" (Isa. 55:3). Spiritual life, if it comes at all, must come from God. God wants to put new life in man, His own life, and this He will do only by the quickening power of the Holy Spirit. The receiving of this life is instantaneous the moment we, by the Spirit, believe the Word. Christ died and came forth from the grave alive; thus the believing sinner receives the life of the Son of God which is both spiritual and eternal.

The second miracle of God's mercy, love, and grace is that He "hath raised us up together . . . in Christ Jesus" (2:6). Dr. A. C. Gaebelein has pointed out that quickening and resurrection are not one and the same thing. Quicken-ings means the giving of life. Resurrection, however, is the placing of that given life into the proper sphere. Having been quickened, or made alive, God has given to us a new position in the world.

When our Lord called Lazarus from death and the grave, "he that was dead came forth, bound hand and foot with grave-clothes: and his face was bound about with a napkin. Jesus saith unto them, Loose him, and let him go" (John 11:43, 44). In contrast to the condition of Lazarus when he received life, John and Peter, upon looking into Christ's tomb, found both the linen clothes and the napkin that was about His head still lying in the tomb (John 20:4-7).

Too many professing Christians are like Lazarus who, while testifying to the fact of having received new life, know nothing of the blessed liberty that accompanies the new life. Many professing Christians are still bound by the grave-clothes of tradition and law and unbelief. You see, the unloosing of the grave-clothes was the condition of exer-cising the life in its proper sphere. Moreover, if the grave-clothes had not been removed, Lazarus would have sunk back into the tomb. When our Lord imparts new life, He delivers the sinner from the grave-clothes, which speak of the bondage of the law and sin. How sad to find so many in our churches cumbered with the death wrappings of those who are spiritually dead in trespasses and sins! "Stand fast therefore in the liberty wherewith Christ hath made us free, and be not entangled again with the yoke of bondage" (Gal. 5:1). The believer's resurrection with Christ is an escape from the bondage of sin, for he is "dead indeed unto sin, but alive unto God through Jesus Christ our Lord" (Rom. 6:11). Our spiritual resurrection is to effect a walk "in newness of life" (Rom. 6:4).

Romans 6 explains how God deals with sin in the believer's nature. The believer's old nature, with its sinful possibili-ties, is never eradicated in this present life. Instead of the false teaching of eradication of sin, the Scriptures affirm the truth of the believer's identification with Christ. Our Lord not only died *for* our sins (1 Cor. 15:3), but "He died *unto* sin" (Rom. 6:10), and in the divine reckoning we died with Christ to sin. However, Christ did not remain in the grave; He was raised from the dead henceforth to walk in a new kind of life. Now "if we [believers] have been planted together in the likeness of His death, we shall be also in the likeness of His resurrection" (Rom. 6:5). No one can share Christ's resurrection life who has not died with Him and who has not been made alive with Him. Judicially, Christ did not die His own death but ours. Likewise, when He was raised from the dead, we were raised with Him.

It is an essential fact that the saved man has been made alive with Christ. By an amazing and mighty act of God He reached down through human history and made His Holy Son one with the entire human race, thereby bringing into a perfect and mysterious union and oneness the life of the perfect Son of God and that of the sin-scarred posterity of Adam. The persons, then, who stand fused in this remarkable coalescence are Jesus Christ and the believing sinner. While some professing believers do not break completely from the fetters of the old life, there is a glorious future awaiting the redeemed. Paul wrote: "For ye are dead, and your life is hid with Christ in God. When Christ, who is our life, shall appear, then shall ye also appear with Him in glory" (Col. 3:3, 4).

Dear reader, do you say that you are a Christian? "If ye then be risen with Christ, seek those things which are above, where Christ sitteth on the right hand of God. Set your affection on things above, not on things on the earth" (Col. 3:1, 2).

The third miracle of God's mercy, love, and grace is that He "made us sit together in heavenly places in Christ Jesus" (2:6). Not only was our Lord made alive and raised from the dead, but He ascended into heaven (Acts 1:10, 11), even

"on high" (Eph. 4:8) where God has highly exalted Him
(Phil. 2:9). So it is with the Christian. He has been delivered from hell to heaven itself. This experience is not
perfected in this present life, but it is very definitely so in a
spiritual sense. As resurrection and quickening are not one
and the same, even so ascension. In Old Testament times
none but the high priest could enter into the holy place and,
when he did, he represented all Israel; for he had their
names upon the breast and shoulders of his garments. Christ
is our "merciful and faithful High Priest" (Heb. 2:17), even
Jesus the Son of God who is passed into the heavens. He
is both understanding and compassionate (Heb. 4:14, 15)
as He intercedes in our behalf.

Now the wonder and glory of it all is that, when the
eternal Son left heaven's heights and descended to man's
lowest depths (Phil. 2:5-8), He paid our debt, delivering us
from death and hell, and took us back with Himself. Here
is the amazing outreach of God's grace and the height of
Christian position. Not only did Christ love us and wash
us from our sins, but He "hath made us kings and priests
unto God" (Rev. 1:6; 5:10). We are as royalty in the
presence of Royalty, since we are both a "holy priesthood"
and a "royal priesthood" (1 Pet. 2:5, 9). Each member of
Christ's true Church is a holy and royal priest called to the
ministry of intercession and of offering up spiritual sacrifices
to God. The saints not only comprise a spiritual house but
the priesthood of that house. Priests were those who carried
on the worship; thus any vested priesthood ordained of men
is contary to the plain teaching of God's Word, since the
saints comprise the only true priesthood.

Are we truly serving as priests, drawing near to God to
offer up sacrifices of praise and intercession? Under the old
covenant no individual ever held the offices of priest and
king simultaneously. Such an honor was reserved for our
Lord Jesus Christ, of whom Zechariah prophesied: "He shall
be a Priest upon His throne" (Zech. 6:13). Now, as priests,

we enter into the Holiest where our great High Priest has gone, and when He comes again to reign we, too, shall reign with Him. And while we wait for that day, let us exercise our priestly privilege. "By Him therefore let us offer the sacrifice of praise to God continually" (Heb. 13:15).

We come now to an important question, namely: "Why has God bestowed upon us the fruits of His mercy, love and grace?" Paul answers: "That in the ages to come He might shew the exceeding riches of His grace in His kindness toward us through Christ Jesus" (2:7). Through all the millenniums to come in eternity, God will exhibit His glory and grace in those whom He has redeemed. The great purpose of God in redemption is not merely the safety and happiness of the redeemed, but His own glory. What a monument it will be! Angels and demons will see and know that God has triumphed through His Son. We look into eternity past and see the divine plan of the Church before the foundation of the world; we look into eternity future and see the perfected Church on exhibition as a trophy of the mercy, love, and grace of God, and that to the praise of His glory. Indeed, the remembrance of such kindness must be hallowed throughout eternity.

And oh, the certainty of it here and now! Not that we hope to be saved eventually, but "by grace *are* ye saved" (2:8). The entire transaction has been signed, sealed, and delivered, for "by grace have ye been saved." The only appropriating agency in salvation is "faith," and even that is not of ourselves: "it is the gift of God." No works of man could put him in right standing with God, for then would he have whereof to boast. But God has justified us by His grace in order that not any one should glory. From start to finish salvation is the gift of God. Faith is the instrument by which we receive the gift, but even faith is a gift which comes to man by the hearing of God's Word (Rom. 10:17). God's plan of salvation for the soul of man is finished, and redemption is free. Therefore you have only to believe, and God will save you for eternity. Praise Him for salvation.

Good works, nevertheless, have an important place in the life of every Christian: "For we are His workmanship, created in Christ Jesus unto good works, which God hath before ordained that we should walk in them" (2:10). The "good works" spoken of here constitute one of the purposes of God in saving us, and these can be performed only by those who have been saved by grace. The word rendered "ordained" may be translated "prepared," suggesting that God has cut out for each of us a special work of His own preparation. There must be an exhibition of the fruits of grace in this life as well as in the ages to come.

Notice, please, that the "good works" assigned to us are not our good works but His. These gifts our ascended Lord distributes to His own, and through the power of the indwelling Holy Spirit we are able to use them. We are His *workmanship* doing His *works*. We may gaze upon the sun, the moon, the stars, the snow-capped mountains, or the beautiful flowers of every season, but these are not the best workmanship of God. The Church is God's masterpiece, and it is the loftiest conception of beauty, unity, and usefulness— above everything else in the earth. God takes rough, crude sinners, dead in trespasses and sins, and produces vessels meet for the Master's use. Sin-marred, defective material is transformed by God into useful instruments of righteousness. Now that we know this, life should be sacred to each of us.

(2) *Separated by Distance* (2:11-12).

The general theme in the verses before us differs little, if at all, from that contained in the preceding verses of this chapter. Here are listed more characteristics of the natural man, proving the need of regeneration. However, the message here seems to be directed in a peculiar way to the Gentiles alone. Before the day of Pentecost, which day was the birthday of the Church, the Gentiles included all people in the earth who were not Jews. Since Pentecost God sees a threefold division of the human race: the Jew, the Gentile, and the Church of God (1 Cor. 10:32), the last being made up of Jew and Gentile who have been saved through faith in the Lord Jesus Christ. Paul's usage of the pronouns "we" and "ye" shows that he had in mind the condition of man in general in verses 1-3, and the condition of the Gentile in particular in verses 11-13.

(a). *The Condition of the Past.* The key phrase in this portion of our study is "far off" (2:13), suggesting separation by distance. Before the Gentile was saved he was separated from God by a great gulf. We were "Gentiles in the flesh . . . called uncircumcision" (2:11). Circumcision was originally a rite enjoined by God upon Abraham as a sign of the covenant God made with him. Later it took on a definite religious and moral significance. Hence the Jews became known as "the circumcision" and looked with reproach upon the Gentiles to whom they referred as "the uncircumcised" (1 Sam. 17:26, 36; 2 Sam. 1:20).

Actually the Gentiles were inferior to the Jews in that they were separated from the sacrifices and religious privileges that united Jewish believers to God. Of course there were those who were Jews in name only; and while they proudly called themselves "the circumcision," they were Jews outwardly and not inwardly, for they lacked that real circumcision of the heart (Rom. 2:25-29). The Gentile at that time stood condemned before God. After the flood God's covenants were all made to Israel, giving Israel hope which the Gentiles lacked.

Then, too, the Gentiles were "without Christ" (2:12). While every unsaved man, both Jew and Gentile, is without Christ, the Gentiles were separated by a greater distance, since the Jew had the types, symbols, and prophecies that pointed to the coming Person and work of the Messiah. When Paul referred to God's dealings with Israel, he said:

"Now all these things happened unto them for ensamples [or types]" (1 Cor. 10:11). In the Old Testament every hope of the Jew centered in the Messiah, for in Him their every expectation was to be fulfilled. All of the pre-incarnate appearances of Christ were to the Jews and, as we shall see later, it was not until His death at Calvary that He became the world's Saviour.

Now when one is "without Christ" he has "no hope." Even as the Gentiles were without hope before Christ came, so is every man today who has not trusted in Christ. There is no hope for the world or for the individual apart from Christ, but in Him God has given "everlasting consolation and good hope" (2 Thess. 2:16). The "blessed hope" of the believer is the appearing of our great God and Saviour Jesus Christ (Titus 2:13). He is Israel's hope and the only hope of the world.

Paul pictures the Gentiles finally as being "without God in the world" (2:12). While they had "gods many, and lords many" (1 Cor. 8:5), they were in a true sense of the word atheists, since they were alienated from any contact with God. No sadder plight can befall a man than that of being in the world without God.

(b). *The Contrasts with the Present.* Again divine intervention marks a transition. When Paul pointed out the sad past of both Jew and Gentile, he contrasted the bright side of the picture by using the conjunction "but"— "But God . . ." (2:4). Here the contrast between the unsaved Gentile and the saved Gentile is marked with the connecting words, "But now . . ." (2:13). From the distressing scene of what the Gentiles had been, Paul turns in vivid phrases to show what had been accomplished for them in Christ. They were "far off . . . but now . . . made nigh." Once distance had separated them *from* Christ; now they are enjoying blessed union *with* Christ.

In antithesis to the Gentile being an alien from the commonwealth of Israel and a stranger from the covenants of promise, he is created a new unity with the believing Jew. Christ became peace, having made both Jew and Gentile one by breaking down the middle wall of partition (2:14). The outer court in the temple for Gentiles was separated from the inner court for Jews, but when Christ came He broke down the partition. At the same time He abolished the enmity, which was the ordinances of the law, the rites, and ceremonies. These unobserved laws had caused the Jews to despise them (2:15). But now "Christ is the end of 'the law for righteousness to every one that believeth" (Rom. 10:4), by which (faith) He has created a union of Jew and Gentile. This new creation does not make a Jew into a Gentile, nor a Gentile into a Jew. Rather did our Lord "make in Himself of twain one new man" (2:15). Here is the true Church, a new organism in which the believing Jew and Gentile are reconciled to God in "one body" (2:16). Thus the whole world is blessed in Abraham according to promise, "that the blessing of Abraham might come on the Gentiles through Jesus Christ" (Gal. 3:14). Now the believing Gentile has received every spiritual privilege that Israel has, including spiritual circumcision (Col. 2:11).

Sin separated man not only from God but also from man. Man needed to be reconciled to God, but there had to be a conciliation between man and man also. Our Lord Jesus Christ is that Conciliator to abolish enmity and make peace, and we know of no other meeting-place where man can be at peace with man. You see, both Jew and Gentile had to be at peace with God before they could be at peace with each other, and only in Christ can the Jew forget that he is a Jew and the Gentile that he is a Gentile. Thank God that neither Jew nor Gentile can boast of one having had a better patch-up job than the other. This new man is not the result of any mere outward putting on, but is a "new creation" (2 Cor. 5:17) in Christ Jesus.

Now "through Him we both have access by one Spirit

unto the Father" (2:18). There can be no boast as to which man's religion or church gives him access to God. There are no advantages in being a Jew or a Gentile now. Christ is the Mediator of the new covenant and only "through Him" can there be access to the Father. The Lord Jesus said: "No man cometh unto the Father but by Me" (John 14:6), and that through the present ministry of the Holy Spirit.

The believing Jew and Gentile constitute one household: "Now therefore ye are no more strangers and foreigners, but fellowcitizens with the saints, and of the household of God" (2:19). We are both in one family, hence we are no longer strangers, no longer unknown to one another. There is now the intimate association of family life; we are brothers in Christ. We possess the same citizenship, not living as neighbors but as the saints and sons of God in the same house with God.

The believing Jew and Gentile constitute one holy temple: "And are built upon the foundation of the apostles and prophets, Jesus Christ Himself being the chief corner stone; In whom all the building fitly framed together groweth unto an holy temple in the Lord" (2:20, 21). Paul adds that the Church is a building, a holy temple, the New Testament prophets and apostles forming the foundation and Jesus Christ Himself being the chief corner stone. It is Christ Himself who holds together the foundation and the superstructure. Think of it, dear Christian, we are the habitation of God (2:22), His dwelling place on earth. Does your heart enter into this blessed truth? God has taken up His residence in the Church, in each believer. The true Church is of perfect and harmonious design, its beauty and holiness surpassing any shrine or building made with human hands. The most sacred spot on earth is no towering cathedral with stained glass windows, but the believer's heart where God has come to dwell. While the building is not now complete, it will be one day, and then all creation will view its splendor and give praise and glory to its Creator and Designer.

(c). *The Cross as the Power.* Before we conclude our meditation on these verses we would do well to ponder the method whereby our awful past has been blotted out and our present position made possible. In Christ alone we find the basis of reconciliation to God and man. "But now in Christ Jesus ye who sometimes were far off are made nigh by the Blood of Christ" (2:13). Reconciliation could be accomplished only by the finished work of God's Son on the cross. "For Christ also hath once suffered for sins, the Just for the unjust, that He might bring us to God . . ." (1 Peter 3:18). Aaron made an atonement once a year with blood which he offered to God for the people. Even so Jesus Christ, our great High Priest, entered into the holy place, having obtained eternal redemption for us (Heb. 9:11, 12). "Having therefore, brethren, boldness to enter into the holiest by the blood of Jesus . . . Let us draw near with a true heart in full assurance of faith" (Heb. 10:19, 22).

"In His flesh" He made peace, "having made peace through the blood of His cross" (Col. 1:20). Christ Himself is our peace, and he who has the Son of God enjoys peace with God and with all them that are in Christ. Let us thank God for accomplishing redemption and making our peace through the blood of His cross, for apart from His substitutionary death we would still be at enmity with God and man. It was at the cross where Jew and Gentile were condemned as sinners and united to God through faith in the blood of His Son. At the cross every enmity was slain and every provision made for redemption and reconciliation. The shedding of the blood of our Lord Jesus Christ is the plea of the sinner and the praise of the saint. In heaven we shall sing: "Thou wast slain, and hast redeemed us to God by Thy blood, out of every kindred, and tongue, and people, and nation" (Rev. 5:9).

If you are reading these lines and you are yet in your sins, Christ has removed the enmity between God and you by His propitiatory sacrifice at Calvary. You have only to acknowledge that your sin nailed Him there, and then receive Him as your Substitute and Saviour. You need not remain afar off, for even "now" you can be made nigh, as near to God as Christ Himself, but trusting in His blood.

C. *The Christian's Place in the Divine Plan* (Chap. 3)

In our approach to a new chapter of any book in the Bible we need to take care lest we lose the thought in the preceding chapter. There is sometimes the danger of missing the continuity of some particular idea or even a doctrine when we break up our reading and study-periods by chapters. If we keep in mind that the first three chapters in Ephesians have to do with the creation and design of the Church, we can look for the progress of thought in that connection as we begin our study of chapter three.

1. *Paul's Part in the Mystery* (3:1-13)

Chapter one describes the Church under the imagery of "His body" (1:23). In chapter two, the Church is seen as "the building" (2:21). The body is possessed of His life; the building is inhabited by His very Presence. Under the Old Covenant, God met with man in a temporary temple specially designed for such a meeting; under the New Covenant the body of the believer is that temple (1 Cor. 6:19).

Chapter two depicts the mystical body of Christ, the building, as made up of both believing Jew and Gentile. The position of Jew and Gentile in the body of Christ is here referred to as a "mystery." The divine plan and purpose are revealed in the magnificent scope of uniting Jew and Gentile to Christ in the Church. Now the building is in process, and for the completed project God has a definite purpose. It is our prospective place in God's future plan that is before us.

(a). *The Meaning of the Mystery Explained* (3:1-6). Paul, the converted Hebrew, informs his readers that for their sakes he is the Lord's prisoner: "For this cause I Paul, the prisoner of Jesus Christ for you Gentiles" (3:1). The reference to his imprisonment leads to a subject which, to Paul, was of greatest import. He went as God's witness to the uncircumcised knowing what would befall him (Act 9:15, 16). Later he testified of this as his experience (Acts 22:21, 22). Paul was "the prisoner of Jesus Christ." He had been imprisoned at least three times before; therefore this was not new to him. Yet he knew the blessing and comfort of his Lord's fellowship. If Christ wants a man in prison with Himself, that lends dignity to the occasion. A point not to be overlooked, however, is that the great apostle had been imprisoned because he preached the gospel to the Gentiles. His countrymen hated him because he affirmed that the Gentile had equal privileges in Christ with the Jew. Every Gentile believer should pause to give thanks to God for this fearless missionary to the Gentiles.

To Paul were entrusted in a special way hitherto unrevealed truths of this "mystery." He speaks of it as "the dispensation of the grace of God which is given me to youward" (3:2). Here the word "dispensation" means *the management, or stewardship of a household*. The grace of God had now reached out beyond the limit of the Jew to the Gentile, and this trusteeship had been given to Paul in order that he might dispense it to the Gentiles. The household of God must be managed according to a particular plan; therefore it was a high honor bestowed upon Paul when God entrusted His plan to him. The apostle was a steward, holding something in trust for another. In this case he held in trust the divine bestowal of saving grace to the Gentiles. The prime requisite of a steward is "that a man be found faithful" (1 Cor. 4:1, 2), hence the Apostle Peter writes: "As every man hath received the gift, even so minister the same one to another, as good stewards of the manifold grace of God" (1 Pet. 4:10). Every gift is a trust from God and must be exercised according to divine plan. Thus Paul recognized the source and character of his mission as well as the responsibility to faithfulness.

Under what circumstances did the apostle receive this truth? Paul himself says: ". . . by revelation He made known unto me the mystery" (3:3). A special dispensation had been arranged by God which included Paul. It was planned in past eternity, and Paul writes: "It pleased God, who separated me from my mother's womb, and called me by His grace, to reveal His Son in me . . ." (Gal. 1:15, 16).

A "mystery" (hitherto unrevealed truth) cannot be found out by the searching of men. God alone must reveal it. Human wisdom never stumbled on such a plan. A veil of secrecy had covered the truth of the dispensation of grace to the Gentiles until God revealed it in Paul's day. The apostle reminds them that he mentioned the mystery "afore in few words," referring, I take it, to his words in 1:9. The subject received only a passing notice in the early part of the epistle but, because of its source (revelation from God) and Paul's stewardship, he will now plead its cause the more earnestly. He felt that God had highly honored him in the divine appointment and special commission to preach His grace to the heathen.

This revelation was not vouchsafed to Paul that he might merely ponder it in His own heart but, he continues: "Whereby, when ye read, ye may understand my knowledge in the mystery of Christ" (3:4). What earnest watchfulness Paul displayed over the saints of God! The body of truth in his possession must be passed on to others; the world must know. There was no time to be lost. Others must not *read* it merely but *understand* it as well. May God give unto the ministers and teachers of His Word such earnestness and fervency of spirit that none will rest until every eager listener has a clear understanding of the divine message. The message is "the mystery of Christ," which means that it all centers in the Person and work of the risen and ascended Lord. It is Christ Himself who composes the body of believing Jews and Gentiles. To prepare Paul for this ministry God had given to him a supernatural revelation, and now he must not rest until men hear and understand its meaning. When we will not allow anything to overshadow the blessed work of God, then are we His servants indeed. The writer of these lines has been guilty of repeating truth when he himself did not understand, much less was able to make it plain to others; but when Paul preached and wrote, he did it as a divinely-inspired man who comprehended the subject under discussion and had a right to be heard.

This mystery "in other ages was not made known unto the sons of men, as it is now revealed unto His holy apostles and prophets by the Spirit" (3:5). Here the word "ages" suggests the idea of *generations,* so that Paul is emphasizing the fact that the mystery was given to him by revelation and was not the subject of any of God's previous servants. One searches in vain in the early Scriptures to find this distinctive truth "that the Gentiles should be fellowheirs, and of the same body, and partakers of His promise in Christ by the gospel" (3:6). From Moses to Malachi there is nothing to be found on the subject. It was "hid in God," to be passed on through the New Testament apostles and prophets, Paul having himself received it "by the Spirit."

In this mystery there are no vagaries which savor of the mysterious, but the glorious revelation that *in Christ* both Jew and Gentile "should be fellowheirs." God had said to Abraham: "In thee shall all families of the earth be blessed" (Gen. 12:3). Before Christ came, the Gentile depended on the Jew for his spiritual blessing. Now that Christ has come, who is Abraham's Seed (Gal. 3:16), the believing Gentile becomes a fellow-heir with the Jew.

It probably would have astounded any Old Testament prophet were he told that there would be one day a special dispensation of grace in which the Jew and Gentile would be fellow-heirs, and of the same body and partakers of the promises of God. And yet this is the mystery. Certainly Abraham, who believed God, knew that in his Seed all families of the earth would receive the blessing of the promise; but what he and the rest of the Old Testament saints did not know was that God purposed and planned to create this "new man" out of Jew and Gentile, thus constituting them one body, the Gentile being co-equal with the Jew in every respect. Certainly God must despise with holy hatred not only the anti-Semitism among Gentile-Christians but also the Hebrew-Christian cliques which shut out the Gentile believer. The distinctive feature of the gospel in this dispensation is found in the words of the angel of the Lord, who announced: "Behold, I bring you good tidings of great joy, which shall be to *all* people" (Luke 2:10). Gentiles as well as Jews are to receive this good news. Remember, the mystery is not that the Gentiles should be saved. Rather it is that a thorough and entire change wrought by the creating of a new entity would make the believing Gentiles co-heirs and co-sharers with the Jews. Such is the power of "the Gospel."

(b) *The Minister of the Mystery as an Example* (3:7-13). Of this gospel, Paul continues: "Whereof I was made a minister, according to the gift of the grace of God given unto me by the effectual working of His power" (3:7). The greatness of his task and the sublimity of the trust must have humbled Paul. His divinely-given ministry he calls "the gift of the grace of God." He marveled that God would choose him and make him a messenger of so deep a mystery. There was no other way of explaining it; it was given to him by the unmerited kindness of God. That such a persecutor and blasphemer as Paul was entrusted with so lofty a mission is a clear demonstration of divine grace.

Some men in the ministry speak of having "earned" certain degrees and diplomas which qualify them for the ministry. God save us from such pride! As famous as Paul became as an able and honored servant of God, he never forgot for a moment that the ministry was a gracious gift from God. It is not unusual for us to comment on the sacrifice of money, energy, and time that we spend in preparation for some work for God. Yet this humble messenger of the mystery looked upon it all as a gift of grace. Paul made no claims for himself.

Add to this the fact that the discharge of his ministry was "by the effectual working of His [God's] power." To make a saint out of a sinner shows the effectual working of His power. To make a divine messenger out of a deliberate murderer shows the effectual working of His power. The arrogant Pharisee had become a witness of the Gospel to the Gentiles. The secret of his success lay in the effectual working of the power of God in him. He could testify: "And my speech and my preaching was not with enticing words of man's wisdom, but in demonstration of the Spirit and of power" (1 Cor. 2:4). When will some of us learn this lesson?

"Unto me, who am less than the least of all saints, is this grace given . . ." (3:8). H. S. Miller has written: "Paul is so full of his wonderful subject and sees so clearly the awful sin of self-righteousness and bigotry and cruelty from which he has been saved, that he breaks the rules of grammar and piles a comparative upon a superlative and calls himself 'less than the least' [*leaster,* if such a word were allowable] of all saints." If one is the least of all he can hardly be less than that. Since pride is much reflected in the ministry, it is refreshing to hear of men, greatly used in God's work, full of the grace of humility. When Paul stood in the presence of Jesus Christ he felt such terrible guilt, because of his past pride and other sins, that he was consciously aware of his unfitness and unworthiness for the task. He remembered his thorn in the flesh lest he should be exalted above measure through the abundance of the revelations made known to him (2 Cor. 12:7). How unlike some today! A smattering of truth comes to some of us and we are carried away with conceit and an attitude of superiority. But not so Paul! As he went about preaching he took the lowest place among the saints.

It was to this humble messenger that God entrusted the

mystery, that he "should preach among the Gentiles the un-searchable riches of Christ." Some translate "unsearchable" to mean *inexhaustible;* others like to use *intraceable.* Both are suggestive and proper. Certainly the truth could not be traced back to any man since it had been "hid in God" from the beginning of the world (3:9). Then, too, the mystery of Christ is unmeasurable, "great" and "without controversy" (1 Tim. 3:16).

The writer has read seventeen commentaries on Paul's Epistle to the Ephesians, all written by well-known men of God, yet each man has placed emphasis where another has not, and very often each is correct. Think of it! For nineteen centuries men have been searching out riches from this one epistle, and still there are riches in it which can never be traced out or comprehended. "The riches" are "past finding out" (Rom. 11:33). Since they are not fully discoverable they are incalculable. Calvin calls them "the astonishing and boundless treasures of grace."

Paul felt keenly his responsibility "to make all men see what is the fellowship of the mystery, which from the beginning of the word hath been hid in God, who created all things by Jesus Christ" (3:9). Notice the end in view—to make all see, or to pass on spiritual illumination to all. The Church's commission is to "all the world" and "to every creature" in order that all might be enlightened as to God's purpose in the mystery, namely, the calling out from among the Gentiles a people for His name. God's plan is to give light to all the world through the world-wide distribution of the gospel. This Paul saw clearly. We conclude then that the evangelization of the world formed a part of God's plan when He created the universe. When will the Church realize this?

The purpose of the mystery reaches above and beyond the world of men: "To the intent that now unto the principalities and powers in heavenly places might be known by the church the manifold wisdom of God" (3:10). Here Paul is stating simply that God intended that principalities and powers, including the angelic beings of heaven and the demons of the air, should see *"now"* in the true Church *"the manifold wisdom of God."* You see, even the angels, fallen and unfallen, had no knowledge of the mystery until it was given by God to the Church through Paul. Now God wants the vast unseen hosts to see what He is doing here on earth in His Church. The angels beheld the wisdom of God in many ways, but *now* only in the Church can they see His manifold (many-sided) wisdom. Only because the angels see God's purpose in the Church do they rejoice whenever a sinner repents (Luke 15:7). They know now what it means to God and to Christ every time another sinner is saved and added to His body. Here the believer catches a glimpse of his place in God's perfect plan. "According to the eternal purpose which He purposed in Christ Jesus our Lord" (3:11), the Church occupies a key position on the earth. We marvel at the very thought of our important share in God's perfect plan. Our confidence in the Lord Jesus Christ and in all that He accomplished for us makes us bold to declare our faith in the plan (3:12).

Were those saints in the early Church losing heart because the apostle was a prisoner in Rome? Did they fear that now God's great plan would be hindered? Paul did not so reason. He added: "Wherefore I desire that ye faint not at my tribulations for you, which is your glory" (3:13). Paul is not telling them to rejoice because he is suffering but to rejoice in the fact that, through his sufferings, he was carrying out his responsibility in God's great plan. This indeed was cause for rejoicing.

As we labor in His cause, let us not give up when we are made to suffer, but let us praise God and rejoice that He counted us worthy to suffer for His name. If any of us are alive to see the day when we are called upon to suffer for Christ, may God give us grace to find occasion to glory in our sufferings. "If so be that we suffer with Him, that we may be also glorified together" (Rom. 8:17).

2. *Paul's Prayer as a Minister* (3:14-21)

The prison prayers of the Apostle Paul call for deepest reverence and devoted study. One does not read in a hurry these solemn words between God and Paul. It is a remarkable thing that the Holy Spirit was pleased to preserve these prayers as a necessary part of the Canon of Holy Scripture. There are two prayers of Paul in this epistle. In the first, the apostle petitions God for knowledge; and in the second, he prays for love. The first is a prayer for revelation; the second is for realization. The first prayer is for enlightenment; the second is for enablement. It is not enough merely to *know;* we must *be*. The fruit of divine knowledge is the expression of divine life.

(a) "For this cause I bow my knees unto the Father of our Lord Jesus Christ, of whom the whole family in heaven and earth is named" (3:14, 15). Did Paul pray because he had nothing else to do or because he was in difficult straits? Neither. Paul prayed *"for this cause."* Then we must conclude that the prayer relates to something he had already written and is, thus, a necessary part of the epistle.

Immediately our minds inquire: "For what cause?" The prayer is a continuation of the thought in the first half of this chapter. He had explained the meaning of the mystery and his own responsibility as its minister. Having shown how believing Jews and Gentiles are fellow-heirs, of the same body and partakers of God's promises in Christ by the gospel, he now longs for the Ephesians to experience the power and love of Christ in their relationships with one another. His desire is that they might live the life of the believer. Then, too, he reminds them of his sufferings and imprisonment for their sakes in order that they should know and understand the mystery. Having said all of this Paul felt that the Ephesians might lose courage because of his tribulations, so "for this cause" he prayed.

Paul's attitude before God was one of deepest reverence and humility. He said: "I bow my knees unto the Father of our

Lord Jesus Christ." The posture here suggests utter submission to and dependence upon God. From certain passages of Scripture we know that standing was a common posture in prayer (see 1 Samuel 1:26; Matthew 6:5; Mark 11:25; Luke 18:11). Yet we know that to bow before God befits all of His subjects whom He has saved by sovereign grace. Paul no doubt dictated this epistle to an amanuensis, but he was so overwhelmed with the majesty of his great theme and the miracle of his call to minister it that he fell upon his knees as he continued to dictate. The Ephesians would know that this was no mere outburst of emotion, for the elders of the church were with him at the dock when "he kneeled down and prayed with them all" (Acts 20:36). Prayer can be made to God sitting or standing, but when something has gripped and stirred you intensely, you have found yourself almost helplessly brought to your knees. Though not necessary to prayer, kneeling expresses adoration and confidence as we come to our Father and the Father of our Lord Jesus Christ.

When speaking of God as Father, Paul says it is He "of whom the whole family in heaven and earth is named" (3:15). Here we do not understand the "whole family" to mean the entire human race. Christ taught only His followers to address God as their Father. It is revealed in chapter two that the believing Jew and Gentile form one household of which God is the Father. The reference is to that spiritual family of the redeemed who through faith in the Lord Jesus Christ are made the sons of God.

The modernist cannot turn to Paul to support his ideas of the universal fatherhood of God. There is no such thought in Paul's mind. There is that true spiritual family life which has its origin in the Father, but it includes only those who have put faith in Jesus Christ (Gal. 3:26).

No sound basis can be found for the teaching which says that "the whole family in heaven and earth" suggests a mutual family relationship between the angels and redeemed men. Rather would such a statement strengthen the general teaching of the context, namely, that there is no distinction between Jews and Gentiles in the family of God. Jews have no ground to boast that they are the children of Abraham or that they belong to a certain tribe, but there is one relationship to God for all believers, whether they be the saints in heaven of a former dispensation or saints on earth.

(b) This brings us to the appeal of Paul: "That He would grant you, according to the riches of His glory, to be strengthened with might by His Spirit in the inner man" (3:16). Paul knew the weakness of the flesh. He testified: "For the good that I would I do not: but the evil which I would not, that I do" (Rom. 7:19). So he prays that believers might be strengthened with might by His Spirit in the inner man.

We need not fear to ask God for strength. We can never ask Him for too much. He gives "according to the riches of His glory." Our Father knows our need, and as we petition Him He promises to supply all our need "according to His riches in glory by Christ Jesus" (Phil. 4:19). How often we have felt limited, weak, and powerless, accomplishing very little for our Lord! Beloved, the power is not of ourselves but of God. The outworking of all of God's purposes for us is the result of the Spirit's inworking. The Christian needs to be made strong with a power outside of himself, and the Holy Spirit indwelling him is present to strengthen and empower him with divine energy. His power cannot be acquired or purchased; it is a "grant" through the Person and work of the Holy Spirit.

The sphere in which His strength is realized is "the inner man." Every Christian needs to see his human weakness and pray daily for spiritual strength, so that he can say: "Though our outward man perish, yet the inward man is renewed day by day" (2 Cor. 4:16). It is possible for the inward man to grow stronger while the body becomes weaker. When the servants of God learn the secret of spiritual strength they can face tremendous difficulties and work under severe handicaps. The measure of such strength is the measure of our daily contact with God.

Paul continues: "That Christ may dwell in your hearts by faith . . ." (3:17). The apostle was not praying for the Ephesian Christians to accept Christ by faith. They already had done this, else they could not be rightly called "saints." He was praying here that they might appropriate His indwelling Presence. Do not miss this blessed truth! There is far more in appropriating His Presence than any of us have ever yet realized. The more we appropriate Him the more we become "rooted and grounded in love." A tree that is well rooted is stable and productive. If the believer is to be strong and bear fruit he must practice the Presence of Christ in his life. Calvin has written: "Our roots ought to be so deeply planted, and our foundation so firmly laid in love, that nothing will be able to shake us."

The more firmly we are established and planted, the more able we are "to comprehend with all saints what is the breadth, and length, and depth, and height; and to know the love of Christ, which passeth knowledge . . ." (3:18, 19). Here is a great text of which the interpretations and applications are so many and varied that the present writer hesitates to attempt anything on this profound subject of divine love in four dimensions. W. M. Clow has written a sermon on this text in which he associates with it John 3:16. His outline follows:

1. The *breadth* of the love of God—"God so loved the world."
2. The *length* of the love of God—"He gave His only begotten Son."
3. The *depth* of the love of God—"That whosoever believeth in Him should not perish."
4. The *height* of the love of God—"But have everlasting life."

How broad is the love of God? Broad enough to include all men of every race, color, and tongue. How long is the love of God? It removes our transgressions as far as the east is from the west. How deep is the love of God? The immeasurable distance from heaven's highest heights to hell's deepest depths.

How high is the love of God? High enough to lift every believing sinner into the very presence of God.

Dr. Nathan R. Wood has said: "The Fourth Dimension, so much sought and so much desired, is Reality." It is experience. Comprehending the cube of God's love can never be accomplished in the span of one natural lifetime. "Keep on studying, thinking, praying, meditating, conversing, learning, knowing, and at the end of life you will know much, yet not much as compared with what there is to know, of the matchless, boundless, fathomless love of Christ." (H. S. Miller). Paul adds that it "passeth knowledge."

Oh, the wonder of God's grace and wisdom! He enables us to know something of the unknowable and to comprehend something of the incomprehensible. O beloved Christian, let us stay close by our great God in order that the indwelling Spirit may make us strong to share that blessed privilege of the few, namely, to comprehend by experience the love of Christ! It is not a matter of knowledge in our heads; it is the experiential knowledge of the heart for which Paul is praying. It can come only to those who have fellowship with Him.

Now to the doxology. In the following words Paul concludes the doctrinal half of the letter. Keep your heart warm until you hear him say the "Amen." He has been praying in the Holy Spirit, and now he concludes with an ascription of praise "unto Him that is able to do exceeding abundantly above all that we ask or think, according to the power that worketh in us" (3:20). Yes, He is able to do *all* that we ask or think; He is able to do *above all* that we ask or think; He is able to do *abundantly above all* that we ask or think; He is able to do *exceeding abundantly above all* that we ask or think. Think of it! the power and ability of God surpasses by far our highest aspirations, our most concentrated thinking, and our most earnest petitions.

And what God can do, He will do; but only *"according to the power that worketh in us."* He will never bestow upon us anything above our capacity to receive and to exercise.

Divine power must be controlled by the indwelling of the Holy Spirit, thus according to the measure of our faith in, and our yieldedness to Him will He impart that power to us. He will do as much *for* us and *through* us as we let Him *in* us. "According to the power that worketh in us" do we experience the measure of His limitless ability to do for us and through us far more than our tongues can ask or our minds conceive.

A fitting word of praise concludes the prayer: "Unto Him be glory in the church by Christ Jesus throughout all ages, world without end. Amen" (3:21). To the Master-Builder, who is building His Church by Christ Jesus His Son, Paul ascribes glory. This is the highest privilege and possibility of the Church now, and it will be unto all generations forever and ever. Glory in the Church! "Amen"—let it be so.

II. THE CONDUCT AND
DUTY OF THE CHURCH
(Chapters 4-6)

In the study so far, we have finished the first half of this great epistle with its clear and blessed revelation of the calling and design of the Church. We have learned something of how God planned the Church before the foundation of the world, how that, in the fullness of time, the Son of God purchased it with His own blood, and finally, how the Holy Spirit came as the deposit, or pledge, that the whole transaction will be satisfactorily completed.

The first part of the epistle is doctrinal. The fact of God's love to us ere we were ever born is propounded. The great doctrines of salvation are set forth in the first three chapters. Now Paul is ready to enumerate the duties of the Christian.

Proper conduct springs from a correct undertanding of one's calling; duty springs from doctrine. Dr. N. B. Harrison writes: "To harangue people into better living is one thing; to root our appeal in a relationship we sustain to Christ through the eternal purposes of grace is quite another." A babe in Christ must lay hold of some God-given revelation as to the dignity of his calling before he will lay hold of his duty as a Christian.

This order we expect in Paul's epistles: it is typical of his writings. He teaches doctrine before deportment, calling before conduct, wealth before walk, position before practice, revelation before responsibility. The believer, having realized his high calling, is now ready to be led into a life of holy conduct. If you believe in doctrinal Christianity, you will desire practical Christianity. If your heart said, "Amen" (3:21), to the doctrine, you will yield as readily to the deportment. The way God sees us in Christ in the heavenlies is the way men should see us in action on the earth.

Two great truths stand out in this part of the epistle:

the believer's *walk,* and the believer's *warfare.* The teaching deals at length with these two thoughts, referred to by some as conduct and conflict. The larger part of the last three chapters has to do with the former (4:1-6:9).

A. *The Christian Is to Walk Characteristically* (4:1-16)

Certain distinguishing traits of character mark the believer in Christ. Having set forth the believer's position doctrinally, Paul now calls upon him to prove the reality of his calling through right conduct: "I therefore, the prisoner of the Lord, beseech you that ye walk worthy of the vocation wherewith ye are called" (4:1).

The "therefore's" of Paul are significant. Here the "therefore" stands as a signboard to tell us that there is no divorcement of Christian doctrine from Christian duty. Wherever there is faith, there will works be found also.

For the second time Paul mentions the fact that he is "the prisoner of the Lord" (see 3:1). This is not a plea for sympathy. The man who was about to expound the walk and warfare of the believer knew whereof he spoke. It was for their sakes that he was a made a prisoner; and if his bonds did anything at all, they added dignity to his position. True he was the prisoner of the Roman state, but more exactly he was "the prisoner of the Lord."

On the ground of the believer's calling, Paul would "beseech" him—not scold or command. Doubtless the Ephesians were touched by such an earnest entreaty from one who was suffering for their sakes. While his bondage was permitted by Christ, it was the direct result of his having preached Christ's Gospel to them, as well as to others. These "beseechings" were not human commands but divine compulsions. Having received the authority of apostleship from God, Paul had a right to command, but he had a heart to beseech. To command is law; to beseech is grace. Elsewhere Paul wrote: "Wherefore, though I might be much bold in Christ to enjoin [command] thee that which is convenient, yet for love's sake I rather *beseech* thee . . . " (Philem. 8-10). This humble servant of God chose to entreat them, to desire God's best for them, to pray for them.

Paul besought them to walk worthy of the vocation wherewith they were called. One's vocation is one's calling. Paul is saying: "I entreat you to live your life worthy of the call you have received." The saint's calling is described in Scripture as high (Phil. 3:14), holy (2 Tim. 1:9), and heavenly (Heb. 3:1). Recipients of God's mercies, resulting in a miraculous change in heart, should deport themselves consistent with their high position. Beware lest the term "walk" lose its meaning to you. I know that it is a familiar figure of speech. But do not forget that it suggests a course of life; hence we have here solemn exhortations to live in obedience to God's Word lest the steps we take create false impressions in men's minds regarding the Christian life.

1. *The Christian Walk Preserves Unity* (4:1-6)

"*All* lowliness" suggests the idea of *perfect humility*. Genuine humility becomes the Christian at all times under every circumstance. We dare not pretend on the outside that we are lowly while on the inside we are deceitful and haughty. Lowliness might be despised by the world, but it is esteemed by God. Humility is the first step to unity.

"Meekness" is next mentioned as a characteristic virtue of the believer's walk. The incarnation and earthly life of our Lord echoed "lowliness and meekness." He said: "Take My yoke upon you, and learn of Me; for I am *meek,* and *lowly* in heart" (Matt. 11:29). And "he that saith he abideth in Him ought himself also so to walk, even as He walked" (1 John 2:6). Meekness in heart is that fruit of the Spirit that esteems the brethren higher than one's self. In meekness, envy, malice, or an underestimate of another's gifts and ability finds no place. Meekness is the next step to unity.

"Longsuffering" follows. This is a gracious tolerance that never desires revenge. Pride and self-seeking, with a revengeful spirit, show that one has never taken one's rightful place before God. Are you long-tempered or short-tempered? Do you get in a heat easily or do you remain calm and serene under fire? Longsuffering is another step toward unity.

"Forbearing one another in love." This expression appears also in Colossians 3:13 and signifies *to bear with, to endure*—an extraordinary patience, with restraint of one's feelings. One of the early lessons we learn as Christians is how to get along with one another. Mutual forbearance among us means that we pray one for the other in each other's weaknesses and offenses, and while we are called upon to forbear it is to forbear *in love*.

All of these virtues contribute toward keeping "the unity of the Spirit in the bond of peace" (4:3). Notice, please, what we are *not* asked to do here. We are not asked to *make* unity. God Himself has made unity already, both of the Spirit and of the body of Christ created by God. When we were born again the Holy Spirit united us to that body, and nothing can ever sever us from it. Believing Jews and believing Gentiles have been made a new unity by God, thus forming the body in its unity. This was explained in the first part of the epistle.

Within the Church, differences in wealth, education, race, color, and social standing create the temptation to deny that unity. But God warns His people to guard the unity which He provided. Dr. A. C. Gaebelein has said: "We keep the unity of the Spirit when we recognize in every true believer a member of the same body." Preservation of an ecclesiastical or organizational unity is not implied. This plea of the apostle does not apply to any ecumenical movement in church history, present or past.

Commenting on "the unity of the Spirit," Dr. H. J. Ockenga wrote: "But this spiritual unity is more difficult to keep than organizational unity. It is easy to exercise authority, to discipline, to rule, to excommunicate those who agree not with us, but it is difficult to preserve love, respect, faith, humility, mutual honor one of another, which is necessary in a spiritual unity. The latter becomes a matter of self-discipline, in which most of us are lacking. We are always willing to discipline others, but very unwilling to discipline ourselves. For this reason the indwelling Spirit is the principle of unity among Christians, and this may be promoted or disturbed." Hence the need to walk worthily with all lowliness and meekness, with longsuffering, forbearing one another in love as the Scriptures enjoin.

The basis of spiritual unity in the Church follows in verses 4-6. It is sevenfold. Observe the seven "one's."

(a) *"One body."* Here is the oneness of the Church itself. This mystical body of Christ (the Church) already exists. It originated on the day of Pentecost and answered the Lord's prayer when He prayed: "That they all may be one: as Thou, Father, art in Me, and I in Thee, that they also may be one in Us: that the world may believe that Thou hast sent Me" (John 17:21). There are many denominations, many churches, many forms of administration, many gifts, but only one body, one true Church. The members of this body differ in color, nationality, ability, mentality, and outlook; but through faith in the Lord Jesus Christ, and by the power of the Holy Spirit, "are we all baptized into one body" (1 Cor. 12:13). "So we, being many, are one body in Christ, and every one members one of another" (Rom. 12:5). Beloved Christian, we *are* one body. Therefore our lives must be lived in the light of our vital relationship with other fellow Christians.

(b) *"One Spirit."* Doubtless Paul means the Holy Spirit. The unity is of His begetting. It is called "the unity of the Spirit." By His operation men are born again and added to the body. The individual member who is led by the Holy Spirit is thereby preserving the unity. Beware of other spirits. "Beloved, believe not every spirit, but try the spirits whether they are of God" (1 John 4:1). Watch out for "the spirit of error" (1 John 4:6). None but the Holy Spirit is the activating power in the body; hence, a sin against the body is a sin against the Holy Spirit. When the Holy Spirit came down on the day of Pentecost to form that body, the disciples "were all with one accord in one place" (Acts 2:1). Such is the unity of the Spirit.

. (c) *"One hope."* In Chapter 1:18, Paul wrote about "the hope of *His* calling"; here it is "one hope of *your* calling." It has been mentioned that the believer's calling is high, holy, and heavenly. The hope of such a calling is our final glorification when we shall be like the Lord and be forever with Him. The saints have a rich inheritance in the Person of our Lord Jesus Christ. While we will not enter fully into our inheritance until Christ returns, we have the earnest of the Holy Spirit to strengthen our hope. He keeps that hope alive. There is no hope like it in all the world, and in this one hope all Christians share. Think of it: millions having the same hope! This one thing in itself is a bond of unity. One body, one Spirit, one hope—what a powerful incentive to keep the unity of the Spirit!

(d) *"One Lord."* The one Lord is God's eternal Son, our Lord Jesus Christ. Jude speaks of ungodly men who deny Him (Jude 4). The believer owns Him and walks in obedience to His will. Jesus Christ is our Saviour; but He is more: He is our Lord. It is the recognition of His Lordship that preserves the unity of the Spirit. When each individual Christian acknowledges Jesus Christ as his sovereign Head, there can be no schism in the Church. Elsewhere Paul writes: "And there are differences of administrations, but the same Lord" (1 Cor. 12:5). There are many gifts but one Giver. There are many ways of exercising and administering those gifts, but the same Sovereignty owns and rules over all.

The Lord spoke these solemn words: "Not every one that saith unto Me, Lord, Lord, shall enter into the kingdom of heaven; but he that doeth the will of My Father which is in heaven. Many will say to Me in that day, Lord, Lord, have we not prophesied in Thy name? And in Thy name have cast out devils [demons]? And in Thy name done many wonderful works? And then I will profess unto them, I never knew you:

depart from Me, ye that work iniquity" (Matt. 7:21-23). How fitting a climax to the Sermon on the Mount! The day of judgment will bring to light some unusual things. Some profess His Lordship but do not practice submission to Him. Sad will be the day of reckoning for all such! In that day "every tongue should confess that Jesus Christ is Lord, to the glory of God the Father" (Phil. 2:11), but then there will be neither joy nor reward.

(e) *"One faith."* There is only one system of truth; it is *"the faith* which was once delivered unto the saints" (Jude 3). One may possess the right attitude of faith but the wrong object of faith. It matters not *how* one believes if he does not embrace the one saving object of faith, the Lord Jesus Christ. The Apostle Paul testified that he preached "the faith" (Gal. 1:23). Christian faith has the Word of God as a standard; hence it recognizes one access to God, and that through believing on the Lord Jesus Christ. When anyone embraces the faith, he immediately is made a part of the body, thereby becoming a contributing factor in keeping the unity of the Spirit.

(f) *"One baptism."* Because of the existence of various schools of thought on the subject of baptism, we can expect divergent interpretations on the "one baptism" mentioned here. I do not believe that baptism in the Spirit is meant in this verse. Baptism in the Spirit has already been dealt with in the preceding verse. Here the apostle refers to water baptism. It is that ordinance which, according to the New Testament, should follow one's acceptance of the "one faith" and one's embracing of the "one Lord." It is sad to meet those who have submitted to the rite of Christian baptism but who have not been born again through faith in the Lord Jesus Christ. There is but one outward rite whereby the believer declares his faith in, and union with, Jesus Christ; it is the "one baptism."

(g) *"One God and Father of all, who is above all, and through all, and in you all"* (4:6). The message of this verse recognizes the Trinity actively engaged in forming the unity.

Looking back from verse six, we have the Father, the Son, and the Holy Spirit. The triune God is sovereign in the Church. His Presence is all that we need and all that we should desire. He is the Father of all of us who have accepted Christ; hence we believers bear the same relation to Him and to one another. As we recognize Him as "above all," we preserve the unity of the Spirit. "In Him we live, and move, and have our being" (Acts 17:28).

2. *The Christian Walk Promotes Usefulness* (4:7-16)

Unity is a pre-requisite to usefulness, especially in the Church, where one finds the widest variety of personalities and the greatest diversity of gifts. But no matter how striking and winsome the personality, or how capable one might be in the exercise of gifts, grace is needed. And so, writes Paul: "Unto every one of us is given grace according to the measure of the gift of Christ" (4:7).

In the verses before us attention is drawn to the gifts that our ascended Lord has bestowed upon the members of His Church which is His body.

Before examining the various gifts and the contribution that each member makes to the whole, Paul tells us that every one has been the recipient of the gift of grace. Each gift is a bestowment of grace, each comes from the same divine source, and each is in proportion as the Lord Himself is pleased to bestow. The gifts are given by measure, each member receiving his gift from the same Person. As we shall see later, there is a difference in gifts (Rom. 12:6) as well as a difference in the ministration of them, but each member functions to preserve the unity of the Spirit in the body.

In support of his statement that the ascended Christ gives gifts unto men, the apostle dips back into the Old Testament and brings forward, with some alterations, a quotation from Psalm 68:18. Paul writes: "Wherefore He saith, When He ascended up on high, He led captivity captive, and gave gifts unto men" (4:8). Upon examining the words of the Psalmist it is apparent that when Paul quotes the words, he introduces some changes. The quotation from the Psalm reads:

> Thou hast ascended on high, Thou hast led captivity captive; Thou hast received gifts for men; yea, for the rebellious also, that the Lord God might dwell among them (Psalm 68:18).

Apparently David writes in this Psalm of an historic incident during his own reign as king over Israel, perhaps of the conquests over his enemies when he led as captives those who had attacked his people. Which of the battles David had in mind we cannot be certain of, but it would seem that, upon the conquering king's return from battle, the giving of gifts was a part of the celebration. We are not here attempting to show whether the king gave gifts to his subjects, or the subjects gifts to the king. The point for us to observe is that Paul saw in this Old Testament Scripture our Lord Jesus Christ, the Antitype of the story, in His incarnation, death, burial, resurrection, and ascension (4:9, 10). In the conquest of the Old Testament king, Paul saw our Lord's triumph over death as well as over him that had the power of death, even Satan (Heb. 2:14). Upon His triumphant return to His Father's house, He distributes gifts to His subjects. All of this Peter must have understood when he said at Pentecost: "Therefore being by the right hand of God exalted, and having received of the Father the Holy Ghost, He hath shed forth this, which ye now see and hear" (Acts 2:33). Pentecost was the first great display of the exercise of gifts. The main thought in these four verses (7-10), then, is the bestowal of gifts by the ascended Christ.

The mighty victories which God wrought for Israel were noble triumphs. But, says Calvin: "The noblest triumph which God ever gained was when Christ, after subduing sin, conquering death, and putting Satan to flight, rose majestically to heaven, that He might exercise His glorious reign over the Church." Now the Church on earth has a goal toward which she moves, and Christ as the Church's Head determines her actions. The duty of the Church is to evangelize the world, to preach the gospel to every creature. The enablement and equipment for the task is supplied by the Head, for, says Paul: He "gave gifts unto men" (4:8). The proper exercise of the gifts will preserve unity and promote usefulness in the Church.

"And He gave some, apostles" (4:11). To some He gave the gift of the apostolate. No individual could choose or decide to become an apostle. The choosing of the man and the bestowal of the gift were of God. I consider this to be of extreme importance, for God did not merely confer upon a man the name of "apostle"; He endowed him with the gift and enabled him to discharge the office. This office of an apostle was a highly exalted one appointed directly by Christ. These specially-called spokesmen for God were missionaries in a peculiar sense in that they had to see the risen Lord and be sent by Him. Because of the very nature of the qualifications, this office could not be passed on to others. Some sects claim "apostolic succession." In the very beginning of the Christian Church some claimed to be apostles but, under trial, were found to be liars (Rev. 2:2).

"And some, prophets." The New Testament prophets were men who received revelation from God for the time, and announced the same in power for the edifying of the body of Christ. Sometimes the prophet was a fore-teller of predictive prophecy; at other times he was a forthteller (preacher) of a divinely-revealed truth for the present, pertaining to doctrinal instruction (1 Cor. 14:3). There are neither apostles nor prophets today. Their work was to lay the foundation for the Church (Eph. 2:20).

"And some, evangelists." The evangelist is the bearer of the glad tidings of the gospel to a lost world. The gift of evangelism is a remarkable thing indeed, since evangelism is essential to the growth of the Church. Philip was a successful evangelist in the early Church (Acts 8:26-40). Paul must have recognized in Timothy this gift, for he wrote: "Do the work of an evangelist" (2 Tim. 4:5). Teaching the Word of God and building up the saints is an important phase of Christian service, but the taking of the gospel to those who have not heard is an unique privilege.

"And some, pastors and teachers." Not some as pastors and some as teachers, but rather the combined office of pastor-teacher. He is a ruler and feeder of the flock. The pastor needs a heart to shepherd the sheep as well as a mind to teach them. This dual function he performs as minister of a particular congregation. His gift is divinely bestowed; so no Bible school, or seminary, or college can make a man a pastor-teacher.

The purpose of the gifts is "for the perfecting of the saints for the work of the ministry, for the edifying of the body of Christ" (4:12). Special gifts were bestowed to equip the saints to do the service, and the intent of this service is the building up of the body of Christ. Each gift is a contribution to the whole body. From these special gifts responsibility passes to each member.

This service continues "till we all come in the unity of the faith, and of the knowledge of the Son of God, unto a perfect man, unto the measure of the stature of the fulness of Christ" (4:13). Our blessed Lord gave these gifts that each of His followers should serve Him, and that service must continue as long as the Church remains on the earth.

When Christ returns to take us home to heaven, we shall see the full expression of unity and possess complete knowledge of Him. There will be no need for the apostle, the prophet, the evangelist, the teacher, or the pastor, because we will have attained perfection in unity and knowledge. The members of the Church will not be as many members in that day, but as "a perfect [fullgrown] man." We shall be like our Lord, having attained that standard of perfection of Christ Himself, "unto the measure of the stature of the fulness of Christ." This is God's goal for the Church.

A. C. Gaebelein writes: "The measure of the stature of the

fulness of Christ will be reached when the body is joined to the Head." Until the Head returns He will continue to give gifts to His own. Faithfulness in the proper exercise of these gifts will result in others being added to the body and trained to carry on Christ's work on earth till He comes.

Furthermore, the purpose of the gifts is "That we henceforth be no more children, tossed to and fro, and carried about with every wind of doctrine, by the sleight of men, and cunning craftiness, whereby they lie in wait to deceive" (4:14). False doctrine abounds. Satan has his sleight-of-hand men who, with cunning craftiness, prey upon babes in Christ. These spiritual babes are sometimes powerless to resist and are tossed about by varying winds of doctrine. Hence the need for Christians to walk in unity and usefulness. Lack of unity and laxity in usefulness reveal a condition of spiritual infancy and immaturity. We must grow in grace and in the knowledge of our Lord Jesus Christ. In order to do this we need to be established in the great doctrinal teachings of God's Word. God has chosen to edify and instruct His people with special gifts. There is no substitute for a careful study of the Word.

Having said that we ought not to remain children, immature and untaught, Paul now exhorts the believer to grow up: "But speaking the truth in love, may grow up into Him in all things, which is the head, even Christ" (4:15). The gifts were given by the ascended Christ to edify the body so that believers might manifest the truth in love. It is not enough to know and speak the truth; it must be manifested *in love*. While we insist upon a good confession we must live the truth in love. One can be fearless in standing for the truth and at the same time gentle and kind. Truth declared in a cold, contentious manner will neither preserve unity nor promote usefulness.

An aid to perfecting the positive purpose of the gifts is doing (living) the truth in love. Truth must be spoken but never harshly or bitterly. No amount of loyalty to the truth, however eloquently and forcefully expressed, signifies spiritual maturity unless spoken in charitable sincerity. It is not enough that our tongues hold to the truth; the truth must hold our tongues in love.

Elsewhere in the epistle the Chrurch is called "His body" (1:23), "the body of Christ" (4:12), of which He is "the Head" (4:15). When each member functions in its proper order "according to the effectual working in the measure of every part," nourishment is added to the body, and "maketh increase of the body unto the edifying of itself in love" (4:16). As each member looks to the Head, he finds there are no gift-less and useless parts, but that each part is a gifted and useful member in a relation of interdependence to every other part. As the incapacitation of one member of the human body robs strength and limits the usefulness of the whole body, even so a believer who is dwarfed spiritually holds down the increase of the body of Christ unto the edifying of itself in love. Each member receives grace and gifts from the Lord, and all members are so constructed to join together fitly. God planned this to be so in the human body and, as it is in the human body, so it is with the body of Christ.

In conclusion, I refer you to a phrase used by Paul in verse 12, namely, "for the perfecting of the saints." Sometimes the word from which "perfecting" is derived is used to mean *to mend*. Such is the case in Matthew 4:21, where James and John are seen in a ship with their father "mending their nets." The saints are saved to engage in harmonious and happy service with the other members of the body. Some of the saints are like broken nets that need mending, or like fallen brothers needing to be "restored" (Gal. 6:1). At some time we all have been acquainted with some Christian (perhaps you were that Christian) who, like a net torn and full of holes, had lapsed into a state of disrepair in need of mending. Christ's gifts to the individual believer, and to the Church as a body, are the media through which He works to mend the saints. When the saints are mended they are fit for the work of the ministry.

They edify the body of Christ, they preserve Christian unity, they promote maturity, and they speak the truth in love.

Beloved Christian, do you need some repair or adjustment? Is your net torn or full of holes so that you are no longer a fisher of men? God in His mercy has saved you, to be sure, but He also has made wondrous provision for any adjustments that are necessary in Christian experience. Let Him mend you and cast you out upon life's sea where souls wait to be rescued.

B. *The Christian Is to Walk Consistently* (4:17-5:14)

Sometimes a believer's acts and his profession are in discord. A man may testify to certain beliefs and purposes and yet be incongruous in his life, his speech and his deeds not fitting well together. He is inconsistent. Such incompatibility should not be found in a child of God. The Christian is to walk differently, in outward manifestation of the indwelling Holy Spirit. The spiritual garments of the "new man" must be worn in exchange for the natural clothing of the "old man." This teaching is now before us.

1. *The Consistent Walk Is in Separation* (4:17-32)

Paul turns now to warn his readers against returning to any form of the old pagan mode of life. If they were truly saved, then they should be living as those having a true knowledge and clear understanding of God's way of salvation in Jesus Christ. If they continued in the practices of the unsaved, they were only giving evidence that their understanding was still darkened.

"This I say therefore, and testify in the Lord, that ye henceforth walk not as other Gentiles walk, in the vanity of their mind" (4:17). The Scriptures do not waste words. Paul is not merely talking; he is testifying, that is, making a solemn appeal in the name of Jesus Christ. As followers of Christ they would at once recognize the mark of divine authority in his speech and would, therefore, heed what he had to say. They would give proof by a consistent walk. They would not walk as other Gentiles walk, in the vanity of their mind. The life of the Christian, no longer regarded as a Gentile or a Jew, is in contrast to the life of Gentiles or Jews who are not Christians.

C. R. Erdman emphasizes the fact that Paul is not comparing his readers with "other Gentiles." Paul indicates that his readers are now fellow-citizens with the saints and of the household of God. They were surrounded by pagan associates and heathen customs, hence they would be tempted and even enticed to fall back into those sinful practices of the past. But if their minds were not empty of the truth, like the minds of the "other Gentiles," and if they were no longer vain in their imaginations (Rom. 1:21), their lives would conform to their Christian profession.

A reprobate mind (Rom. 1:28) may hear the gospel, but such a mind is unreceptive. Now an unreceptive mind may give assent to the truth, yet it never can result in a changed life. By the consistent walk of the Ephesian believers they would prove that they understood and received the truth of God. A consistent walk in righteousness is the only outward evidence that one has been born again. To this end God had sent Paul to the Gentiles, "to open their eyes, and to turn them from darkness to light, and from the power of Satan unto God, that they may receive forgiveness of sins, and inheritance among them which are sanctified by faith that is in Me" (Acts 26:17, 18). So testified the mighty apostle to Agrippa. How disappointing to Paul if the walk of the Ephesians was no different from that of other Gentiles!

The condition of the unconverted Gentiles is expressed further as "Having the understanding darkened, being alienated from the life of God through the ignorance that is in them, because of the blindness of their heart" (4:18). There is not so much as a spark of divine life in an unregenerated man. He is the natural man and, as such, he cannot understand, or discern, spiritual truth (1 Cor. 2:14). The unsaved man may boast of his knowledge and understanding of the things of this world, but he is unable of himself to discover spiritual truth. His mind is irresponsive to the things of God. Before a man sees his lost condition and exercises heart faith in the Lord Jesus Christ, his powers of thought are darkened so that he cannot receive divine truth but remains in mental darkness.

Next, unsaved persons are in a state of spiritual death, "being alienated from the life of God through the ignorance that is in them, because of the blindness of their heart." Sin has both a blinding and deadening effect upon people. The marginal rendering for "blindness" is "hardness." It really means a dullness as though one were drugged. Such willful blindness has produced an impotence whereby the sinner can continue in sin with little sense of shame or need. Because of ignorance and the hardness of their hearts, the unsaved are cut off from the life of God. When a man continues in this state the blame is all his own. God has given His Word and His Spirit to deliver from death and darkness, but so long as one resists the truth, one chooses to remain spiritually blind and spiritually dead. The knowledge of God is true light and life. God never refuses it to the believing heart which casts itself on His mercy. Only a consistent walk in righteousness would prove that the Ephesians no longer had their understanding darkened.

This condition of mental darkness and spiritual death leaves the sinner in a state of awful degradation. Such are described as those "Who being past feeling have given themselves over unto lasciviousness, to work all uncleanness with greediness" (4:19). What an awful condition to be in! "Past feeling"—a calloused heart, a seared conscience; abandoned to wallow in gross sensuality and to indulge greedily in all sorts of uncleanness. There are those in the world for whom there is little hope of ever refining their feelings or raising their moral standards. Certainly such a state is not true of every unsaved person, but it is of many unsaved, and it shows just how far one can go if he resists the truth. Let us not dull the senses of our hearts lest we drift into indulgence of the pleasures of sin without restraint. How sad when one's conscience is *past feeling!* How awful to be delivered up to all manner of uncleanness!

When one walks consistently in righteousness, he proves that he has understood spiritual truth. When Paul labored among the Ephesians he taught and preached Christ. In the apostle's life and labors they "learned Christ," "heard Him," and were "taught by Him." All that the Ephesians knew about God they learned in and through His Son. Paul had preached Christ to them and they had learned that to become a Christian one had to receive Christ. Paul here contrasts the inconsistent life of an unsaved man with the consistent character of the man in Christ. The Gentiles walked in darkness but the Ephesian Christians had learned Christ and were therefore different.

To be "in Christ" means that the believer is a new creation (2 Cor. 5:17), in a new order of things, with a new standard for living. This calls for a laying aside of the old ways and a putting on of the new. Since the Ephesians had been taught as the truth is in Jesus, they are exhorted to "put off concerning the former conversation the old man, which is corrupt according to the deceitful lusts" (4:22). The new life calls for the laying aside of the old garments which label the unbeliever. The "old man" is the unregenerate, natural man, and his manner of life is corrupt, deceitful, and lustful.

Just as the coming of light dispels darkness, so the presence of Jesus Christ in one's heart dismisses corruption. At no time did our Lord ever call upon the "old man" to put off his manner of life. The old man has neither the desire nor the power to lay aside his polluted garments of self-righteousness. Trying to get the "old man" to lay aside his corrupt garments and replace them with the garments of righteousness is like sewing a new patch on a worn-out garment, or like pouring new wine into an old wine skin about to burst (Luke 5:36-38). Christianity cannot be comprehended, much less apprehended, by the "old man." He does not want the new life. The Lord Jesus read this in the heart of the Pharisee, when He said: "No man also having drunk old wine straightway desireth new: for he saith, The old is better" (Luke 5:39). To the worldling, the Christian is a kill-joy; the former has no desire to do the things that the Christian does. Like the Pharisee who would go away saying, "We do not want the new wine; the old is better," even so the worldling is content to enjoy the pleasures of sin, though they be but for a season.

The demand upon the "new man" continues: "and be renewed in the spirit of your mind" (4:23). The spirit of man is that part of him that is born anew (John 3:6) and which worships God (John 4:24). When man's spirit is regenerated it feeds the mind with pure desires and motives. As we surrender moment by moment to the Holy Spirit and feed on God's Word, He renews our spirit and enables us to do those things that please God.

Now, in contrast to putting off "the old man" we are urged to "put on the new man, which after God is created in righteousness and true holiness" (4:24). The words "righteousness" and "holiness" sum up the believer's walk before man and God. "Righteousness" expresses the right behavior of the Christian before men; "holiness," his behavior before God. The former is an outward attitude expressed in words and deeds; the latter is the attitude of heart and mind toward God. Since we are a new creation we are to wear the garments of the "new man," a new conversation, and a new conduct. The desire of every Christian should be like that of Zacharias, who said: "That He would grant unto us, that we . . . might serve Him without fear, In holiness and righteousness before Him, all the days of our life" (Luke 1:74, 75).

Have you put off the old man and put on the new? Have you exchanged your old life for the new? God wants to make you a new creation now.

Further proof that one has been renewed in the spirit of his mind is seen in the putting off the garments of the "old man," some of which are mentioned in the closing verses of

our present chapter. The first of these is the garment of un-
truthfulness: "Wherefore putting away lying, speak every man
truth with his neighbour: for we are members one of another"
(4:25). The garment of falsehood must be put away, since it
does not become the new man in Christ. Since we are all members of the same body we are exhorted to give expression to
truth when dealing with one another. Honest dealing in word
and deed, and not deceit and hypocrisy, should characterize
every saint. Let sincerity mark every form of communication
among us. Misrepresentation, half-truth, pretense, and deceit
are practices of the "old man." They are characteristic of the
devil and his children (John 8:44). Since lying is a part of the
deeds of the "old man," Paul writes: "Lie not one to another,
seeing that ye have put off the old man with his deeds" (Col.
3:9). Dr. Erdman wrote: "Nothing so divides and separates
Christians as falsehood, misrepresentations, suspicion, and un-
scrupulous partisanship. Mutual confidence is the essential
bond of Christian fellowship."

The second exhortation follows: "Be ye angry, and sin not:
let not the sun go down upon your wrath: Neither give place
to the devil" (4:26, 27). Verse 26 might be translated: "If you
do get angry, you must not sin in your anger." This verse
suggests that one can be angry apart from sinning. There is a
righteous anger that is not sinful, referred to sometimes as
"righteous indignation" or "righteous resentment."

Our Lord was angry at different times and always apart from
sinning. He showed a deep, moral resentment against those who
turned the temple into a house of merchandise (John 2:13-16).
He spoke in strong language against all who neglect the spiritual needs of children, thereby causing the little ones to stumble
(Matt. 18:6; see also Mark 3:15).

But Paul is exhorting against sinful anger particularly
among God's children. He is warning against permitting a
hidden malice or a smouldering resentment to remain in the
heart of any one of us. Anger, when allowed to linger in the
heart, is a mighty weapon in Satan's hands. It is a dangerous

state of mind and becomes a wedge for more open and damaging forms of sin. When I am wrong, I must show patience. I accept with literalness the words, "Let not the sun go down upon your wrath." Resentment must not be cherished beyond the sunset, "For the wrath of man worketh not the righteousness of God" (James 1:20). Let us never retire to our beds angry; let us kneel first and confess to God the sin in the anger.

"Neither give place to the devil" (4:27). These words, along with those of verse 26, are all a part of one sentence. Satan works through that heart which cherishes anger. It is a part of his scheme to get Christians to act in malice against other believers. Elsewhere Paul said that we were to forgive one another "Lest Satan should get an advantage of us" (2 Cor. 2:10, 11). Oh, that we Christians might learn the strategy of Satan in his evil work among the saints of God! The devil has no place in the life of a Christian, so let us beware lest we give him something to lay hold of.

Paul turns now from the sin of anger to the sin of theft: "Let him that stole steal no more: but rather let him labour, working with his hands the thing which is good, that he may have to give to him that needeth" (4:28). The present form is suggested in the translation of J. N. Darby: "Let the stealer steal no more." It is addressed to those in the church at Ephesus, or any church, who may yet be guilty of this sin. The Christians in Paul's day were new converts from a heathenism that practiced such sins. Their knowledge of God's Word was limited; they might yield, therefore, to the temptation to obtain something dishonestly, or at the expense of another.

There are various forms of stealing. One may steal time from his employer. Another may steal someone's good name and reputation. The misuse of another's funds, even when practiced with the intention of replacing the "borrowed" money, is accounted stealing in a court of law. Gambling, unpaid debts, deception in some business transaction, misrepresentation of facts on one's income tax return, withholding from God that which should have been given to Him, graft in politics, pleading want—these all are forms of stealing.

Opposed to the vice of stealing is the virtue of service to others: "Let him labour, working with his hands the thing which is good, that he may have to give to him that needeth." It is not enough that we engage in honest labor merely to satisfy our own needs and wants, but we are to toil diligently so that we might render service to others. Our Lord Jesus Christ came to minister and not to be ministered unto, and if I have accepted Him as Saviour and Lord, then His standard of life should be my highest aim. The "new man" expresses himself most genuinely when he ministers to him who has need. Dr. Ironside has said: "I could live up to the righteousness that is in the Law if I refrained from taking what is another's, but I cannot live up to the holiness of grace except I share with others what God in His kindness gives to me." The joy of the giver is far deeper and richer than that of the receiver. It is more blessed to give than to receive. "Whoso hath this world's goods, and seeth his brother have need, and shutteth up his bowels of compassion from him, how dwelleth the love of God in him?" (1 John 3:17).

Unholy speech is dealt with next: "Let no corrupt communication proceed out of your mouth, but that which is good to the use of edifying, that it may minister grace unto the hearers" (4:29). Worthless thoughts ought never to be expressed. We need to pray with David: "Set a watch, O Lord, before my mouth; keep the door of my lips" (Psa. 141:3). The wise man makes God the Doorkeeper of his mouth (Prov. 4:24) that he might be preserved from lip sins. "Let your speech be alway with grace, seasoned with salt, that ye may know how ye ought to answer every man" (Col. 4:6). When our speech is seasoned with salt, our words have a gracious flavor; and when we have salt in ourselves, we have peace one with another (Mark 9:50). Wrong words reveal a wrong heart. Bitter water comes from a bitter fountain. Worthless conversation is a misrepresentation of true Christianity.

Over against the vice of corrupt communication Paul presents the virtue of "that which is good to the use of edifying, that it may minister grace to the hearers." How delightful to be in the presence of one whose words are helpful to others according to the need of the occasion! How refreshing to see the x-ray of a pure heart in the words that emanate therefrom! "For out of the abundance of the heart the mouth speaketh" (Matt. 12:34). As the Word of Christ dwells in us richly (Col. 3:16), our words will be guided by His Word, and this will build up the body of Christ, bringing to others the blessing of grace.

"And grieve not the Holy Spirit of God, whereby ye are sealed unto the day of redemption" (4:30). Perhaps there is no passage so worthy of being lifted out of its context as this. It is an established fact, attested by both Scripture and experience, that at the time of the new birth the Holy Spirit enters the believing sinner to take up permanent residence. The initial work of the Spirit, after having wrought conviction to the heart, is to create a new nature within. His full title is the *Holy* Spirit, and His divine nature grieves when any wrong thought, word, or deed occupies the mind or body of the believer. He abhors those sins just mentioned by Paul: lying, anger, stealing, and evil speaking. The Holy Spirit is a Person with personal feelings. Hence He may be grieved. We cannot now enter into a study of the many phases of His ministry, but since He has made secure our eternal redemption, we will be most ungrateful if we cause Him to grieve. His Presence with us should make us want to lay aside all that is ungodlike. Sin wounds and pains the Holy Spirit. Grieving Him is synonymous with backsliding. Only when we give the Holy Spirit His rightful place can we expect a revival in the body of Christ. As we yield our human spirit to Him, He makes us holy.

The blessed assurance is here added that the believers "are sealed unto the day of redemption." Paul had said: "Ye were sealed with that Holy Spirit of promise, Which is the earnest of our inheritance until the redemption of the purchased possession" (Eph. 1:13, 14). Here again, in chapter four, he tells us how long we are sealed—"unto the day of redemption." The day of redemption is not the day Christ died to redeem us. Christ's death was the payment for our redemption and His finished work at Calvary paid in full the penalty of our sins. But the believers' redemption will not be fully experienced until Christ comes back for His own and redeems our bodies. We are "waiting . . . for the redemption of our body" (Rom. 8:22, 23).

When our Lord returns He will recognize all of the redeemed, since God has impressed His Spirit upon us as the seal and mark of ownership. There is not the slightest danger of a single true believer being left behind at the rapture of the Church. Jesus gave certain signs whereby the saved on earth could know that His appearing would not be far hence, and then He added: "And when these things begin to come to pass, then look up, and lift up your heads; for your redemption draweth nigh" (Luke 21:28). The seal of the Spirit is the stamp of divine likeness upon the heart of the believer and is, thereby, the mark of ownership and security.

 In view of the Spirit's sensitiveness to sin and the approaching day of redemption, a list of sins follows which should be put away from us: "Let all bitterness, and wrath, and anger, and clamour, and evil speaking, be put away from you with all malice" (4:31). Bitterness is the opposite of sweetness. Bitterness suggests the acrid, sharp, severe, sarcastic. Bitter words and actions show that the heart is not right, for only the mouth of the unrighteous is full of bitterness (Rom. 3:14). Believers must take heed "lest any root of bitterness springing up trouble you, and thereby many be defiled" (Heb. 12:15). No fountain can send forth at the same place sweet water and bitter. Therefore, if we have bitter envying and strife in our hearts, it is earthly, sensual and devilish (James 3:11-15).

What is clamour?

We are to put away "clamour." Clamour is the audible expression of anger, wrath, and bitterness in the heart. It is the cry of one's passions in railing against others while asserting one's own rights.

All evil speaking must be put away, with all malice. "Speak not evil one of another, brethren" (James 4:11). Yes, dear Christian, let it all be put away from you. Put away bitterness. Put away wrath. Put away anger. Put away clamour. Put away evil speaking. Put away all malice. These things defile the believer even as commercialism defiled the temple in our Lord's day, so that He said to them that sold doves: "Take these things hence" (John 2:16).

Our chapter concludes with an exhortation to a virtue which, if cultivated, will drive out those sins that grieve the Spirit: "And be ye kind one to another, tenderhearted, forgiving one another, even as God for Christ's sake hath forgiven you" (4:32). Kindness should characterize believers in their relationships with one another. Kindness is that gentle, gracious, easy-to-be-entreated manner that permits others to be at ease in our presence. The word "kind" comes from such words as "kin" and "kindred," so that to deal kindly with others is to deal with them as our own kin. And after all, believers are brethren. Kindness and tenderheartedness go together. They express a warm sympathy and love for all men, both the righteous and evil doers. I fear that sometimes we are not very pitiful and compassionate toward others.

Kindness and compassion find expression in forgiveness: "forgiving one another, even as God for Christ's sake hath forgiven you." Divine forgiveness is our greatest example: sin is the only ugly, hateful thing that separates man from God. And still God forgives all our sins when we come to Him for salvation because Christ, the sinner's Substitute, paid our penalty. This is the example we are to follow. Perhaps the one who wronged you does not deserve your forgiveness. Neither did you deserve God's forgiveness.

No one could ever wrong us as much as we have wronged God. Still He loves us and forgives us all our sins. This, beloved, should be the measure of our forgiveness.

2. *The Consistent Walk Is in Love* (5:1-7)

The division of chapters at this point seems unfortunate, for the exhortation at the beginning of the fifth chapter is inseparably linked with that of the preceding verses. The words, "Be ye therefore . . ." show the close relation between 4:32 and 5:1, 2. Having exhorted believers to be kind, tenderhearted, and forgiving of one another, even as God for Christ's sake has forgiven us, Paul adds: "Be ye therefore followers of God, as dear children" (5:1).

The word, "followers," is most generally translated "imitators." To imitate is *to duplicate, to mimic, to impersonate*. Children learn by imitation. Since God is the best educator, He used the method of imitation to teach His creatures.

The exhortation to imitate God is addressed to Christians only. It is useless to plead with an unregenerate man to follow "in His steps." To walk in His steps is not the means of our redemption but the result of our having been redeemed. Until one becomes a partaker of the divine nature through being born again, any attempt on the part of a lost sinner to imitate God is futile. It is only as "dear children" that we can begin a true imitation of Him. The children of the devil find it quite natural to imitate their father. Our Lord said as much (John 8:44). We have often heard it said: "Like father, like son." We have seen in our own children how they love to imitate their parents. Now when God saved us He gave to each believing sinner His own life and nature; therefore He expects that we will pattern our habits and manner of life after His. It is expected that children will resemble their parents.

God Himself is the standard of every thought, word, and act of His children. This was so in the life of Israel. "And the Lord spake unto Moses, saying, Speak unto all the congregation of the children of Israel, and say unto them, *Ye shall be holy: for I the Lord your God am holy*" (Lev. 19:1, 2). The object of the whole ceremonial and moral law under the Old Covenant was the same as the purpose of Christ's coming under the New, namely, to make men like God. The Apostle Peter wrote: "As obedient children, not fashioning yourselves according to the former lusts in your ignorance: But as He which hath called you is holy, so be ye holy in all manner of conversation; Because it is written, Be ye holy; for I am holy" (1 Pet. 1:14-16). This mandate of God seems an impossibility, as far as our producing holiness is concerned.

The practice of holiness does not happen all at once. As we read the Word of God, and pray, and exercise ourselves to obey His will, we are conformed to His image. The eternally productive seed of holiness, which is God's very nature, is in us as believers (1 Pet. 1:4). As we behold our blessed Lord in the mirror of God's Word, the seed develops, and we "are changed into the same image from glory to glory even as by the Spirit of the Lord" (2 Cor. 3:18). Since God commands us to be holy, we may be certain that He is ready to minister the needed grace and strength. God intends every believer to be like Himself, so He has given us His nature to get us started, and in this one sense the Christian is perfectly sanctified positionally now (1 Cor. 1:2). But in a more practical sense holiness is progressive. Therefore, we are exhorted to "*become* holy."

The whole plan of redemption has this for its ultimate purpose. "God hath not called us unto uncleanness, but unto holiness" (1 Thess. 4:7); "[He] hath saved us, and called us with an holy calling" (2 Tim. 1:9). Holiness is the property of God, but He has placed it within our reach. As He possesses the whole man, the transformation takes place.

Does the command to be holy, as God is holy, appear

unfair since we are asked to imitate Him whom we have never seen? The satisfying answer to such reasoning is found in the Person and work of our Lord Jesus Christ. He came to reveal the Father (John 1:18), and in His holy life He demonstrated in a practical way how we should walk. Christ is God, "for in Him dwelleth all the fulness of the Godhead bodily" (Col. 2:9). His flawless life was a demonstration of divine holiness. Now when a man receives Jesus Christ, it is not merely that he is brought into *relationship* with the Holy One but also into participation in His holiness. Once we accept the salvation which is in Jesus Christ, we are empowered by the divine Presence in us to imitate Him.

There follows next in Paul's teaching three ways by which we are to imitate God. It is done by our "walk." We are to walk in love (5:2), walk in light (5:8) and walk circumspectly (5:15).

First, we are exhorted to "walk in love, as Christ also hath loved us, and hath given Himself for us an offering and a sacrifice to God for a sweetsmelling savour" (5:2). Before one can walk in the sphere of love he must get into that sphere. Do we know the love of Christ? We were poor, wretched sinners, and "while we were yet sinners, Christ died for us" (Rom. 5:8). One of the attributes of God is love. That love reached us at Calvary, and the moment we believed, the love of God was shed abroad in our hearts by the Holy Spirit who was given to us (Rom. 5:5). Since Pentecost, God's love has been reaching out to others through those of His children who walk in love. Here is one of the strongest evidences of our regeneration:

By this shall all men know that ye are My disciples, if ye have *love* one to another (John 13:35).

We know that we have passed from death unto life, because we *love* the brethren. He that *loveth* not his brother abideth in death (1 John 3:14).

Beloved, let us *love* one another: for *love* is of God; and every one that *loveth* is born of God, and knoweth God. He that *loveth* not knoweth not God; for God is *love* (1 John 4:7, 8).

The true believer will imitate God in love, and God in love is God in action: "As Christ also hath loved us, and hath given Himself for us . . ." We are to *walk* in love. "Let us not love in word, neither in tongue; but in deed and in truth" (1 John 3:18). We can never give ourselves as Christ gave Himself, but we can imitate Him in self-sacrificing love for the good of our brethren. Such love is unto God "a sweetsmelling savour." Such sacrifice, described in terms of the Old Testament ritual in the whole burnt offering, is "a sweet savour [smell] unto the Lord" (Lev. 1:9). It indicates something well pleasing to God. Our Lord Jesus Christ is the great Burnt Offering, a sacrifice of a sweet odor to God. And since we have been redeemed, we too can be "unto God a sweet savour of Christ" (2 Cor. 2:15).

If we are to walk in love, there are those things that must not be a part of us in any way. There is "fornication." He who is not walking in love might readily succumb to this degrading and corrupt form of lust. In the circle of the unsaved, "fornication" and "uncleanness" are regarded as common practices without scruple. The old nature, which is present in every believer, is subject to every form of impurity. Added to these is "covetousness," seen in either an unlawful desire for gain or in that vile greed for sensual gratification. Unmentionable vileness is prevalent all around us, on newsstands, on billboards, on the cinema screen; yes, the very air we breathe is polluted with it. Of all such Paul adds: "Let it not be once named among you, as becometh saints." It is not enough that we do not engage in such vile things; they should not even be talked about among saints. Obscenity and indecency are not becoming to "saints," hence they should not even be mentioned. Beloved, let us guard against lust of every form and description, and let us not so much as indulge our thinking in them. Saints should remain free from every appearance of evil.

"Neither filthiness, nor foolish talking, nor jesting, which are not convenient: but rather giving of thanks" (5:4). We are to shun "filthiness," which is everything inconsistent with the modesty of a saint. Filthy words and filthy deeds bring dishonor and shame. Next the apostle deals with "foolish talking" and "jesting." Paul is not here condemning a sense of humor. I have always been quite careful not to become too intimate with these very pious folks who are too holy to engage in laughter. H. A. Ironside said: "God meant man to laugh. That is the one thing that distinguishes him from all the other creatures. Until scientists can find a monkey who can laugh, they will never find the missing link."

Notice that filthiness, foolish talking, and jesting are linked together. I believe we are being warned here against taking any part in the telling of or listening to "dirty jokes." People who engage in such buffoonery act like fools. It is a sign of degeneracy when one must take part in immoral pleasantry in order to laugh. Laughter at the expense of decency is sinful. Some persons cannot be witty without using double talk and suggestive phrases. Many a Christian has spoiled his testimony with such low frivolity. It is never "convenient" (befitting) to make light of sin. Instead of using our speech in a scurrilous way, we should exercise ourselves in "giving of thanks." Walking in love and talking in lust are incompatible. If we are grateful to God for saving us, then we should use our lips to honor and glorify Him.

Paul reminds his readers that he is not telling them anything new: "For this ye know, that no whoremonger, nor unclean person, nor covetous man, who is an idolater, hath any inheritance in the kingdom of Christ and of God" (5:5). The words and deeds of the vile man are just as empty as his heart is of the grace and love of God. The dwellers in darkness are doomed to spend eternity with the devil and his own. Some church members and some professing Christians feel that they will get to heaven in spite of their sinful words and deeds. To all such Paul would add: "Let no man deceive you with vain words: for because of these things cometh the wrath of God upon the children of disobedience" (5:6). Where there is genuine faith in Christ, fruit follows. "The Lord knoweth them that are His. And, let every one that nameth the name of Christ depart from iniquity" (2 Tim. 2:19). Society is corrupted by immorality, and the end of every immoral person is the wrath of God. "Be ye not therefore partakers with them" (5:7). You cannot afford to be deceived in this all-important matter.

3. *The Consistent Walk Is in Light* (5:6-14)

"For ye were sometimes darkness, but now are ye light in the Lord: walk as children of light" (5:8). Here Paul again contrasts the believer's past with his present. Earlier in the epistle the contrast was between death and life (2:1); here the contrast is between darkness and light. The appeal is made to what we now are in contrast to what we once were. We were darkness but now are we light in the Lord; hence we are not to be partakers with the children of disobedience.

There are two great kingdoms, in one of which every man is to be found. There is the kingdom of Satan, which is the kingdom of darkness; and there is the kingdom of our Lord, which is the kingdom of light. The unsaved man is by choice under the dominion of the rulers of the darkness of this world (Eph. 6:12). He prefers the darkness to the light because his deeds are evil (John 3:19). He is not merely in the dark, but he is darkness. Darkness is ignorance, and every unsaved man is ignorant of the things of God. They are foolishness to him, nor can he know them, because they are spiritually discerned (1 Cor. 2:14). He practices the works of darkness by choice, since that is all he knows.

Every Christian was at one time in darkness. But when Christ, who is the Light of the world (John 8:12), came into our hearts, we were immediately delivered from the power of darkness and translated into the kingdom of God's dear

Son (Col. 1:13). Now since "God, who commanded the light to shine out of darkness, hath shined in our hearts, to give the light of the knowledge of the glory of God in the face of Jesus Christ" (2 Cor. 4:6), we walk as children of light, no longer practicing those things of which we are now ashamed. The coming of the Light has dispelled the darkness, so that engaging in those things for which the wrath of God now cometh upon the children of disobedience has long since passed. The actions of the believer should differ widely from those of the unbeliever; hence Paul refreshes the remembrance of the Christians by contrasting their former position with the present: "Ye were darkness; ye are light."

Our Lord said to His disciples: "Ye are the light of the world . . . Let your light so shine before men, that they may see your good works, and glorify your Father which is in heaven" (Matt. 5:14, 16). Many kinds of darkness abound in the world—sin, suffering, and sorrow. Instead of complaining that we must live in the midst of such darkness, we should thank God that He has placed us here as the light of the world, to shine in the midst of such conditions and circumstances.

The light must be securely fixed in a conspicuous place, not under a bushel, "but on a candlestick," or lampstand (Matt. 5:15). We will need to be kept filled with the oil of the Holy Spirit and kept trimmed, not that we should be looked at, but that He might be seen and the Father glorified. It was the glory of the Father that Christ ever had in mind all during His earthly life. Guy H. King has said: "The shining of our light is not to say 'Look at me!' but 'Look at Him!' " Never allow the bushel of cowardice or compromise or carelessness to hide the light, for "if our gospel be hid, it is hid to them that are lost" (2 Cor. 4:3). Of John the Baptist our Lord said: "He was a burning and a shining light" (John 5:35).

Do you want to shine? If so, you must be willing to burn.

Shining calls for sacrifice. What a blessed privilege is ours as Christians! He who said, "I am the Light of the world," said to His own, "Ye are the light of the world." In His absence we are to shine for Him as lights, "blameless and harmless, the sons of God, without rebuke, in the midst of a crooked and perverse nation, among whom ye shine as lights in the world" (Phil. 2:15). The wise man has said: "The path of the just is as the shining light, that shineth more and more unto the perfect day" (Prov. 4:18).

The apostle gives three features of a walk in the light which he calls, "The fruit of the light" (A.S.V.). They are "goodness and righteousness and truth" (5:9). *Goodness* is kindness in action, beneficence. This grace should characterize the children of the light. It is a fruit whereby believers are distinguished from those who dwell in darkness. Active goodness is the natural result of light. Let something come between you and the Light of the world, and your life will no longer be controlled by selflessness.

The fruit of the light is in *righteousness*. Here the word "righteousness" is the same as that in 4:24, and is simply thinking right and doing right. Moral uprightness is a scarce commodity among the children of darkness, in spite of wishful thinking among theologians and statesmen. More and more the selfishness of the unregenerate heart shows itself. In the world today the rule of life seems to be "every man for himself." But where men are walking in the light they have fellowship (communion) one with another (1 John 1:7). They share things commonly.

Finally, this verse reveals that the fruit of life is in *truth*. This is truth in "the inward parts" (Psa. 51:6) as opposed to sham and hypocrisy. The fruit of the light permits no secret compromise with evil. Moreover, there is abstinence from every appearance of evil (1 Thess. 5:22).

He who walks in the light is daily "proving what is acceptable unto the Lord" (5:10). To prove is *to test by experience*, not before the eyes of man but before God. We dare not test our conduct by the standards of certain denominations and churches, nor by the things everyone does. The test of the light is that "ye may prove [test] what is that good, and acceptable, and perfect, will of God" (Rom. 12:2). If our words, thoughts, and acts are "all to the glory of God" (1 Cor. 10:31), we may be certain that we are walking in the light.

Then, too, we are to "have no fellowship with the unfruitful works of darkness, but rather reprove them" (5:11).

The Christian cannot have fellowship with those in darkness and expect to escape the pollution of evil. Paul's epistles sound the warning repeatedly against Christians keeping company with unbelievers. "I wrote unto you in an epistle not to company with fornicators" (1 Cor. 5:9); "Be ye not unequally yoked together with unbelievers: for what fellowship hath righteousness with unrighteousness? And what communion hath light with darkness?" (2 Cor. 6:14). The unequal yoke in marriage, business, lodges, secret societies, or even churches, is forbidden God's children, for "God is Light, and in Him is no darkness at all. If we say that we have fellowship with Him, and walk in darkness, we lie, and do not the truth" (1 John 1:5, 6). Our negative action is to have no fellowship with the unfruitful works of darkness; the positive action is that we must "reprove them" both by our lives and our lips. We are not to deal lightly with sin. The appearance of our Lord exposed the darkness in men's thoughts and deeds. It must be so with His own. "For it is a shame even to speak of those things which are done of them in secret" (5:12). Dr. Erdman warns against Christians acting as moral detectives to spy out the sins of their fellow men. A further warning is given against making public such sins.

Verses 13 and 14 teach us that when the light is turned on, the vices of those who walk in darkness are revealed in their odious character. All things, when they are discovered, are made manifest by the Light, for whatsoever doth make manifest is light (5:13). Light is the very nature of God, and when we let the light shine by a Christlike life, the sinner sees himself in the pure light of God's holiness.

Dear Christian, do our lives expose the foulness of the evil in others? Are the unsaved being transformed by the illumination of our words and actions? If not, we are not worthy of the name Christian. May God use us to make sin appear sinful.

There follows next a strong exhortation: "Awake thou that sleepest, and arise from the dead, and Christ shall give thee light" (5:14). Paul quotes in part from Isaiah 60:1, 2, applying it to the Church. In view of the sin all about the people of God, through the Prophet Isaiah He called upon His own to put on the light of Jehovah's glory in the midst of the surrounding darkness. Israel's light had not been shining, so that they were as those who were dead; hence the call to arise and stand out as lights in the midst of those who were dead.

Many Christians today are as those who are still in death and darkness. Some of you have not been letting your light shine. You are scarcely discernible from the unsaved. If you will arise from your slumber, Christ will bless you and cause His light to shine through you to others.

C. *The Christian Is to Walk Carefully* (5:15-6:9)

1. *The Careful Walk Is in Sagacity* (5:15-21)

This is the last appearance of the word "walk" in this epistle, and it is not without significance. Paul writes: "See then that ye walk circumspectly, not as fools, but as wise" (5:15). The consistent walk of the believer, that is, his daily deportment, is with full knowledge of the temptations that surround him. Still he is not as the unwise but as the wise. He looks carefully how he walks, not ignorant of Satan's devices. The wise Christian is strict with himself about his walk. He watches each step as he goes, certain where the next step will lead him. Strictest consistency is essential lest one wrong step prove fatal. The unwise person is the unthinking person who follows the line of least resistance and very often surrenders his convictions.

Christian, you are not to go along with the crowd; you are not to do something because every one else is doing it. Be careful where you walk. Look about you before you put down your feet. The word "circumspectly" carries the idea of strictness and exactness based on careful observation. He is a wise man who looks all around him as he walks.

The reason for walking in wisdom is expressed in the following words: "Redeeming the time, because the days are evil" (5:16). Paul lived in evil days when there was bitter opposition to the gospel, but the days in which we live are no less evil. This whole present age is evil (Gal. 1:4), the one difference, I believe, being the increase of wickedness as the age nears its end. With evil waxing worse, the opportunities to do good become less. Therefore, we are to be "redeeming the time," which means simply that we are to seize upon every opportunity and avail ourselves of every means to spread the gospel of our Lord Jesus Christ. As a wise shopper would go bargain-hunting to buy up every scarce commodity, so must the Christian lay hold of every fleeting moment of time to advance Christ's cause in the earth. The doors in some countries are closing to the gospel. Communism and Romanism are suppressing the spread of the Truth. It is quite possible some of us may live to see the day when opportunities to preach the gospel, apart from persecution and even death, will be scarce. Beloved, make every moment count for God and for lost souls.

Because the days are evil, Paul adds: "Be ye not unwise, but understanding what the will of the Lord is" (5:17). We are not to allow the evil days to cause us to become foolish. Too often the Christian acts without intelligence in the face of sin. He needs true wisdom to discern between right and wrong as well as knowledge to deal with the wrong-doers.

A walk in wisdom is defined as "understanding what the will of the Lord is." When God asks us to walk wisely, it means that He has made provision for such a walk. We can know what His will is, and the wise and thoughtful Christian will give prayerful attention daily to "the will of the Lord."

The only way that we can be delivered from the foolishness of the natural mind is to be divinely enlightened. Let us not make the foolish mistake of becoming worldly-wise, "for the wisdom of this world is foolishness with God" (1 Cor. 3:19). "This wisdom descendeth not from above, but is earthly, sensual, devilish . . . But the wisdom that is from above is first pure, then peaceable, gentle, and easy to be intreated, full of mercy and good fruits, without partiality, and without hypocrisy" (Jas. 3:15, 17). "The wisdom that is from above" is "the will of the Lord" and it is given to those who earnestly seek it. Prayer and the careful reading of the Bible will make clear to any Christian what the will of the Lord is. "If any of you lack wisdom, let him ask of God, that giveth to all men liberally, and upbraideth not; and it shall be given him" (Jas. 1:5).

The shame of the Christian church is the sad and tragic neglect of thoughtful Bible reading on the part of its members. Quite often we are faced with decisions. What shall we do about such and such a thing? Beloved, if we use the Bible aright, we can turn to God's Word to see what He says about it. The Word of the Lord reveals the will of the Lord. The Bible is the Christian's rule of faith and practice, so that "he is no superficial optimist nor is he a despairing pessimist but a confirmed Biblicist." Acquaintance with the Book and its Author is the secret to a knowledge and understanding of God's will. But basic to all else is the matter of my heart. Am I willing and ready to obey God's will?

The thought in verse 18 is connected with that in verse 17 by use of the word "and." "Be ye not unwise . . . and be not drunk with wine, wherein is excess; but be filled with the Spirit." An unwise and senseless man will become drunk with wine, but a wise and sensible Christian will be filled with the Spirit. The worldly man and woman seek exhilaration in excess indulgences of various forms, but the Christian reaches the height of safe and divinely-guided exhilaration by being filled with the Holy Spirit. To be under the control of the Holy Spirit, so that one walks wisely in the will of God, is not an exceptional experience for any one Christian or any one special group of believers; it is the normal experience for all who know our Lord Jesus Christ.

While the evil of intemperance is surely before us in verse 18, the weightier matter is the positive command to all Christians to allow the Spirit of God to have full control of their lives. However, let a solemn warning be sounded. It is an easy thing to mistake a fleshly enthuiasm for the filling of the Spirit. Of the disciples on the day of Pentecost the Scripture says: "They were all filled with the Holy Ghost" (Acts 2:4). However, the unbelievers said of the Spirit-filled followers of Christ: "These men are full of new wine" (Acts 2:13).

Beware of the false intoxication of Satan! He has his counterfeit in many of the so-called "holiness" movements. The command to be filled with the Spirit does not mean that we are to pray for the baptism of the Spirit to seek some kind of experience. Every true believer in the Lord Jesus Christ has been baptized in the Holy Spirit, hence he is indwelt by the blessed Third Person in the Godhead. Our being "filled with the Spirit" means that the Holy Spirit has complete control of our whole being. It is possible that some Christians who read these lines have never reached that crisis in life where the whole personality was surrendered to

God. When a man is drunk, he is completely given over to the influence of liquor and has no self-control; when a Christian is filled with the Spirit, he is completely given over to the Spirit and makes no attempt to please self.

The fruit of walking in wisdom is a heart overflowing with praise to the Lord: "Speaking to yourselves in psalms and hymns and spiritual songs, singing and making melody in your heart to the Lord" (5:19). The song of a man reflects his soul. Let me hear a man sing and I will be guided somewhat in determining where his devotion lies. Please do not misunderstand me. Mere vocalizing in itself may determine nothing. Every Sunday there are hypocrites who sing praises to God with their lips while their hearts are not right before Him. It is true that we sing together to praise God in unison and to encourage one another, but such singing glorifies God only when we are singing and making melody in our hearts "*to the Lord.*" Such singing begets vocalizing that honors God.

Not all of us can sing well with our voices. Some of us cannot make melody on a musical instrument, but every child of God can make melody in his heart to the Lord. The secret of the singing heart is to be Spirit-filled, and when we are controlled by the Holy Spirit we will not be singing to entertain ourselves or others, but to please the Lord. When the believing sinner receives a new heart, he should be able to say with David: "And He hath put a new song in my mouth, even praise unto our God" (Psa. 40:3). Only the Spirit can cause us to sing songs that are in harmony with the purposes of God. Is there a song in your heart just for the Lord?

Further evidence of walking in wisdom is the giving of "thanks always for *all things* unto God and the Father in the name of our Lord Jesus Christ" (5:20). Thankfulness goes along with spirituality and godliness. Would you understand what the will of the Lord is? Listen to the Scriptures:

"In *every thing* give thanks: for this is the will of God in Christ Jesus concerning you" (1 Thess. 5:18); "Be careful for nothing; but in *every thing* by prayer and supplication *with thanksgiving* let your requests be made known unto God" (Phil. 4:6). As we surrender to the Holy Spirit, He causes us to see that "*all things* work together for good to them that love God" (Rom. 8:28). Do we thank God for all things? Do we thank Him for the sobs as well as for the songs? We all can thank God for some things! But for "all things," and "*always*"—let it be to our shame that we have grumbled and complained about our little ailments. God has wonderfully provided for us in this life and in the next, and He has willed that we praise Him for all things. "By Him therefore let us offer the sacrifice of praise to God continually, that is, the fruit of our lips giving thanks to His name" (Heb. 13:15). We may not know now why all the difficult things of life come our way, but we do know that all things are for our good. God sees the end from the beginning and He will not permit us to be tested beyond that which we are able to bear. May God deliver us from the thankless spirit.

The Spirit-filled Christian is submissive: "Submitting yourselves one to another in the fear of God" (5:21). Mutual subjection is sorely lacking among us. When it is too hard to admit our wrong, or when it is too difficult to give place to another, we may be certain we are not filled with the Spirit. In a church whose members are Spirit-controlled, one sees no dissension, no quarreling, no selfishness, no jealousy. Loving submission to our Lord will make us subject to one another. Let us seek to cultivate that genuine lowliness that esteems others better than ourselves. When the wills of two persons are yielded to the will of God, there will be mutual subjection. The Spirit-filled believer, then, is joyful (verse 19), thankful (verse 20), and submissive (verse 21). Indeed, this is the test of spirituality. A profession which lacks these things is false.

2. *The Careful Walk Is in Submissiveness* (5:22-6:9)

a. *The Husband-Wife Relationship* (5:22-33). The apostle has just finished stating that we are to submit ourselves one to another in the fear of God. Here he presents some concrete, down-to-earth teaching about reciprocal relations in the home. He begins with the relationship between husband and wife. Let it be said here that submission in the home is not something enjoined upon the woman only; it is a mutual relationship.

Paul begins: "Wives, submit yourselves unto your own husbands, as unto the Lord" (5:22). This is a subject which, in our day, is not easy to teach. Woman suffrage groups and woman's rights leagues are opposed to the plain teaching of Scripture on the subject of female submission. Some educated women have been quite vociferous in their rebellion against the headship of the man. But let every woman keep her mind and heart open to the plain teaching of Scripture on this subject as well as any other. God has spoken. To Eve He said: "Thy desire shall be to thy husband, and he shall rule over thee" (Gen. 3:16). Eve overstepped her bounds when she yielded to Satan, thereby giving evidence that she should not be free but instead subject to her husband and dependent upon him. This divinely-instituted subordination of the woman was the result of her display of her own weakness. Paul states elsewhere: "Let the woman learn in silence with all subjection. But I suffer not a woman to teach, nor to usurp authority over the man, but to be in silence. For Adam was first formed, then Eve. And Adam was not deceived, but the woman being deceived was in the transgression. Notwithstanding she shall be saved in childbearing, if they continue in faith and charity and holiness with sobriety" (1 Tim. 2:11-14). Paul insists upon the subjection of the woman on Scriptural grounds. Adam ate the forbidden fruit by his own choice, with his eyes open; on the other hand, Eve was deceived. There is not the slightest inference here that man is, or ever was, mentally, morally, or spiritually superior to woman; but the woman, because of her greater trustfulness, is controlled by her heart more than her head.

Women enjoy the highest happiness in Christian communities and in Christian homes where the Bible, with its Christian principles, is accepted and obeyed. The subjection of a wife to her husband is "*as unto the Lord.*" There is nothing here that would suggest the husband's authority to be equal to Christ's authority, but that in subjecting themselves to their husbands wives are subjecting themselves to the Lord, since the command to do so came first from Him. In another place Paul writes: "Wives, submit yourselves unto your own husbands, as it is fit in the Lord" (Col. 3:18). The submission here is not always, but the submission of loyalty and obedience to a God-given arrangement. Such submission of a wife to her husband is part of her obedience to the Lord.

There is a reason why such a command is given to women: "For the husband is the head of the wife, even as Christ is the head of the church: and He is the Saviour of the body. Therefore as the church is subject unto Christ, so let the wives be to their own husbands in every thing" (5:23, 24).

At once it becomes obvious that the Apostle Paul has drawn an analogy between the relationship of Christ and the Church on the one hand, and the marriage relationship of husband and wife on the other. Frequently in the Old Testament we see the relationship between Jehovah and Israel discussed in a similar way. Israel is referred to as "the wife of Jehovah." Isaiah wrote: "as the bridegroom rejoiceth over the bride, so shall thy God rejoice over thee" (Isa. 62:5). And in the New Testament, speaking of his own relationship to the Lord, John the Baptist referred to himself as "the friend of the Bridegroom" (John 3:29). Paul, writing to the Corinthians, said: "For I am jealous over you with godly jealousy: for I have espoused you to one husband, that I may present you as a chaste virgin to Christ" (2 Cor. 11:2).

It is quite clear, then, that the people of God in every dispensation stand to Him in the relation analogous to that of a husband and wife. Whenever His people transferred their love and allegiance to another, He was moved with deep displeasure. The marriage relation is exclusive, hence all violators of the marriage vow, such as fornicators and adulterers, will be judged by God. Even as our loyalty and allegiance can be sustained to one God only, so with every wife to her own husband. So sacred and binding is the marriage union between a husband and wife that Paul uses it as a fit symbol of the blessed relation between Christ and His Church. Christ is the Saviour of the body. The right of responsibility and leadership of the Church is Christ's; the right of responsibility and leadership of the wife is the husband's. The union of husband and wife is a vital and enduring one, like the union between Christ and the believer. The sinner is in bondage until he comes to Christ, but, said the Lord Jesus: "If the Son therefore shall make you free, ye shall be free indeed" (John 8:36). The subjection of a wife to her husband is not that of force and fear and slavery, but of loving subjection which comes from freedom. "Therefore as the Church is subject unto Christ, so let the wives be to their own husbands in every thing." A body with two heads is a monstrosity; a Church with two heads cannot prosper; a house with two heads cannot stand. Wife, be subject to your husband in a sweet spirit of reasonableness, and do it "as unto the Lord."

Now in the verses that follow we have the reciprocal relationship brought out in the duties of the husband. "Husbands, love your wives, even as Christ also loved the church, and gave Himself for it" (5:25). Just as Paul used Christ and the Church to illustrate the submission of the wife to her husband, here again Christ and the Church are mentioned, this time to illustrate the responsibility of the husband to the wife. Christ loved the Church enough to die for it, and when a husband manifests such love for his wife, submission on her part will be a joy and delight. The Christian husband who bears the image of Christ will be like his Lord in the exercise of sacrificial love. No Christian wife can dispute the ruling place in the home when her husband displays such love. Every right of husbands to headship in the home must be exercised in love toward their wives, "and be not bitter against them" (Col. 3:19). The wife is not told to submit to "bitterness"; on the other hand, she will readily submit to love. Husband, does your action in the home give expression of the redeeming love of Christ? Is yours a selfless, sympathetic, sacrificial care of your wife?

Christ gave Himself for the Church "That He might sanctify and cleanse it with the washing of water by the Word" (5:26). His redeeming love precludes the ultimate holiness of the Church to the end "That He might present it to Himself a glorious church, not having spot, or wrinkle, or any such thing; but that it should be holy and without blemish" (5:27). A dirty bride is unthinkable. The purpose of Christ for His own, as expressed in verse 26, is to be accomplished in the present. As we read and study the Bible carefully we are kept cleansed of the defilements we are apt to gather day by day. This verse does not mean that the cleansing is effected by water baptism, but by the "Word," of which the water here is but a symbol. The holy Bridegroom must have a holy bride; so, as her Head, He must provide everything for her now as well as prepare her for the marriage feast when she will be presented to Him at His return. By His love He saved her; by His Word He sanctifies her; at His coming He will glorify her. He took the form of a Servant for her and become obedient unto the death of the cross, and until now He continues to serve her from His position in heaven so that the Church, His bride, gladly yields in willing submission to Him. When a husband's love toward his wife is expressed in sacrificial service in her behalf, "giving honour unto the wife, an unto the weaker vessel" (1 Pet. 3:7), then will she willingly become subject to her godly and Christlike husband.

Already in Ephesians we have seen that the Church is Christ's body (1:23) as well as His bride. Even so a man's wife is both his bride and his body. After vividly describing how God made woman from the side of man, Moses adds: "Therefore [because of this conjugal relation] shall a man leave his father and his mother, and shall cleave unto his wife: and they shall be one flesh" (Gen. 2:24). So Paul writes: "So ought men to love their wives as their own bodies. He that loveth his wife loveth himself" (5:28). A man who would injure his wife is as one who would injure himself. While Adam slept God removed a bone from his body and, from it, made woman, so that Adam said: "This is now bone of my bones, and flesh of my flesh" (Gen. 2:23). Let every husband and wife learn the truth that both are one flesh. Then will they experience the joy and blessing of kneeling together to bring their problems to the Lord in prayer and of walking together in mutual love and subjection. The mind of the modern world is opposed to this teaching from God's Word, but the sacred relationship between husband and wife, and Christian doctrine concerning it, still stand. Adulterers and adulteresses are strangers to the grace of our Lord Jesus Christ, for while the state may sanction immorality, God will judge it.

By nature every man loves himself. In both the Old and New Testaments we read: "Thou shalt love thy neighbour as thyself" (Lev. 19:18; cf. Matt. 19:19; Rom. 13:9; Gal. 5:14). Now no man in his right mind will do or say anything to hurt himself. If he did he would be a monster at heart. Between a man and his wife there is a oneness by the bond of marriage illustrated by the weighty example of Christ and His Church. By becoming partakers of the divine nature, believers "are members of His body, of His flesh, and of His bones" (5:30). Christ is the Head of His own body; therefore He cherishes and nourishes it with tender love. He will do nothing to injure it. Since the husband is the head of the wife, she is as his own body; therefore he cherishes and nourishes her with tender love. Our Lord supplies everything for our comfort and happiness; so does the husband care for his wife.

When the soldiers pierced the side of our Lord "and forthwith came there out blood and water" (John 19:34), the bride of Christ was being taken from His side, for "without shedding of blood is no remission" (Heb. 9:22). Beloved, that was the greatest demonstration of love the world has ever seen, or ever will see. When God pierced the side of Adam, He did it to take Adam's bride from his side. Thus she became bone of his bone and flesh of his flesh. Adam "is the figure of Him [Christ] that was to come" (Rom. 5:14). Eve is a type of the Church. Let every Christian husband be to his wife what Christ is to His own. Marriage is a union for life between one man and one woman. Therefore let the husband be the complement of the wife, and the wife the complement of her husband, for "they are no more twain, but one flesh. What therefore God hath joined together, let not man put asunder" (Matt. 19:6). "For this cause shall a man leave his father and mother, and shall be joined unto his wife, and they two shall be one flesh" (5:31). What can be added to this? Certainly we can conclude that the husband-wife relationship is more intimate than any other earthly union, even than that between parents and children. As the Son of God left His Father's house to claim and care for His bride, even so the husband his wife. Beloved, Christ will never cast off His Church. Husband, take good care of the wife God has given you.

Perhaps more has been left unsaid about these verses than what we have written. But Paul himself realized and declared the fact of the mystical union between Christ and His Church to be a great mystery: "This is a great mystery:

but I speak concerning Christ and the church" (5:32). The relationship between Christ and His Church, and its analogy, namely, the relationship between husband and wife, have hidden meaning, the import of which is beyond human knowledge. For my own part I am overwhelmed at the depth of revelation and I acknowledge that in my own life there is room for improvement. I readily accept Paul's closing word of admonition to husbands: "Nevertheless let every one of you in particular so love his wife even as himself . . ." (5:33). In every way, I am far below par, yet I have thought well of myself and have put up with myself quite nicely. I know my wife is far from perfect, but I desire to do equally as well, and perhaps better, in caring for her than I have for myself. The whole context presents challenging truth to both husband and wife, so let "the wife see that she reverence her husband." When people see these truths practiced by us in our homes, they may begin to realize the power of the gospel of Jesus Christ. The Christian home is the most sacred institution on earth. Let us guard it with the greatest of care.

b. *The Parent-Child Relationship* (6:1-4). The main thought in the last part of the preceding chapter, namely, *submission*, continues in the first part of chapter six. Paul has been dealing with the thought of submission on the part of the Christian. In chapter 5:22-33 the apostle showed that when the child of God is walking carefully, the relationship between husband and wife is one of love and subjection. Now he applies the same lessons in parent-children relationships (6:1-4).

"Children, obey your parents in the Lord: for this is right" (6:1). The command to children is to obedience. To obey means *to submit to*, or *to comply with*, a command.

There is an obedience which comes not by willing submission to authority but as a result of force. Examples of this are recorded in Scripture. When a great tempest arose while our Lord and His disciples were in a ship, He rebuked the winds and the sea and they *obeyed* Him (Matt. 8:27). Natural elements are forced to obey their Creator. Elsewhere demons are forced by Christ into submission: "for with authority commandeth He even the unclean spirits, and they do *obey* Him" (Mark 1:27). Such submission will characterize man and beasts during the Millennium.

However, the obedience of which Paul speaks in Ephesians is the glad and ready willingness to hearken to and heed the divine commands. According to the Word of God, "to obey is better than sacrifice, and to hearken than the fat of rams" (1 Sam. 15:22). Obedience is the first law between the Creator and His creation. The whole world is regulated by the law of obedience. The millions of stars, the seasons—all are under this law. Man must exercise obedience in every sphere of life, beginning as a child in the home, then as a citizen of the state, as an employee at work, and as a member of the church. We are subject to the laws of life.

The first lessons in obedience must be learned in childhood. The home is where basic training begins and, if there is to be harmony in the home, submission must be practiced. Before ever the child is born the wife learns subjection to her husband and the husband loves his wife as himself. Then as the children follow, they too must learn obedience. Perhaps there never has been such a day as ours for lawlessness on the part of children and a reckless disregard for parental instruction. In too many houses the children's word is law. There is little respect for parents. The revolt of American youth has caused the breakdown of many homes. Since the family is the strength of the church and of the state, a fresh study of respective rights and reciprocal responsibilities in the home demands the attention of Christians everywhere.

Here the command is to "children." When applied to the human race the child is regarded as such from birth to maturity. Children are the fruit of marriage, and in a certain sense they are held responsible to their parents. Every child should learn from its parents by instruction and by parental example that children will become the parents of the next generation. Obedience is one of the first lessons a child must learn. In two lists of sins, one list describing the godless pagan world of the past (Rom. 1:29-31) and the other predicting the perilous times of the last days (2 Tim. 3:2), Paul mentions the sin of "disobedience to parents."

Is it not significant that the Holy Spirit should mention this sin in such a striking manner? Evolution teaches the moral and spiritual ascent of man. God shows the heart of the natural man in the end of the age to be no better than it was among the heathen. As we read the Bible we might imagine ourselves reading the newspaper or standing in a juvenile court. There is scarcely room to house the juvenile delinquents in the reformatories and prisons of our country. A child honoring its parents in obedience is a rare sight these days. And yet the command is clear: "Children, obey your parents in the Lord: for this is right."

The basis for Paul's teaching on the parent-child relationship is found in the words, "in the Lord." He is addressing his remarks to Christians, not to the unsaved. We cannot hope to see Christian principles practiced in a home if its members are not Christians. The manner of obedience is "in the Lord," and before a child can *obey* in the Lord, he or she must *be* in the Lord.

While a child might not be mature enough to understand his need for salvation and how one becomes saved, he must see the Lord in the lives of his parents before he will learn to obey the Lord. The children's obedience should arise out of the conviction that such submission is the will of God. The family altar, where the Bible is read together and prayer is offered for each other, will be a daily reminder of our responsibilities in the Lord. Happy the family that worships together day by day! Obedience to parents, then, is one of the ways in which children can glorify God.

Two reasons are given in Scripture for this command. First, it is the right thing to do: *"for this is right."* Second, children are to obey their parents "in all things: *for this is well pleasing unto the Lord*" (Col. 3:20). Children, recognize parental authority in your own home. If you have trusted the Lord Jesus Christ as your personal Saviour, be subject to your mother and father and in loving-kindness obey them. The greatest example of this was our blessed Lord Himself, of whom it is written concerning His relationship to His mother Mary and Joseph, his foster-father: "He went down with them, and came to Nazareth, and was subject unto them" (Luke 2:51). Let every young person reading these lines be quick to hear and willing to heed the counsel of parents. Do it, not merely to please your parents but because in God's sight "this is right." Since it is right to obey, it is wrong not to obey.

The command to obey is followed by that to honor: "Honour thy father and mother; which is the first commandment with promise; That it may be well with thee, and thou mayest live long on the earth" (6:2, 3). To honor means *to esteem with deference or respect.* The estimate of parents in the mind of a child should be the very highest, for this "is the first commandment with promise." God gave to Moses ten commandments, and the offer of a reward is peculiar to the fifth one (Exod. 20:12). Obviously God attaches much importance to children honoring their parents. To those children who obey this command He assures prosperity, good health, and length of days. This promise is to be taken literally. Children, respect the judgment of your parents and pay them deference because it is the right thing to do. For it you will receive a rich reward. To reverence our parents stands at the top of the list of social duties.

Children need to learn that, in their parents, God has made wonderful provision for the child. How grateful we should be for the gift of parenthood! The experience and superior knowledge of parents over children must be recognized by the child. And if a child persists in pursuing a wrong course in spite of parental guidance, disciplinary measures should be taken. Following is a word of wisdom to parents: "He that spareth his rod hateth his son: but he that loveth him chasteneth him betimes" (Prov. 13:24.) Let parents pattern their discipline in the home after the divine order, as taught in Hebrews 12:5-11. Then esteem and respect from children will be forthcoming in a larger measure.

We have an example of the tragic end of the sons of Eli and of God's judgment upon Eli's house "because his sons made themselves vile, and he restrained them not" (1 Sam. 3:12, 13). Here is a case where both the children and parents failed, the children refusing to obey and honor their parents (1 Samuel 2:22-25), and the parents failing to chasten the children.

The apostle continues with a word to parents. "And, ye fathers, provoke not your children to wrath: but bring them up in the nurture and admonition of the Lord" (6:4). While we parents must insist upon obedience and honor from our children, we must guard against treating them harshly and burdening them needlessly. Parents must rule the home well under the guidance and power of the Holy Spirit, so that even when firmness and chastening are necessary, it will be with a loving desire for the welfare of the children.

Some parents are known for their harsh and hasty judgment of their children. One father I know repeatedly strikes his child in heated anger. Certainly God never chastens that man in such a way. This father has been a stumbling block to his child, so much so that the child has lost heart and has become discouraged. Elsewhere Paul warns parents against irritating their children by unreasonable severity "lest they be discouraged" (Col. 3:21). Never quarrel with a child and lose your temper; never give a command unless it is given in loving consideration of the child's good; do not chafe your child by needless fault-finding, for if you do these things you will only arouse resentment. In the exercise of parental authority there is great need for an understanding of the child.

There is also the positive command in verse 4: "but bring them up in the nurture and admonition of the Lord." Let us parents remember that we were children once. Patience was needed to instruct and educate us in the way we ought to go. And what problem-children some of us were! We needed nursing, fostering, training, and the repeated exhorting and warnings of parents. Our children need it too. We must pray for them, exercise watchful care daily, admonish and correct them. Fathers should take time to sit down with their sons, and mothers with their daughters, to counsel them regarding the temptations of life, the books they read, the hobbies they choose, and the friendships they form. In all that we seek to do for them, it must be "of the Lord." In other words, parents are to give their children Christian education, and for this there is no substitute. Point the child to what the Bible teaches about conduct. Certainly do not leave this sacred task to the Sunday school or church. Plant the seed of God's Word in that tender heart, and ere many years are passed you will have the joy of seeing your children decide for Jesus Christ. Any earthly inheritance we leave our children is worthless if we have failed to bring them up in the nurture and admonition of the Lord.

Our Lord said: "Even so it is not the will of your Father which is in heaven, that one of these little ones should perish" (Matt. 18:14); "Suffer little children, and forbid them not, to come unto Me: for of such is the kingdom of heaven" (Matt. 19:14).

We have an excellent example of the fruit of Christian education in the home in the person of Timothy. Paul wrote: "But continue thou in the things which thou has learned and hast been assured of, knowing of whom thou hast learned them; And that from a child thou hast known the Holy Scriptures, which are able to make thee wise unto salvation through faith which is in Christ Jesus" (2 Tim. 3:14, 15). As a child Timothy had learned obedience and honor from the Scriptures at the knees of his mother and grandmother (2 Timothy 1:5). Having been equipped for life and service when he was but a child, Timothy needed to have no fear of the evil men and seducers. Timothy's parents had brought him up in the nurture and admonition of the Lord. He was taught the Holy Scriptures in the home; therefore he was well furnished and fortified against evil temptations. I feel certain that Timothy's parents and grandparents will be richly rewarded at the judgment seat of Christ.

c. *The Servant-Master Relationship* (6:5-9). Paul's teaching on submission continues. However, in the five verses before us he deals with the duties involved in the relation between servants and masters, or between employee and employer. Here is truth which, if applied, can solve some of the industrial problems today. The relations between labor and management are very often bitter, and in some instances open hostility has resulted. Paul's problem in the Orient was quite different from ours. In the apostle's day there were servants in the household, and while the servant was counted a part of the household in which he served, he was a slave nevertheless. The abolition of slavery in most countries has become effective since Paul's day. However, we are all servants to some extent.

In our day, when social "thinkers" are stirring up the masses to rethink their relationships to management and to the state, and inciting them to demand equality and security, the teaching of Scripture on the subject must be brought to the attention of the Christian. Bear in mind the fact that the servants and masters here exhorted are Christians, members of one body in which there is neither bond nor free. Moreover, verse eight makes it clear that Paul is not thinking merely of those slaves purchased in the slave market, for he says: "Knowing that whatsoever good thing any man doeth, the same shall he receive of the Lord, whether he be bond or free." Dr. Ironside has well written: "The instruction which of old was given to slaves now applies to all employees. Slaves were purchased with the money of a master, or born into the house and raised up by the master, but today we enter into an agreement, we sell our labor, and in that way enter into a certain relationship which makes us just as responsible to heed the admonition given here."

Of course we are not attempting here to apply this admonition to the unsaved. We agree with Dr. A. C. Gaebelein, who has pointed out that the slavery existing throughout the Roman Empire when this epistle was written was never attacked by Paul, not even in his beautifully written and courteous letter to Philemon, which letter was all about Onesimus, the runaway slave. Reforming the world and improving social conditions is nowhere included in the Biblical definitions of the gospel. We are not to preach social reform to the unsaved. Here is the message for Christians.

"Servants, be obedient to them that are your masters according to the flesh, with fear and trembling, in singleness of your heart, as unto Christ" (6:5). A man who hires himself out for a stipulated wage has a responsibility to his employer. Certain rules and regulations issued by the employer are to be obeyed. Each employee should go about his daily work "with fear and trembling," which means, of course, the fear of wilfully neglecting his responsibility, which not only robs his employer but makes him chargeable to God. It was "in fear and in much trembling" that Paul came among the Corinthians as the servant of Christ (1 Cor. 2:3), lest he fail both them and his Lord. Thus all true believers are called upon to "work out your own salvation with fear and trembling" (Phil. 2:12). Christianity is not something we work *for* but something we work *out*. Whether in a factory, coal mine, field, office, classroom, or pulpit, the Christian renders proper service, fearing nought but God.

Because we are already saved we demonstrate in every phase of our labors the Christian life by the indwelling power of the Holy Spirit. Your pastor, your church, or your wife cannot be a Christian for you. If you are truly saved, you will fear God and render faithful, obedient service to your employer. Let every man do his work "in singleness of heart," which means without duplicity, no tricky doubleness, not pretending to be a friend of the "boss" to his face while speaking ill of him behind his back. There must be no hypocrisy or pretense. True, those who are over us, whether in domestic, civil, industrial, or legal relationships, are "masters according to the flesh" as distinct from our Master in heaven; nevertheless obedience to them is rendered by the Christian "as unto Christ." In other words, when we obey those in authority over us, we obey our Lord Jesus Christ. When Christians are consistent in doing what is right, more unsaved persons will be won to Jesus Christ.

Paul continues: "Not with eyeservice, as men-pleasers; but as the servants of Christ, doing the will of God from the heart" (6:6). "Eyeservice" is service done when the boss is watching. Those who slow down their pace when not under the eye of the foreman or manager, but who work well when being watched, are guilty of seeking favor that they do not deserve. All such Paul calls "men-pleasers," those who seek to curry favor with men in authority. Such standards not only rob labor of its dignity but are far beneath the dignity of the Christian. The Christian worker does not go to his daily task in a spirit of bitterness, but "with good will doing service, as to the Lord, and not to men" (6:7). When a saved person goes to his job "doing the will of God from the heart," he has his employer's interest at heart; hence he will seek to do him good.

When you return home from your day's work, do you merit the approbation of your Lord? If my employment is digging ditches, I am to dig ditches from my heart as unto the Lord. When the ditch-digger sets to work with his pick and shovel, and digs as unto God, he need not be concerned as to whether or not his employer is recognizing him. Since I am the servant of Christ, my desire is to please Him. This makes my obedience a matter of the heart.

There is encouragement and consolation for all who heed this teaching of Scripture: "Knowing that whatsoever good thing any man doeth, the same shall he receive of the Lord, whether he be bond or free" (6:8). The promise given here applies to all that Paul has been teaching about the servant-master relationship. The Christian who obeys those in authority over him has the assurance that God keeps an accurate record of all faithful service and that no act of service done as unto Him will go unrewarded. If my employer does not appreciate my sincerity and faithfulness, I know that God does. "Be not deceived; God is not mocked: for whatsoever a man soweth, that shall he also reap" (Gal. 6:7).

The Christian stands or falls before God, and no matter what his status in the world, he will receive his reward both in this life and in the life to come. In this world some men are rich and some are poor, some men are masters and some are servants, some men are honest and some are dishonest; in the next world there will be no such distinctions. "For we must all appear before the judgment seat of Christ; that every one may receive the things done in his body, according to that he hath done, whether it be good or bad" (2 Cor. 5:10). The question then will not be whether you were servant or master, foreman or laborer. In that day the commonest slave may hear the Lord Jesus Christ say: "Well done, good and faithful servant; thou hast been faithful over a few things, I will make thee ruler over many things: enter thou into the joy of thy Lord" (Matt. 25:23). When our Lord spoke the parable in which we read these words, He likened it unto the kingdom of heaven. Let the poor but faithful servant be comforted. However ungrateful your master down here may be, God will not allow your faithfulness to go unrecognized and unrewarded. You may even be blamed and punished unjustly, as was Joseph (Gen. 39), but God will reward you if you are faithful (Matt. 6:1-4).

In bringing to a close this section on The Christian Family (5:22-6:9), with its admonition to submission and obedience, Paul is consistent in that he teaches mutual and reciprocal responsibility in each case. In the wife-husband relationship, submission is required of the wife, and self-sacrificing love on the part of the husband. In the child-parent relationship, obedience is enjoined upon children, and tender, loving care is required of parents. And now, in the servant-master relationship, obedience and loyalty are expected of the servant and kindly consideration of the master.

"And, ye masters, do the same things unto them, forbearing threatening: knowing that your Master also is in heaven; neither is there respect of persons with Him" (6:9). The Lord to whom the servant must answer is the same Lord before whom the master must stand. Both will reap reward or suffer loss before a common Master. The same Lord who owns the employee owns the employer. False promises or threatenings ought never to be engaged in by Christian employers. Charles R. Erdman has said: "The obligation of right conduct and fair dealing rests upon the master quite as truly as upon the slave, and upon the employer as well as upon the employee."

Masters are exhorted to act upon the same Christian principles as are the servants: "Ye, masters, do the same things unto them." This means that masters are to rule their servants as unto the Lord, with regard to the will of God. If loyalty and fairness are enjoined upon servants, such virtues are required of masters in a greater measure, since masters and employers are in a position of greater privilege and authority.

The key to this entire section is verse 9. As the servant serves his master looking after his master's interest, so the master serves the servant in looking after his welfare. A master must never seek to rule his servant by threatening but by kindness. When Boaz came to the fields to meet with his employees, he greeted them in the morning with the words: "The Lord be with you"; and they answered: "The Lord bless thee" (Ruth 2:4). When Christ comes into a man's heart, such an attitude should prevail. Then the perplexing problem between capital and labor will be solved.

Let every one of us who is in a position of authority be reminded that he has a Master in heaven, our Lord Jesus Christ, who is touched with the feeling of our infirmities, and let us perform graciously toward those under us even as we are ministered unto by Him. If those under us are placed under our authority, by the same law we are under the authority of our Master in heaven. As we insist upon those under us rendering an account to us, so must we give an account at the judgment seat of Christ. Our rank on earth will not influence Him at the day of judgment. He will condemn the inconsiderate and unkind master as severely as He will the disloyal servant. These truths need to be brought to our attention with regularity, lest we cause those outside of Christ to stumble.

D. *The Christian Is to War Courageously* (6:10-21)

In the last two chapters, the main burden of Paul's message has been the believer's walk. Now he is to deal with the Christian's warfare. It is a subject sadly neglected in the pulpit ministry today. The silence concerning the continual conflict in the Christian life is responsible for a passive acceptance of the depressions and defeats which are so prevalent in the majority of professing believers. There are those who have confessed Christ and yet have no knowledge of the continual spiritual warfare that is relentlessly being pressed against the children of God.

When one reads through Ephesians at one sitting he is jolted somewhat as he meets the sudden change in chapter 6:10. The first half of the epistle portrays vividly the wonders of predestinating grace in the divine selection of hell-deserving sinners. We were held in ecstasy as we beheld our present possessions in Christ, our past position in the world, and our prospective place in heaven. With what rapture we read of the creation and design of the Church. Then we moved into the practical side of the epistle. Knowing we were reading one of Paul's letters, we fully expected Christian responsibility to be set before us. We were not surprised to learn of the conduct and duty of the Church. But here is a call to arms, and we learn that we are not only saved and the servants of Christ, but soldiers as well. From the calm of Christian home life, where wives and husbands, children and parents, and servants and masters live together in Christ, we are removed to the battlefield where we are brought face to face with our infernal foe.

Although the redemption that is ours in Christ is complete and free, our inheritance, which we receive here and now, is contested by the enemy. Satan does not want to see the Christian possessing his possessions. The moment we begin to appropriate our blessings in Christ, we discover at once how hostile Satan is toward Christ's own. When the Israelites entered Canaan, they discovered the enemy in the land and, before they could possess the land, they had to conquer it. The experiences of Israel in Canaan have their counterpart in the spiritual experiences of every Christian. With Israel, the land had been entered, but the enemy was there to contest them: with the believer, the new life has been entered into, but the enemy seeks to keep from us those precious experiences and spiritual blessings that await the redeemed in this life; hence, the Christian's walk merges into a warfare.

We are not caught unawares. As Paul put it, we are warned "Lest Satan should get an advantage of us: for we are not ignorant of his devices" (2 Cor. 2:11). Having no hope of salvation for themselves, Satan and his fallen angels seek to render man's redemption ineffective in individuals. But where men are being saved, there Satan intensifies his warfare in the heavenlies against the newly-begotten children of God. Satan has so shaped his present program to include a furious onslaught against all true believers. He has become the "accuser of the brethren" (Rev. 12:10). Now that God's plan of salvation has been perfected and consummated, and Satan knows his certain forthcoming doom, he carries on an uninterrupted warfare of spoiling men and women by seducing them to neglect the necessary spiritual exercises of prayer, Bible study, and fellowship with other believers, while he spreads the table of the world's "dainties" to attract and to appeal to the children of God. Satan knows that he can never remove a child of God from the nail-pierced hands of Jesus Christ (John 10:28-30), but he continues to wage his warfare in the heavenlies against God's own. If he can weaken our allegiance to Christ, he has gained an advantage. Hence the need for Paul's message in the closing part of Ephesians.

1. *The Encounter* 6:10-13)

"Finally, my brethren, be strong in the Lord, and in the power of His might" (6:10). The word "finally" suggests both the conclusion and a commencement. While the word itself means *the remainder, the rest,* it introduces something new in this epistle. The balance of the message will discuss the struggle which, to many believers, will be something new. The struggle is certain, however. None who is Christ's can escape it. The apostle addresses it to "my brethren," an all-inclusive term which included the saints of Paul's day and ours. Satan aims his darts at the whole body of Christ, so that all brethren are conscripted for the battle. Walking, working, and witnessing do not make up the sum total of Christian activity. As brothers, we are called to the battle to stand side by side against our common foe. We are warriors.

Now it is common knowledge that the best of the "brethren" are ill-fitted to face the foe in their own strength, so Paul exhorts all to "be strong in the Lord, and in the power of His might." Weapons must be taken up, and this will call for strength. No weaklings can stand against our infernal foe. The warfare is not "a mere moral conflict between reason and conscience on the one side, and evil passions on the other" (Hodge), but between the devil himself and the saints. Since the enemy possesses supernatural strength, our source of strength is not in nature. It is "in the Lord, and in the power of His might." Thank God, victory is not dependent upon our own strength, else we would fall; but we are assured of conquest by *His mighty power*.

It is good for us when we recognize our deficiency and His sufficiency. We need to be endued with His strength, and such is available if we are "in" the Lord. It is our position "in" the Lord which makes us strong, just as the vigor of an arm is its position in the body. For *His* strength there is no substitute.

Paul was always cognizant of his own weakness. He wrote: "I was with you in weakness" (1 Cor. 2:3). But he added: "when I am weak, then am I strong" (2 Cor. 12:10). When we are conscious of human weakness and emptied of self, then it is that God endues us with His mighty power.

When Paul said, "When I am weak, then am I strong," he was speaking of a time of great suffering and physical infirmity in his own body. There was no question about the reality of the thorn in his flesh, but his attitude of heart toward God in the hour of his suffering was the secret to his strength. He accepted God's will for his life, and he discovered that the infirmity was, in the divine plan, to be the medium of strength. Strength in weakness is one of the paradoxes of Christian experience.

Paul testified to the Philippians that, in spite of his own weakness, he had strength for all things. Said he: "I can do all things through Christ which strengtheneth me" (Phil. 4:13). If Paul attempted to withstand Satan in his own strength, he failed utterly. But he knew better than to try. He had learned that strength for spiritual battles lay in Christ's presence within him. Our Lord does not defer us from the battle, but He does make Himself responsible to equip us with His strength to fight. His presence in us is the secret of victory. We need not be spiritual weaklings. If we are "in the Lord" we can be strong.

The exhortation to be strong in the Lord is followed by another, namely: "Put on the whole armour of God, that ye may be able to stand against the wiles of the devil" (6:11). Here our adversary is named. He is the "devil," and his weapons are referred to as "wiles." He wages his warfare with cunning and deception; therefore the believer must put on *all* of the armor which God supplies.

In chapter four we are told to put on clothing suited to the saint; here we are told to put on clothing suited to the soldier. God knows the strategems of Satan, and He alone can provide a panoply to protect His own. Satan can easily outwit us but never God. So the wise Christian will put on God's armor and keep it on.

In the verses that follow, Paul explains the armor piece by piece, but here he calls all saints to see their need of armor of God's providing. If we clothe ourselves with God's full armor we will "be able" (*dunamai*), be powerful to stand and not fall. Many a young believer who has failed to heed this command to put on the whole armor of God has fallen "by the sleight of men, and cunning craftiness, whereby they lie in wait to deceive" (4:14). Satan and his emissaries are too clever for us. He beguiles young believers from the simplicity of the gospel (2 Cor. 11:2, 3), transforms himself into an angel of light when it serves his purpose (2 Cor. 11:14, 15), and deceives with all power, signs, and lying wonders (2 Thess. 2:9). Thus we are told to "resist" him (James 4:7; 1 Pet. 5:9).

By submitting to God and clothing ourselves with the divine armor, we are able to resist the devil. The only safe protection against Satan's methods is God's armor. Our enemy is a master in the art of deceit. If our adversary was a man possessing nothing more than human strength, then we might attempt to face him and defend ourselves by human means. But since we are dealing, not with flesh and blood, but with principalities and powers, "we do not war after the flesh: (For the weapons of our warfare are not carnal, but mighty through God to the pulling down of strong holds)" (2 Cor. 10:3, 4). While we walk in a body of flesh we do not war after the flesh, that is, we do not rely on the principles of the unsaved. We are compelled to live as men live, by sight and sound and strength; but when we are fighting spiritual battles, the weak weapons of the flesh will not suffice. How foolish to turn from heaven's arsenal to the puny, ineffectual weapons of the flesh! Only God's weapons can batter down the bulwarks of hell.

"For we wrestle not against flesh and blood, but against principalities, against powers, against the rulers of the darkness of this world, against spiritual wickedness in high places" (6:12). Here it is obvious why carnal weapons are useless in this warfare. *Who* our enemies are and *where* they are is given as the reason for needing God's armor. We are not contending with mortal men but against superhuman authorities who rule the sphere of the world's moral darkness. These forces of evil have access to where we are. The believer is in the "heavenlies" where Christ and His Church are, and into this sphere Satan comes to attack the children of God. Christian, our difficulties are far greater than if we were merely fighting men like Hitler and Stalin. On the battlefields of earth we can match the enemy man for man and plane for plane, for here we resist human strength. But the struggle against Satan is not a physical one; it is against *wicked spirits* and *darkness,* against a superhuman foe we cannot see. No soldier has ever entered a more difficult and dangerous war. To be ignorant of the nature of the conflict and the enemy is to invite calamity in our spiritual lives. Satan and his kingdom are arrayed against us. If you have not realized it before, learn it now.

"Wherefore take unto you the whole armour of God, that ye may be able to withstand in the evil day, and having done all, to stand" (6:13). The repetition of this twofold injunction to put on the whole armor of God, and to stand, is significant. God expects us to heed it. Our day is evil and, as the age nears its end, evil will wax worse. But no matter what the extent of the evil or the fierceness of Satan's attacks, the Christian must stand. We are not to flee but to stand; we are not to hide but to stand.

The days are becoming increasingly perilous, so that the whole armor of God must therefore be put on. Then, too, an evil day may dawn upon any one of us individually, a day of fierce persecution, a day of severe testing resulting from some crisis in our lives, a day of moral peril. Unless we are properly protected with God's panoply, we may fall instead of stand. So to the least and the lowliest, Paul says: *"Stand."* Never retreat! The battle is not ours but the Lord's. If we fully equip ourselves according to divine direction, we shall be standing firm after the smoke of battle has cleared away. If the enemy returns to attack again, keep on standing. Remember, there is no standing in the strength of the flesh; so then, "let him that thinketh he standeth take heed lest he fall." It is in Christ that we maintain our position. There seems to be a promise here that, if we will put on the whole armor of God, we shall be able to stand and there will be no attack of the enemy that we shall not be able to meet successfully by the power of God.

2. *The Equipment* (6:14-20)

Since we are engaged in warfare, equipment for both defensive and offensive purposes is essential. Paul calls the equipment "armor," a metaphor he uses on other occasions. In Romans he writes: "The night is far spent, the day is at hand: let us therefore cast off the works of darkness, and let us put on the armour of light" (Rom. 13:12). The thought here is that of a change of dress. The believer not only casts off the garments of darkness (which is sin) but he puts on the armor of light, the idea being that he is now engaged in offensive warfare against the powers of darkness which are evil. Elsewhere Paul writes that we approve "ourselves as the ministers of God . . . by the armor of righteousness on the right hand and on the left" (2 Cor. 6:4, 7). In this latter Scripture he has in mind the armor of right living and right doing, the practical rectitude and uprightness which should result when we are justified through faith in Christ, having had God's righteousness in Him imputed unto us.

Here in Ephesians the different pieces of the armor are explained in greater detail. There is, first, the girdle of truth: "Stand therefore, having your loins girt about with truth" (6:14). In the dress of the oriental, the belt or girdle was used to strengthen and support the body, as well as to hold in place other pieces of apparel. The girdle is therefore mentioned first, and it is called the girdle of *truth*.

The "truth" here is not alone perfect sincerity and truthfulness; for one may be perfectly sincere and truthful, yet still be wrong. But it means truth subjectively considered; that is, the knowledge and belief of the truth revealed in God's written Word. Of course, such knowledge and belief result in perfect sincerity and truthfulness. The girdle of truth is something, then, that the believer is exhorted to "put on." The loin-cloth of truth must be girt about us so that our progress is not impeded and our vital parts are not exposed to the enemy.

A careful reading and study of the Bible, therefore, are essential to victory over the devil and his wiles. Peter writes: "Wherefore gird up the loins of your mind" (1 Pet. 1:13). This means simply that we are to have our minds girt about with the truth of God's Word. The mind of the Christian must be clear and discerning, unhampered by selfish, sinful thoughts, guarding against error and the making of wrong decisions. The believer's warfare is dangerous and strenuous and will not permit of mental sluggishness. We need to have controlled minds girt firmly about with the Scriptures of truth.

Beloved, do some hard, calm, deliberate thinking on the ways of God as revealed in the Word of God. Bible study is essential to victory over Satan. Novels and magazines may have their place, but far too little time is being given to studying the truths of God's Word. As the girdle on one's body lends strength to vital organs, so the study of the Word of God girds and strengthens the inner man. In the warfare against Satan we cannot afford to become entangled with the affairs of this life; therefore we need God's Word to govern our conduct and guide our course of life. Many professing Christians are "tossed to and fro, and carried about with every wind of doctrine, by the sleight of men, and cunning craftiness, whereby they lie in wait to deceive" (4:14), simply because they fail to appropriate and comprehend the "truth." When our Lord was tempted of the devil, He answered the enemy with the truth of Scripture: "It is written . . ." (Matt. 4:4, 7, 10). So let us give first place to the "truth." "Stand therefore having your loins girt about with truth," the truth of Bible doctrine, even the Word of truth (1:13).

The second piece of the Christian's armor follows: "and having on the breastplate of righteousness" (6:14). This piece of defensive armor covered the body, both front and back, from the neck to the thighs. It offered special protection for the heart. A warrior without his breastplate was dangerously exposed to the thrust of the enemy.

Now we can think of no better protection for the heart than a walk in righteousness consistent with our position in Christ. Paul is not referring alone to that imputed positional righteousness which is the possession of all true believers, but the practical righteousness which results from the positional. It is the righteousness of both standing and state. It is not enough that we have the imputed righteousness of Jesus Christ; our walk must be consistent with our position. Most certainly no man can live righteously who has not had the righteousness of God in Christ communicated unto him. All the righteousnesses of the natural man are as filthy rags (Isa. 64:6), so that we must say with Paul: "That I may . . . be found in Him, not having mine own righteousness, which is of the law, but that which is through the faith of Christ, the righteousness which is of God by faith" (Phil. 3:8, 9).

The righteous ones are the redeemed ones, and to all such God says: "yield yourselves unto God, as those that are alive from the dead, and your members as instruments of righteousness unto God" (Rom. 6:13). If we are not living righteously we are easy targets for the enemy's darts. Sinning saints cannot stand in the day of adversity when Satan attacks. Right living is wound-proof; therefore, "we should live soberly, *righteously,* and godly, in this present world" (Titus 2:12). If we fall instead of stand when Satan attacks, it is because we have not been living right. Let every one with unconfessed sin in his life confess it here and now, lest the devil gain an advantage over any one of us.

Dr. Charles R. Erdman writes: "One who binds himself about with a determined loyalty to the holy will and law of God is secure against the deadly thrusts of the tempter. A man who is conscious of being in the wrong is usually a coward; a man who knows that he is right can withstand a multitude and enters the conflict without fear." Righteousness is a matter of the heart continually; it is not something we piously and fraudulently parade one day a week. Strictest integrity must be maintained at all times, the heart being kept purged of every lustful desire and the mind clear of every unholy thought. Notice the words, "having on." Christians are expected to *be* ethical and righteous. None but the righteous can stand. Righteousness is Jehovah's breastplate (Isa. 59:17). Make it yours.

Next, there is something for our feet: "And your feet shod with the preparation of the gospel of peace" (6:15). In any warfare, ancient or modern, messengers who are swift of foot, as well as soldiers who can stand firmly, are needed.

Two ideas are suggested in this verse. First, the believer must stand firmly confirmed in the gospel. Second, he must be ready to carry the good news of salvation with speed. Paul bore witness to this twofold experience in his own life. He stood firmly for the gospel when he testified: "I am not ashamed of the gospel of Christ" (Rom. 1:16), and he expressed a readiness to spread the gospel to the Greeks, the Barbarians, and even to those at Rome also (Rom. 1:14, 15). Paul's feet were shod with the preparation of the gospel of peace. Are yours? Are you resting firmly with confidence in the gospel, in the finished work of our Lord Jesus Christ through His death and resurrection? Here, beloved, is a good standing-place where we can rest undisturbed amid the battles and storms of life. The gospel of Christ is the gospel of peace, and it makes possible a calm in the midst of the storm.

> Blessed quietness, holy quietness,
>   Blest assurance in my soul!
> On the stormy sea Jesus speaks to me,
>   And the billows cease to roll.

Many a Christian warrior has been fearful and restless until he has learned to stand in the gospel shoes. Allow me to refer you to the Israelites eating their first passover. The hard and bitter attacks of Pharoah had the people fearful and well-nigh exhausted. He was their enemy, bent on their destruction. But on the night the death angel appeared over Egypt, the Israelites who were behind blood-sheltered doors were safe. There was no need for any one to be fearful or restless. God had promised protection to all who applied the blood, so that the people could enjoy eating the passover in peace. God had said: "And thus shall ye eat it; with your loins girded, *your shoes on your feet* . . ." (Exod. 12:11). They were to enjoy perfect peace in spite of the worst the enemy could attempt. Let us rest securely and serenely in the good news of our reconciliation to God by the death of His Son, thereby making peace for us.

The gospel shoes not only provide for our security but they also prepare us for active service as well. They speak not only of steadfastness in warfare but swiftness in witnessing. The word "preparation" suggests the idea of "promptness and readiness." There are unsaved men and women who are held in the fear and bondage of Satan and who need our help. Satan holds them as his prisoners. As we "preach the gospel," we "preach deliverance to the captives, and recovering of sight to the blind, to set at liberty them that are bruised" (Luke 4:18). Quoting the prophets Isaiah and Nahum, Paul writes: "How beautiful are the feet of them that preach the gospel of peace, and bring glad tidings of good things" (Rom. 10:15)! Beautiful feet in God's sight are those feet swift to carry the gospel message of deliverance and peace to those held captive by Satan.

Bringing the good news of salvation to the sinner is a vital move in the warfare against evil. Too many Christians are not in a state of preparedness to witness to the lost. They are unshod. Little wonder they become foot-sore, lame and weary!

Some of you who read these words may need a new pair of shoes. You have not that joyful readiness to talk to sinners about the Lord. The soldier's shoes are not the dancing slippers of this world or the lounging slippers of the slothful, but the shoes of the Christian warrior who knows Christ and makes Him known. Readiness to speak a word for the Saviour is one of the noble virtues of every child of God. Put on the gospel shoes. "Be ready always to give an answer to every man that asketh you a reason of the hope that is in you" (1 Pet. 3:15). Be prepared for war or witnessing.

One word further about the gospel shoes. Reference was made to the Israelites eating the first passover. They were told to eat it with their shoes on their feet in readiness for the pilgrim journey. In this connection there is an interesting statement from the Lord, recorded by Moses in Deuteronomy: "And I have led you forty years in the wilderness: your clothes are not waxen old upon you, and thy shoe is not waxen old upon thy foot" (29:5). God had taken care of their shoes so that they lasted throughout the entire journey. The burning desert sands and the sharp stones could not wear them out. Beloved, the gospel has not lost any of its old-time power. Nor will it ever! As we stand firmly for the truth and speak it to others, we shall witness the same mighty victories such as the apostles won in the early Church. Only be thou ready!

> Ready to go, ready to stay,
> Ready my place to fill;
> Ready for service, lowly or great,
> Ready to do His will.

Verse 16 adds to the list of the Christian's armor: "Above all, taking the shield of faith, wherewith ye shall be able to quench all the fiery darts of the wicked." The words "above all" are often translated "in addition to." The girdle of truth, the breastplate of righteousness, and the gospel shoes are necessary pieces of equipment; but, in addition, to these and possibly more important, the Christian warrior must take up the "shield of faith." The design of Satan is to destroy the children of God; hence our need for the kind of armor that will withstand the devil's forces. His weapon is here referred to as "fiery darts," those burning missiles of evil, ablaze with the flames of destruction. There are a thousand and more perils that would

burn themselves into our lives to render us helpless in the
battles of life. Against these satanic, fiery darts of pride, envy,
jealousy, covetousness, worry, unbelief, impurity, and many
others, we need a sure defense. Paul calls that defense "the
shield of faith."

A question arises as to the identity of the shield. The symbolism of the shield is used in the New Testament in Ephesians
alone, so that we must of necessity look at its more frequent
use in the Old Testament for clearer understanding. It seems
to this writer that, in the metaphorical language of the Bible,
the shield generally represents the Person of God in His pro-
tecting care over His children. In other words, God Himself
is the shield of His people.

The first mention of the shield came from God to Abraham
at the close of the patriarch's struggle against the unbelieving
kings who attacked the king of Sodom and his allies. Moses
writing, says: "After these things," that is, after the events
recorded in Genesis 14, "the Word of the Lord came unto
Abram in a vision, saying, Fear not, Abram: *I am thy
shield,* and thy exceeding great reward" (Gen. 15:1). This new
revelation of God was appropriate to the need of the moment,
for the struggle recorded in the previous chapter is the first war
mentioned in the Bible. Undoubtedly there was a measure of
fear in Abraham's heart, else God would not have told him
not to fear. Over against that fear God assured His child that
He was Abraham's protection. If Abraham was alarmed and
apprehensive about any further attacks of Chedorlaomer, he
could now quiet his troubled heart in the assurance that God
would be his shield and defense. You see, beloved, if we have
God for our shield, we need not fear the worst that man or
demons can do to us; for our Shield and Defender will never
suffer His trusting child to be a loser.

The next time the word "shield" is used is in Moses's song
of praise to God for His majesty and excellency in Israel. It
is used in connection with words familiar to us all: "The
eternal God is thy refuge, and underneath are the everlasting

arms: and He shall thrust out the enemy from before thee; and shall say, Destroy them. Israel then shall dwell in safety alone: the fountain of Jacob shall be upon a land of corn and wine; also His heavens shall drop down dew. Happy art thou, O Israel; who is like unto thee, O people saved by *the Lord, the shield of thy help,* and who is the sword of thy excellency! And thine enemies shall be found liars unto thee; and thou shalt tread upon their high places" (Deut. 33:27-29). Again the context makes it obvious that God is revealed as the shield to defend His children against their "enemies." Israel is to be delivered from all her enemies and in that day she will say with the psalmist: "He is our help and our shield" (Psa. 33:20); "O God, our shield" (Psa. 59:11; 84:9); "For the Lord God is a sun and shield" (Psa. 84:11). In all of these passages God Himself is the shield of His people, their sufficient covering and strong tower in the day of trouble (cf. Psa. 61:3).

Now notice that Paul says: "Taking," or "Taking hold of" the shield of faith. God is our shield, but only as we lay hold of Him in faith does He become our protection against the fiery darts of the enemy. The shield is our sovereign God; faith is the human responsibility. The "faith" here is not that system of Christian teaching "which was once delivered unto the saints," and for which we "should earnestly contend" (Jude 3). It is, as Dr. Ironside has said, not *what* you believe but *how* you believe. And to this we might add that it is also *whom* you believe. Faith here is confidence, complete reliance in the Person, purposes, and power of God. Implicit trust in Him alone can quench the enemy's darts.

Flying missiles have always been a weapon of war to destroy or disable the forces of opposition, and Satan has his. These must be staved off and quenched before they can strike us. If we put confidence in the flesh, we can never hope to ward off the devil's darts. Only as we look to our blessed Lord and draw continually upon His strength can we expect to come forth triumphantly. The believer's mighty bulwark is his confidence in almighty God. No arrow of fear, no dart of temptation can penetrate the soul that lays hold of the shield of faith. God has provided for us a shield in the Person and finished work of our Lord Jesus Christ, but you and I must believe.

"And take the helmet of salvation" (6:17). A number of teachers of Greek have pointed out that the word for "take" here is not the same as that used in reference to the shield, but that it means *to accept from the hand of another, as a gift*. God has prepared salvation for all, and He offers it to all as His gift. We need only to accept it in order to possess it.

Now the head is prominent and vulnerable, and it needs plenty of protection. For this protection God has provided a helmet of salvation. A covering for the head is not a modern invention in warfare. Some form of headgear for soldiers dates back to ancient Egypt and Assyria, and replicas of these, as well as some originals, can be seen in many museums. But the helmet of salvation in the Epistle to the Ephesians is God's gift of salvation to man. Unless that salvation is received, man cannot hope to escape the fiery darts of Satan.

The helmet of salvation for the believer is first the knowledge and assurance of salvation. The experience of salvation is not an emotional one merely: it is reasonable and rational as well. The saved man has intelligent understanding and assuring knowledge that God has saved him. He knows whom he has believed. He may not always be able to answer the questions and criticisms of skeptics, yet no one, man or devil, will ever be able to get him away from the fact of his experience of salvation. The knowledge of sins forgiven is a mighty fortress against the attacks of modernism, atheism, communism, and every other ism. If you have the knowledge and assurance of salvation, you have the protection against many of Satan's darts and the solution to many of life's problems. When a man receives the helmet of salvation he can hold up his head with confidence and face the most potent foe.

To be saved and know it can make us "more than conquerors through Him that loved us" (Rom. 8:37). After the man born blind had been given sight by our Lord, the Pharisees, by their questions, sought to get the man to renounce Jesus. To most of their questions, he could only repeat: "I know not"; but they could never tear from him one thing he did know. He said: "One thing I know, that, whereas I was blind, now I see" (John 9:25). The Apostle Paul likewise did not know a lot of things, for there were times when he had to acknowledge that "we see through a glass, darkly" (1 Cor. 13:12); but at no time were the enemies of the gospel able to put Paul to shame, for he could always testify: "I am not ashamed: for I know whom I have believed" (2 Tim. 1:12).

Salvation was Paul's helmet. Is it yours? If you have any doubt as to your being saved, you will not be able to stand with real confidence when facing the foe. An experiential knowledge of salvation removes all sense of doubt and all fear of condemnation, giving to the believer a sense of security in his Lord.

In one other passage Paul mentions the helmet. "But let us, who are of the day, be sober, putting on the breastplate of faith and love; and for an helmet, the hope of salvation" (1 Thess. 5:8). Salvation is not only the beginning of hope for man, it is future also. Salvation touches the past, the present, and the future, saving from the penalty of sin, the power of sin, and the presence of sin. The Scriptures teach that we *are* saved (Eph. 2:8), that we *are being* saved (2 Cor. 1:10), and that we *shall be* saved (Rom. 5:10). The helmet of salvation must be worn at all times for every circumstance and occasion. Every Christian can stand in the calm confidence that the death of Christ has saved him, the resurrected Christ is keeping him, and the coming Christ will preserve him safely throughout eternity. "Being confident of this very thing, that He which hath begun a good work in you will perform it until the day of Jesus Christ" (Phil. 1:6).

Beloved, if you have trusted Christ, you can fight, knowing without any doubt whatever that you are saved. As you wear the helmet of salvation, no power in heaven or on earth can rob you of confidence and boldness in battle. The professing

Christian, without the helmet of salvation, is an easy target for the devil. If you have any doubt that you are saved now, or if you fear that you might not be saved in the next life, you cannot confidently meet the enemy of your soul from day to day. Assurance of salvation that is based upon the Bible protects the believer from false doctrine, doubt, and fear. *Take* the helmet. It is God's gift to you. What an anchor for our thinking!

Every warrior needs a weapon for offensive warfare, and the divinely-provided weapon is "the sword of the Spirit, which is the Word of God" (6:17). The sword here is not the Spirit but the Word spoken by the Spirit, the Bible. When the Christian warrior is thoroughly acquainted with the Word and has acquired skill and ability in its use, he can ward off every attack of the enemy.

This is not the only place in Scripture where the Word of the Lord is referred to in a militant manner. In the Epistle to the Hebrews we read: "For the Word of God is quick, and powerful, and sharper than any twoedged sword, piercing even to the dividing asunder of soul and spirit, and of the joints and marrow, and is a discerner of the thoughts and intents of the heart" (Heb. 4:12). The Sword is quick (living), for the words God speaks are spirit and life (John 6:63). The Sword is active (energetic), for as it pierces the heart it compels men to retreat. The Sword is sharp to pierce, to divide, and to discern. There is no amount of satanic subtilty, there are none of hell's barriers that the Word of God cannot break through when wielded aright. The Word of God is, in the highest sense, the most dreaded weapon we can use against the foe. No doubt the double-edged bronze Roman sword appeared to Paul a fierce and formidable weapon. But how much sharper is the Word of God than weapons of men and demons!

When writing of our ascended Lord, the Apostle John said: "Out of His mouth went a sharp twoedged sword" (Rev. 1:16). The Sword of the Almighty Conqueror is His own resistless Word. He speaks and it is done. One word from Him and His enemies fall back powerless. More than seven hundred years before His birth the prophecy was written: "He hath made My mouth like a sharp sword" (Isa. 49:2).

The Sword is the Word of the Lord. How wonderfully this Book has vindicated itself through the centuries! How marvelously this Book has met the needs of men in every age! How great has been the triumph of the Word wherever it has gone! The Word was the weapon the apostles used when facing the bitter opposition of pagan powers. The prophets in the old dispensation and the saints in the new make up a mighty army of glorious conquerors because they had ready access to the Sword. They were good swordsmen for God. The Word was in their heads and hearts, and they knew how to use it. These faithful warriors for Christ met the enemy in exactly the same way as did our Lord Himself, by the sword-thrusts of His own Word. There was never a time when God's people had greater need for studying and spreading the Scriptures.

As we anticipate our Lord's return, we know that with His coming to the earth to rule, "He shall smite the earth with the rod of His mouth" (Isa. 11:4). Until we see Him, let us wield the Sword of the Spirit, meeting every temptation with a "Thus saith the Lord." The last victory to be won will be won by the Sword of the Spirit. The rider on the white horse will come forth; "His name is called The Word of God . . . and out of His mouth goeth a sharp sword, that with it He should smite the nations" (Rev. 19:13, 15). With this same Sword we, too, can conquer, for the Word of God is the Sword that the Spirit gives and uses.

We have come to the end of the divinely-provided equipment for the Christian's warfare. Last, but not least, the child of God must have recourse to prayer: "Praying always with all prayer and supplication in the Spirit, and watching thereunto with all perseverance and supplication for all saints" (6:18). Some teachers do not regard prayer as a part of the equipment but, rather, that exercise of soul that takes us into the realm of the believer's resource where the whole armor is rendered effective.

Such an interpretation may be right. However, the important truth for us to learn is the absolute necessity of earnest, constant prayer if we are to live triumphantly as Christians. It is not the possession of the armor and the weapons that makes a great warrior. No resource of strength or strategy lies within ourselves. Rather do we need to look to the One who is superior to the enemy's greatest strength and who can outwit his every maneuver. It is by prayer that we come boldly to God's throne of grace to obtain mercy and find grace to help in time of need. Every conquering Christian in every generation has been a prayer warrior. The one necessity of every good soldier of Jesus Christ is to keep in constant touch with his great Captain and Commander.

We must ever keep in mind that the battle is not ours but God's. If we break contact with Him, we have severed ourselves from the One who orders the battle and who alone can empower us to win. Study the wars in the Old Testament in which Israel fought against her enemies, and in every instance you will find the principle of God's working to be the same. When Israel fought in her own strength, she suffered defeat; when she cast herself upon God's mercy and trusted in His might, victory followed. Abraham took his *trained* servants, numbering only 318, and conquered the coalition of kings that fought against the kings of Sodom and Gomorrah (Gen. 14). Gideon, his army reduced from 32,000 to 300, delivered Israel from the yoke of Midianitish slavery (Judg. 7 and 8). Joshua, with the odds against him, led Israel to a mighty conquest over Jericho (Josh. 6). In his first battle, Joshua was much less experienced in warfare, but certainly no less trustful in the power of God to defeat the Amalekites (Exod. 17). These all, along with King Hezekiah who conquered the Assyrians, could testify: "With us is the Lord our God to help us, and to fight our battles" (2 Chron. 32:8).

The Old Testament saints were often outnumbered and ill-equipped when compared with the armies and weapons of their enemies, but when they were on God's side, when they trusted and obeyed Him, they could not lose. We, too, must meet the enemy of the Church and of our souls in the strength and wisdom of Almighty God. It is through prayer that we receive a never-ending supply of strength and wisdom for the battle.

There must be constancy in prayer: "Praying always." At no time dare we break contact with God. The enemy watches for prayerlessness in our lives and then takes advantage of us. We must be constantly in prayer because we are constantly in danger. Do not stop praying when you have health and prosperity, for such neglect will only expose you to Satan's darts. Vigilance in prayer must be maintained at all times, whether the day be an ordinary one or a day of crisis. God is not asking us to do the impossible when He commands us to pray *always*.

Our contact with God should be just as natural as our breathing. We breathe always. Physically, we could not survive without breathing; spiritually, we cannot survive without praying. Certainly we are not expected to be constantly on our knees or in some church, but we are expected to be constantly in contact with God. Prayer will release a power from heaven on our behalf greater than the power of all those which are against us. Daniel prayed for three weeks and learned afterwards that his prayer prevailed over the demon spirits that were against him. Elsewhere Paul exhorts to "Pray without ceasing" (1 Thess. 5:17). Our Lord commanded: "Men ought always to pray and not to faint" (Luke 18:1).

Then, too, we are to pray "with all prayer and supplication." This suggests that we must avail ourselves of every method and approach in prayer. There is private prayer, family prayer, silent prayer, audible prayer, mealtime prayer, church meeting prayer, the set time for prayer, the emergency prayer. A constant sense of God's nearness and a consciousness of our need of Him will make us versatile in our prayer life. At times our prayer will take on one mode; again it will assume a different appeal altogether. There are prayers of commission, prayers of thanksgiving, prayers of intercession, prayers of supplication, and prayers of petition, and the true soldier of Jesus Christ will practice them all from time to time. We should pray at all times, in all places, and under every circumstance.

Third, we are directed to pray "in the Spirit." The opposite to praying in the Spirit is praying in the flesh, the latter being a form of prayer without power. We saw earlier in our study that the weapons of our warfare are not carnal. Even our prayers must be guided by the Spirit of God, "for we know not what we should pray for as we ought" (Rom. 8:26). There are times when we cannot collect our thoughts or express ourselves in words, and yet we desire to pray. Thank God, we may be assured that the Holy Spirit sees the battlefield and knows the position of the enemy, and He will pray for us. If we are not praying "in the Spirit," we had better not pray at all. To pray in the Spirit one must be born of the Spirit and led by the Spirit. There is a lot of spirited praying that is not praying in the Spirit. Those who pray in the Spirit never pray selfishly but always in the will of God; therefore, they get answers to their prayers and they know the blessings of victory over the foe. Praying in the Spirit glorifies God, and where God is glorified victory is assured.

Fourth, we are to pray "watching thereunto with all perseverance and supplication." There must be wakefulness and watchfulness in prayer, never weariness. The disciples slept when they should have been praying, and our Lord said: "What, could ye not watch with Me one hour? Watch and pray, that ye enter not into temptation: the spirit indeed is willing, but the flesh is weak" (Matt. 26:40, 41). Spiritual drowsiness opens the gates to the enemy, so let us attend to our praying, "continuing instant in prayer" (Rom. 12:12).

Finally, we are to pray "for all saints." All true believers in Christ, who make up His body, are Satan's targets, so that we should pray for all saints. We are not alone in the struggle against wickedness. Christ has His soldiers in almost every part of the earth; therefore, we should be making supplication for the whole army of the Lord. Every day is "All Saints Day" for the believer in Christ, for we should pray daily for one another. If you do not have a prayer interest in the saints in India, Asia, Africa, Europe, the Americas, and the islands of the seas, you are omitting from your prayer life a necessary and vital phase of the ministry of prayer. The devil's victories in other lands are sometimes caused by our prayerlessness here at home.

The importance that Paul attached to intercessory prayer is all the more obvious in his words that follow. Having exhorted his readers to pray for all saints, he adds: "And for me, that utterance may be given unto me, that I may open my mouth boldly, to make known the mystery of the gospel, for which I am an ambassador in bonds: that therein I may speak boldly, as I ought to speak" (6:19, 20). Paul was a prisoner in Rome when he spoke of himself as "an ambassador in bonds"; nevertheless he was in the thick of the fray and felt the need for the prayers of other Christians. He was in a prison cell; still he was God's soldier and servant in Rome. If anything, Paul was in the forefront of the battle. What he wanted the Ephesians to pray for, was not for his release from Nero's chains but for liberty and boldness to speak the claims of Christ. He was asking the saints to pray that he would have God's help in preaching. "Keep on praying for me," he writes to his battle-weary friends. He would have the Romans, as well as others, know the glorious revelation of the gospel. No preacher stands above the need of being prayed for. The critics in some of our churches would render a service if they would pray more for the preacher and criticize him less. Dear friend, all of God's servants need help from heaven. None of us has strength and wisdom of his own to carry the battle to the enemy; so pray always, in the Spirit, with all perseverance, for all saints, and please include the writer of these lines.

Having completed the message, Paul sent it to Asia by the hand of "Tychicus, a beloved brother and faithful minister in the Lord" (6:21). Tychicus might have been looked upon by some as Paul's errand boy, but he was more than that. This faithful messenger had the high honor of bearing this inspired and priceless epistle to the Church at Ephesus and to all the saints of succeeding generations. Suppose Tychicus had failed! Have you ever given thought to what a great loss the Church would have suffered? But he did not fail. God bless you, dear brother. You have fulfilled your mission and our hearts have been comforted (6:22). You not only have relieved the anxiety of the Ephesians concerning Paul, but you have brought from Paul the inspired Word that has lifted our burdens.

In closing, Paul turns to the Lord to invoke a twofold benediction upon the saints:

Peace be to the brethren, and love with faith, from God the Father and the Lord Jesus Christ.
Grace be with all them that love our Lord Jesus Christ in sincerity.   Amen.

THE END

BIBLIOGRAPHY

GALATIANS

BISHOP. *Grace in Galatians*. New York: Gospel Publishing House, 1913.

CALVIN, JOHN. *Galatians and Ephesians*. Grand Rapids, Michigan: Eerdmans, 1948.

DARBY, J. N. *Synopsis of the Books of the Bible, Volume IV*. New York: Loizeaux Brothers.

DARMS, ANTON. *Law and Grace, Studies in Galatians*. New York: Loizeaux Brothers, 1946.

ERDMAN, CHARLES R. *The Epistle of Paul to the Galatians*. Philadelphia: Westminster Press, 1930.

HARRISON, NORMAN B. *His Side vs. Our Side*. Wheaton, Illinois: Van Kampen Press, 1950.

HEYDT, HENRY J. *The Gospel in Galatians*. Grand Rapids, Michigan: Zondervan, 1944.

HOGG & VINE. *Galatians*. London, England: Pickering & Inglis.

IRONSIDE, H. A. *Galatians*. New York: Loizeaux Brothers, 1940.

KEEN, CLARENCE M. *Christian Liberty*. Published by the author.

LEE, ROBERT. *The Outlined Galatians*. London, England: Pickering & Inglis.

LUTHER, MARTIN. *Comments on St. Paul's Epistle to the Galatians*. Grand Rapids, Michigan: Zondervan.

MARLIN, CLARENCE. *God's Grace in Galatians*. New York: Fleming H. Revell, 1940.

MOULE, H. C. G. *The Cross and the Spirit*. London, England: Pickering & Inglis.

NEIGHBOR, R. E. *By Grace Alone*. Cleveland, Ohio: Union Gospel Press.

NEWELL, WM. R. *Paul vs. Peter, Galatians I and II*. Chicago, Illinois: Weir Brothers, 1930.

PETTINGILL, WM. L. *By Grace Through Faith Plus Nothing*. Findlay, Ohio: Fundamental Truth Publishers, 1938.

SADLER, M. F. *Galatians*. London, England: George Bell & Sons, 1892.

SIMPSON, A. B. *The Epistles to the Galatians*. Harrisburg, Pennsylvania: Christian Publications.

SUTCLIFFE, B. B. *Galatians, God's Answer to Legalism*. Chicago, Illinois: Moody Press.

TENNEY, MERRILL C. *Galatians*. Grand Rapids, Michigan: Eerdmans, 1951.

EPHESIANS

BROWN, CHARLES. *St. Paul's Epistle to the Ephesians*. London: Religious Tract Society of London.

CALVIN, JOHN. *Commentary on Galatians and Ephesians*. Grand Rapids, Michigan: Eerdmans, 1948.

CHAFER, LEWIS SPERRY. *The Ephesian Letter Doctrinally Considered*. New York, N. Y.: Loizeaux, 1935.

DALE, R. W. *Lectures on Ephesians*. London: Hodder and Stoughton, 1883.

ERDMAN, CHARLES R. *Epistle of Paul to the Ephesians*. Philadelphia, Pa.: Westminster Press.

GAEBELEIN, A. C. *Unsearchable Riches*. Our Hope, 1928.

GURNALL, WILLIAM. *The Christian in Complete Armor*. Glasgow, Scotland: Blackie and Son, 1865.

HARRISON, NORMAN B. *His Very Own*. Chicago, Illinois: Bible Institute Colportage Association, 1930.

HODGE, CHARLES. *Commentary on the Epistle to the Ephesians*. Grand Rapids, Michigan, Eerdmans.

HUGHES, ALBERT. *The Whole Armor of God*. Grand Rapids, Michigan: Zondervan, 1939.

IRONSIDE, H. A. *In the Heavenlies*. New York, N. Y.: Loizeaux Brothers.

LINCOLN, WILLIAM. *Lectures on Ephesians*. Scotland: Ritchie.

MILLER, H. S. *Ephesians*. Houghton, New York: Word-Bearer Press, 1931.

MOULE, H. C. G. *Ephesian Studies*. London: Hodder and Stoughton, 1900.

MEYER, F. B. *Ephesians*. Grand Rapids, Michigan: Zondervan, 1953.

PARKER, JOSEPH. *The People's Bible. Ephesians to Revelation*. New York, N. Y.: Funk and Wagnalls.

PAXSON, RUTH. *The Wealth, Walk and Warfare of the Christian*. New York, N. Y.: Revell, 1939.

RILEY, W. B. *The Bible of the Expositor and the Evangelist. New Testament. Vol. 12.* Cleveland, Ohio: Union Gospel Press, 1928.

SADLER, M. F. *Galatians, Ephesians, Philippians with Notes*. London and New York: George Bell and Sons, 1892.

SEISS, JOSEPH A. *Lectures on the Epistles*. Philadelphia, Pa.: United Lutheran Publishing House, 1885.

SEUME, RICHARD H. *Studies in Ephesians*. 1952.

SIMPSON, A. B. *Christ in the Bible. Galatians and Ephesians*. Harrisburg, Pa.: Christian Publications, 1886.

STEVENS, GEORGE BARKER. *The Messages of Paul*. New York, N. Y.: Charles Scribner's, 1900.

TALBOT, LOUIS T. *Ephesians, An Exposition*. Wheaton, Illinois: Van Kampen Press, 1937.

TUCKER, LEON. *"With Him."* Harrisburg, Pa.: Christian Missionary Alliance Publishing Company, 1928.

WILLIAMS, CHARLES B. *A Commentary on the Pauline Epistles*. Chicago, Illinois: Moody Press, 1953.

WILSON, WALTER L. *Messages on Ephesians*. Grand Rapids, Michigan: Zondervan, 1940.

INDEX OF SCRIPTURE TEXTS